PAUL
McCARTNEY

Yul Brynner presents Paul with an Ivor Novello
award, London, 1980.

The Beatles are presented to Princess Margaret.

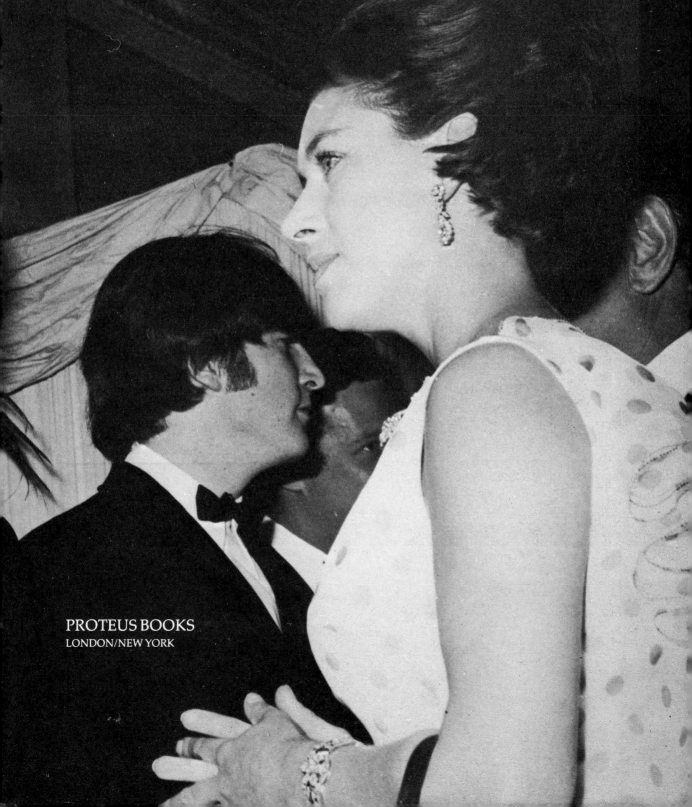

PAUL McCARTNEY:
The Definitive Biography
by Chris Welch

PROTEUS BOOKS

LONDON/NEW YORK

Dedicated to Big Mac.

The author extends grateful thanks to countless legion researchers, and to Marilyne, Tony Brainsby, Bill Harry, Geoff Britton, Robert Ellis for their help and patience.

PROTEUS BOOKS is an imprint of
The Proteus Publishing Group

United States
PROTEUS PUBLISHING COMPANY, INC.
9, West 57th Street, Suite 4503
New York, NY 10019

distributed by:
CHERRY LANE BOOKS COMPANY, INC.
P.O. Box 430
Port Chester, NY 10573

United Kingdom
PROTEUS BOOKS LIMITED
Bremar House, Sale Place
London W2 1PT

distributed by:
J. M. DENT & SONS (DISTRIBUTION) LIMITED,
Dunhams Lane, Letchworth
Herts. SG6 1LF

ISBN 0 86276 125 5 (paperback)
ISBN 0 86276 126 3 (hardback)

First published in U.S. 1984
First published in U.K. 1984

Photocredits:
Aquarius Literary Agency;
British Broadcasting Corporation;
André Csillag;
Chalky Davis;
Keystone Press Agency;
David McGough Incorporated (Ann Clifford);
National Portrait Gallery, London;
Barry Plummer;
Kay Rowley;
Frank Spooner Pictures;
Star File (Kate Simon, Bob Gruen, Vinnie Zuffart
Syndication International.

Editor: Kay Rowley

Designed by: Jill Mumford
Typeset by: SX Composing Ltd, Rayleigh, Essex
Printed and bound in Great Britain by
Blantyre Printing & Binding Co., Glasgow

CONTENTS

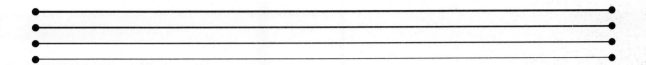

A tousle-haired man wearing a blue pullover, crumpled collar and a weary smile appeared on the British telly in the autumn of 1982, facing the man from the BBC Nine O'Clock News with his defences on standby rather than red alert. It was twenty years to the day since the release of *Love Me Do*, The Beatles' first single and Paul McCartney was being asked, once again, about the pop phenomenon of two decades ago, that had shaped his life and altered and affected countless millions around the world.

It could have been a moment for back slapping nostalgia. Instead Paul parried the questions with the skill born of long practice, the interviewer earnest and unsmiling in his anxiety to get to the nub of the matter for the precious few seconds of peak viewing time. The uncomfortable realisation was beginning to penetrate the heavily edited chat that perhaps it was time to let Paul McCartney off the hook about the old group.

Paul had become the most successful and consistently creative of all the four lads from Liverpool, just as everyone had predicted. He had weathered the storms of antipathy that followed the rows and wrangling of the break up. He set himself the task of creating a group that would outshine the achievements of The Beatles and came within an ace of total success. At the same time, he earned the respect, admiration and downright awe of fans, record buyers, critics and fellow musicians, as the gifted popular songwriter of the age.

The man who created *Yesterday*, *Mull Of Kintyre*, *Eleanor Rigby* and so many more classics, that were part of a planetwide consciousness, was always friendly, outgoing and accessible. And yet to many he remained an enigma, a man who commanded great power and wealth, with a hard manipulative streak feared lurking beneath the soft exterior.

Just who was this man raising his eyebrows in anticipation of the age old question about The Beatles, albeit now put in retrospective form? Who was this scruffy celebrity, his boyish charm still intact, who they say earned more than Queen Elizabeth II of England?

Paul looked like he was on auto-pilot, retelling the story of The Beatles, managing to look concerned about the national interest in a subject long since withered away. He was seated in Abbey Road recording studios, where all the great Beatles songs were made. "John and I started writing a couple of years before we ever got a record contract and we actually used to sag off school – go to my house and we started trying to write songs, and we got together a bunch of songs and *Love Me Do* was one of them...."

It was not the most riveting stuff. The video editor went to work. Cut. 'Was it ever a serious possibility The Beatles would have reformed in the late Seventies?'

'No – while those offers were going on we used to ring each other and say, "Have you heard about this? You're not going to do it are you? No way!" So between the four of us there was never any question we were going to do it. We were just watching the world going mad really and the reason was this chemistry I was talking about had been broken. We'd said right, don't like you, don't want to work with you again and everything had come to such a head, like a divorce....' Paul's eyes rolled downwards as he listened to himself repeating the old phrases.

'But towards the end you were all on better terms?'

'We were on better terms yeah, but no one would pick up the group thing again.... nobody wanted to work with each other. There were moments when we thought, "Ah, it would be great" but we thought if we did it, it would be a let down; one of the things we'd always been very conscious of with The Beatles was to have a great career and leave 'em laughing. So we thought we had done that; we didn't really want to come back as decrepit old rockers.'

Paul suddenly became animated, alive and amused by the thought of The Beatles as old men. His face creased into a grin. 'Remember us? She Loves You Yeah Yeah! Oh dear, they *were* good, honest kids.'

Other groups had survived, it was pointed out, like The Who and The Rolling Stones. Paul adopted a quizzical expression, his eyebrows arched and a finger rested on his chin. 'Yep,' he allowed. Silence. Then he relented. 'Yeah.... but we broke up. It was the natural thing. We were kids, eighteen and growing up.... we had to go our separate ways, to look at life instead of just this group. We had to find women for one thing, which we all did, and then we had to give time to that new life....'

'And now for the main points of the news again....'

The news was that, while McCartney in 1982 was enjoying triumphant sales with his album *Tug Of War* and yet more hit singles with *Ebony And Ivory*, *Take It Away*, *Tug Of War* and *This Girl Is Mine*, the past was still haunting him, courtesy of the EMI promotions department. In November that year the charts once again resounded to a milder but still potent form of Beatlemania. *Love Me Do* made an astonishing reappearance and was joined in the Top Ten by the LP *20 Greatest Hits*. Even so, there were kids who had to be advised that Paul McCartney had once been a member of the group who sprang from a Northern seaport with *Love Me Do*, *She Loves You* and *Please Please Me* and conquered the world.

Theirs was a saga of power and adulation that could have driven each Beatle mad. Indeed, there was a period when it seemed forces were building up to destroy them from within and without. The headlines, the hits, the money and mad scramble to control their destiny and riches, were enough to unbalance any bunch of schoolfriends who had merely started out with a harmless skiffle group in mind.

They had all survived intact, largely fulfilled, apparently happy and quite obviously sane, until that dreadful moment when a spokesperson for the American gun lobby exercised his right to bear arms and shot down John Lennon outside the Dakota Building in New York City on December 11, 1980.

Only then was the symmetry of The Beatles truly and cruelly broken, putting to an end forever the speculation that the greatest group in popular music history would ever reform. But the great clamour for them to try and repeat past glories had nearly always stemmed from the music business and the press. The former made what seemed like huge offers which were really an inducement for The Beatles to pay themselves to play and generate vast sums for entrepreneurs and promoters. The press was miffed at the decision of The Beatles to quit, thus denying them a steady supply of Beatle stories to entice the youth market. The group had not been given permission to break up, and it was rather like the Royal Family packing their possessions into a pantechnicon and pulling out of Buckingham Palace. It rankled, and as Paul McCartney was the most visible and successful of all the ex-Beatles, he found it hardest of all to be accepted and even drum into the heads of commentators that he was no longer a Beatle and now had a group called Wings, that was touring harder and playing to more people with greater efficiency than The Beatles. The Beatles joined The Abdication, The Battle Of Britain and Coronation Street as one of those great Fleet Street stories that refused to die. It was a heavy burden.

The public at large, however, were quite able to cope with the demise of the group. They could see the pressures, understood the reasons for the split and readily accepted each Beatles' attempts at creating his own life as an individual performer.

Lennon, after his astonishing outburst of creativity and anguished soul searching, lapsed into a happier, purged state of contentment. George Harrison broke free from the constraints of his Beatle partners to indulge in his own ideas about life and music, and to make important constructive steps to alleviate some of the distress he saw in the real world, notably with his concerts in aid of Bangla Desh. Ringo Starr dabbled in films and records and seemed to thoroughly enjoy being Ringo Starr.

Paul was left with the odium of being 'the one who broke up The Beatles,' who ditched Jane Asher for an unknown American girl, who took The Beatles to court and caused them to be wound up, and was damned for writing 'silly love songs' and playing the all-round entertainer, while even John Lennon pilloried him in *How Do You Sleep*, on his 1971 album, *Imagine*. It was not a promising set of circumstances in which to start the new decade and his earliest post-Beatles recordings showed him off balance, in an almost trance-like state. If he had ever been guilty of being bossy in The Beatles, he certainly paid the price in the aftermath.

To be publicly attacked in song by his old song writing partner was a mortifying experience that left him as much puzzled as hurt. If he had tried to bring rationality and good sense to The Beatles in the years after Brian Epstein's death, then he was not exactly thanked by the others, who were resentful of his attempts to dominate them or crush them with good advice. In the light of that experience, it was amazingly stupid of people ever to expect them to reform, even for a million dollars. But then only gossip columnists, desperate for an exclusive, ever really thought they would, with fingers crossed and an eye at the deadline.

Paul faced the Seventies, an out-of-work bass guitarist and songwriter. As he paced the lonely Scottish moorlands, he let clean air blow away the smoke and accumulated grime of Liverpool and London and perceived his mission. He was to disengage himself and The Beatles from American adventurers, gain control of his own song writing and create a vehicle for his future musical output. He would become once again a public performer, not a recluse, or fading superstar. He would never be res-

trained, ripped off or made mock of again, and he could count on two important allies. One was his wife Linda and their family; the other was the blank sheet of paper he could convert into scribbled music and song. Anybody he met along the way could be an ally, and with luck a friend. Adversaries could be either converted or shunted aside, along with those who turned out to be failures or disappointments. There could be no avoiding harsh measures. Paul McCartney would rather be hung as a sheep than as a lamb.

Beyond the obvious facts of his triumphs and failures, there is curiously little about Paul McCartney's music that gives much clue to the personality that lies behind the smile, or indeed the scowl. His songs have none of the inward looking, self-gratifying tendencies of the rock singer-songwriter. There is no anguish or recrimination, no condemnation of the world and its people, nor any kind of spite, malice or promiscuity.

Instead, he deals in human frailty, concern for the lonely and old, romance, nostalgia, whimsical humour, rock 'n' roll escapism and something called love. At his most positive and direct he has called for reconciliation and freedom in such songs as *Ebony And Ivory* and *Give Ireland Back To The Irish*. For a man who is usually held to be apolitical and conservative, he has shown himself to be brace, outspoken and radical. It is all part of the McCartney make-up that can appear confusing to those who imagine they have encapsulated him safely into a particular brand of pop star. He is the family man who likes the open air life, but is happiest chain smoking untipped cigarettes, working in the stuffy confines of a recording studio. He is the millionaire who owns the copyright to some of the world's most lucrative hits and controls his own business empire headed by McCartney Productions. But he is a millionaire who prefers to drive a Landrover, wear wellington boots and several days growth of beard, while mucking out the farm. He is the fun-loving organiser of magical mystery tours, parties, and celebrations. He is also the demanding boss who brooks no failures or interference with his plans and will take drastic action to get what he wants.

It is perhaps, then, no wonder that McCartney is held in awe, even by those

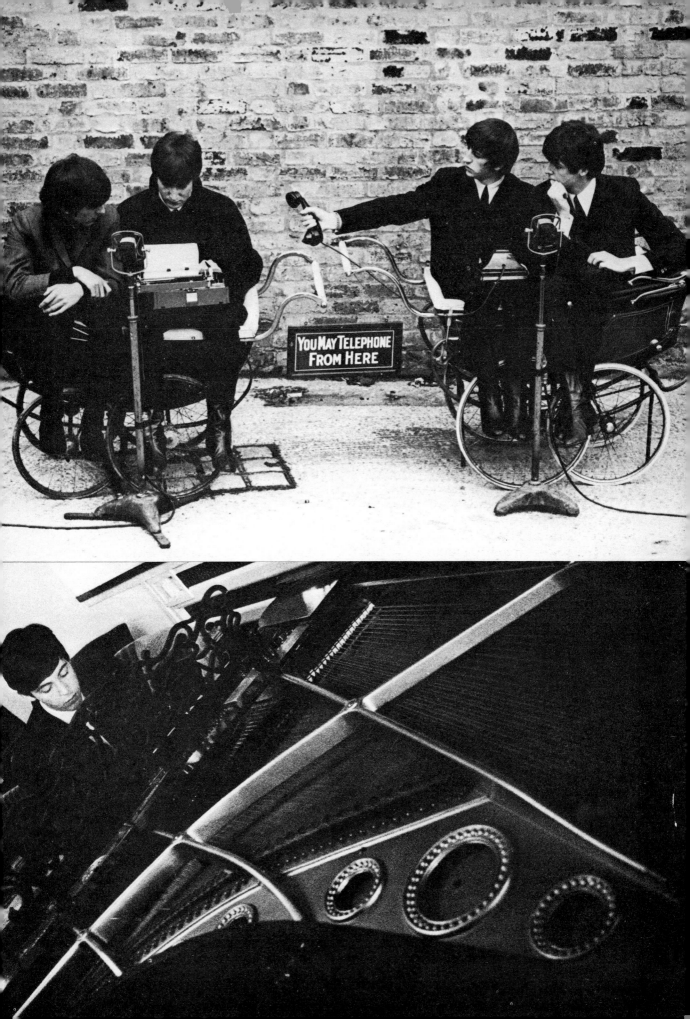

closest to him. The multi-facets of his personality slowly revolve to reveal themselves, some glittering, some opaque, all somewhat mysterious.

McCartney has himself suffered innumerable blows; some through envy, or sheer thoughtlessness. Those who live in the glare of constant publicity come to expect to pay this price for their position and prestige. It does not make them any less immune to the blows when they fall, often with devastating power. In his time, Paul has been accused of writing 'Muzak', of active treachery, nepotism and being dead (following the bizarre campaign of anonymous American freaks). The fact he can still smile a crooked smile after having abuse heaped on his songs, his band and even his wife, says much for the inner comfort provided by the Liverpudlian sense of humour and the stability of a happy childhood. Paul learned early on, as do most middle class children growing up in a tough city environment, that there are plenty ready to knock you down, for whatever reason, without warning, at anytime.

When Paul talks in interviews, on TV, or even through the wry couplets in his lyrics, it is with the accumulated, handed-down wisdom of the British family realists, proud, optimistic and slightly defensive. 'It's alright for some,' Paul will say to cap his own story of some latest extravagance, a wild party, or a trip round the world. And echoing through his 'music hall' songs like *When I'm 64* and *Admiral Halsey* is the memory of family sing songs and the collective fun of childhood. It's a characteristic that enfuriates those who perhaps never knew or enjoyed such security, and found it easier to identify with the angst and confusion of John Lennon. Those who still take sides after all these years, should remember that it all began with a bond of friendship between the unlike poles of John and Paul. Neither could be blamed for the forces that tore them apart.

The Beatles grew up rapidly in an age when most British teenagers remained innocent, often until their twenties. As itinerate rock 'n' rollers, tasting freedom in Germany of the post war boom years, they were already sufficiently worldly wise to prepare them in some measure for the astonishing explosion of Beatlemania.

Even when the pressure was at its greatest, when they were being mobbed, trampled underfoot and idolised, they revelled in it all, laughing and joking and delighted at their good fortune. People could do what they like, abuse them as blasphemers or award them medals of honour. Nothing could take away their ability to go on making hit songs, and they had the collective strength of their shared experience.

But even in the pop group boom, The Beatles were in a sense outsiders, larger than life and strangely ill-equipped to cope when the split came in 1970. The group had been off the road for years and existed only in the studio, on film or TV. Since their touring days, a whole new generation of groups had sprung up, whose music and playing ability seemed far in advance of anything The Beatles had done. In the light of Cream, The Jimi Hendrix Experience and The Mothers Of Invention, The Beatles, even with *Sgt. Pepper* as the shining achievement of the age, had begun to appear rather quaint. Hugely influential, but so far above the mainstream of rock, as to be on a different plain. Indeed, The Beatles were like a huge albatross around the necks of rock musicians, and their passing was almost greeted with a sense of relief. Its removal meant everyone else could get on with their lives.

When Paul crept out into the sunlight of freedom, it is unlikely he felt any sense of competition with the bands who were then busy energising the 'progressive rock' scene like Yes, The Nice, ELP, Jethro Tull, King Crimson and Led Zeppelin.

He was a rocker at heart and a romantic who loved a good tune. There was no chance he would become involved in the heavy rock juggernaut, but he would look closely at the new sound systems the bands were using, their elaborate stage presentations, their appeal to world wide audiences, and the way rock had become a form of mass entertainment. He would absorb, adapt and utilise these ideas, as he gradually fashioned Wings. From hesitant, nervous beginnings, it would eventually rival all the supergroups at their own game.

There was a plan for Wings and it worked. Paul was less successful in finding a firm, cohesive direction for his own career. His

ability to write songs appealing to the broad mass of the public, as well as more specialist and partisan pop fans, meant he had a duty to both audiences which could never be conveniently reconciled. The howls of anguish that greeted *Mull Of Kintyre* from rockers was only matched by the roar of approval from those who couldn't resist a Scottish ballad.

The idea of his becoming an entertainer in the showbusiness tradition was perhaps not entirely unappealing. But when he tried it with a TV spectacular and was rebuffed, he drew back from the allure of the top hat, white tie and tails. His music was beefed up and there was always a rock 'n' roll alternative supplied with the ballads to meet the demands of all his followers.

A new partnership was formed with singer, guitarist and composer, Denny Laine. It would never attain the public recognition of Lennon & McCartney but nevertheless formed a useful and productive team. Paul could not work entirely in a vacuum and the drift together with Denny was almost an act of stealth. No one really noticed Paul had a new partner so they could never accuse Denny of trying to upstage or replace John Lennon. Tough on Denny perhaps, but he proved a sympathetic and stalwart friend, at a time when Paul may have been forgiven for thinking there were few to be found.

The decision to bring Linda into Wings baffled and infuriated Beatle-watchers. As John had involved Yoko in all his projects, so Paul was determined that Linda should not be left at home. She would accompany him on his perilous journey back from post-Beatles hibernation and be given a positive role to play. This descent into apparent amateurism and self-indulgence by both the Lennon and McCartney camps seemed like a slap in the face. And who was this American woman who had not only taken off Britain's most eligible bachelor but now had the audacity to attempt to play in his band? The Royal Family had not only quit Buckingham Palace; they were now holding a campfire knees-up in St. James Park.

Even as the press fulminated against her alleged inability and questioned her right to exist, there was a significant welcoming response by the public and fans. Paul had trusted his own judgement and got it right.

The low-key approach to the start of Wings was absolutely right. Here was the super Beatle prepared to knuckle down and start all over again, going out on the road, playing to students at unpublicised concerts. It may have been avoiding the scrutiny of the music press but it was also building firm foundations of trust and it did Paul's credibility no end of good. While the rest of The Beatles were involved in media campaigns, Indian mysticism or off the wall movie ventures, there was McCartney digging in and playing to whoever would come and listen. It wasn't a ploy, a marketing move, or shrewd PR. It was a genuine desire to get out and do all the things denied The Beatles in their latter years.

Why should the Seventies rock stars have all the fun? Wings would provide his base for operations, give him the chance to present his songs, old and new, in the most appropriate setting, and give him room to manoeuvre outside the group, without being tied down or totally committed. Paul has remained busy, restless and full of ideas throughout his career, always ready to take on new challenges whether writing film music or creating a movie. The burden of prejudice and hostility will always be lurking in the shadows but now he seems past caring what anybody thinks and does what he enjoys. He just hopes somebody else will enjoy it too, and they usually do, in vast numbers.

In the closing months of 1982, Paul announced that he was to star in his own musical drama, *Give My Regards To Broad Street*. It was conceived and written by Paul and based on a day in his life. It marked his first solo acting role and script writing debut, with filming carried out on location in England. A reporter for one of London's commercial radio stations, told of the plan responded tartly: 'It's just a bit of self-indulgence isn't it?'

Most peoples' lives suffer from conflicting pressures on a sliding scale, depending on their good or ill fortune and amount of personal activity. The hyper-active, workaholic is likely to win and lose on a scale that would terrify the average man content to plod along a dull, predictable course. Paul has known great wealth, acclaim and led a life rich in excitement since the day he met John

Lennon back in 1956.

For McCartney, normality is the greatest prize. To have a drink with people he can count on as friends, to watch his family grow up, and to listen to the music of Buddy Holly and favourite rock 'n' roll heroes of his boyhood, counts far more than being an 'ex-Beatle', or an object of public scrutiny, whose every move is examined and whose motives are questioned in a system of positive vetting, that seems far more thorough than anything devised by the nation's security services.

There should never be any doubt that Paul's life is of his own choosing. He could have retired after The Beatles faded away but nothing could have seemed more boring. He was, and is, immensely proud of the old group and its achievements. It was this pride that prevented them from reforming simply for the sake of cash inducements. And the weariness that Paul shows now on the subject is induced not so much by the memory of the band he helped create and guide, as simply by the old controversies constantly dredged up.

Indeed, McCartney will willingly talk about The Beatles and will show visitors to EMI's studios in Abbey Road the very spot where all the old hits were made with great affection. His conflicts are hinted at in the song *Tug Of War*, where he explains that he and John Lennon were trying to outscore each other, and neither had been able to let go.

The unpredictable response of the public and media to his work with conflicting cries of 'genius' and 'self-indulgence', the 'Tug Of War' between himself and those who mean most to him, the need for fulfilment and the wellspring of talent within, have all combined to shape the man in the blue pullover.

We cannot presume to say we know anyone heart and soul. Like the famous tin of sardines mentioned in *Beyond The Fringe*, there is always that little bit in the corner you can't get out. But by telling the story of Paul McCartney, we can examine the evidence, and perhaps learn a little more and gain some modicum of insight and understanding, that is not already provided by Paul's own words and music.

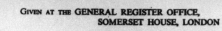
The statutory fee for this certificate is 3s. 9d.
Where a search is necessary to find the entry,
a search fee is payable in addition.

REGISTRATION DISTRICT _____ Liverpool North

1942 BIRTH in the Sub-district of _____ Walton Park _____ in the _____ County Borough of Liverpool

Columns :—	1	2	3	4	5	6	7	8	9	10*
No.	When and where born	Name, if any	Sex	Name, and surname of father	Name, surname, and maiden surname of mother	Occupation of father	Signature, description, and residence of informant	When registered	Signature of registrar	Name entered after registration
240	Eighteenth June 1942. 107 Rice Lane u d	James Paul	Boy	James McCartney	Mary Patricia McCartney formerly Mohin	Centre lathe turner (aircraft factory) of 10 Sunbury Road Liverpool 4.	g. McCartney father. 10 Sunbury Road Liverpool	Fourteenth July 1942.	WSBailey Registrar	

CERTIFIED to be a true copy of an entry in the certified copy of a Register of Births in the District above mentioned.

Given at the GENERAL REGISTER OFFICE, SOMERSET HOUSE, LONDON, under the Seal of the said Office, the 17th day of July 1968

*See note overleaf

BX 524344

Chapter Two

BACK TO THE EGG

Paul McCartney, like millions of teenagers growing up in Britain during the late Fifties, was smitten by a strange disease. It was diagnosed as a severe attack of skiffle-itis, further complicated by a bout of rock 'n' roll. And it presented parents with the alarming spectacle of their sons and daughters apparently losing touch with reality.

The parents were the generation who grew up knowing mass unemployment in the decade before the war, and then a struggle to 'make ends meet', in the grey years of austerity and rationing that followed.

The new generation was poised to reap the benefits of a consumer boom and the era of 'You've never had it so good.' Suddenly, youth discovered they could be 'teenagers' too, just like the Americans they saw in the movies, wearing garish clothes and listening to popnetrate the heavily edited chat that perhaps it was time to let Paul McCartney off the hook about the old group.

Faded snapshots of yesteryear show youth in the Fifties as mirror images of their parents, in the same conservative suits and frocks. There were dances and bands and punch-ups and even proto Teddy Boys, who appeared as far back as 1951, during the Festival of Britain. But with National Service waiting to whisk any potential juvenile delinquents off to Cyprus or Malaya, there was no sign of a teenage culture with money to burn.

The war babies were due for a pleasant surprise. Conscription ended officially in 1963, but most of those who left school in 1958 knew they no longer faced the threat of being called up and made to undergo the discipline and brutalisation of Second World War training methods. If it had not been phased out, then we would doubtless be listening still to Vera Lynn and The Beatles would have never existed.

James Paul McCartney, MBE, was born in Walton Hospital, Liverpool on the 18th of June, 1942, not long after the Blitz and a few years before the arrival of the Flying Bombs and V1 Rockets. He was the son of James and Mary McCartney. Paul also has a younger brother, Michael, who later achieved fame as Mike McGear with Scaffold, the poetry and satire group.

Paul went to Stockton Road Primary School and then to Joseph Williams Primary. Passing his 11-plus examination, he went to the Liverpool Institute – a grammar school. It must have been a source of great pride to Mr. McCartney and Mary that their son had started life so well.

Jim had begun work at the age of 14 in the cotton trade. During the war, Jim got married and took a job at a local engineering works. Michael was born in 1944 and early on the two brothers displayed different characteristics. Paul was quiet and mischievous; Michael was noisy and argumentative. Both were good looking, although Paul was prone to podginess at odd stages, as man and boy. Jim hoped his eldest would go to university but reckoned without the disruptive influence of pop music. Music and rebellious tendencies – the result was a career that would astonish the world as well as his family.

The McCartney's moved from Speke to Allerton and lived happily until Paul's mother, who had worked as a midwife, died suddenly from cancer at the age of forty-five,

1948 photograph of Paul and his brother Mike, aged six and eight respectively. Mike is Mike McGear of The Scaffold.

just a few weeks after developing pains. Paul was fourteen years old. It was a devastating blow and when Paul took up playing guitar with an almost fanatical devotion, it led some to suspect the guitar was a substitute for his loss. Certainly for a bright, teenager, the guitar was a passport to freedom and a totem for individuality.

Unless you are going to be a folk singer, playing in the bedroom is a lonely business. It wasn't long before Paul looked around for a group to play with.

At least he had the example of his father to encourage him in his growing interest in performing. Jim McCartney had led a dance band before the war, known somewhat cutely as The Jim Mac Jazz Band. He played the piano and trumpet and his band supplied music for dances and even the silent movies. He rather hoped that Paul, who had done so well in exams, would pursue an academic rather than musical career, but nevertheless gave him a trumpet for his birthday.

Paul had been brought up to enjoy music of all kinds. His father played the piano at home a lot and Paul liked to sing songs from the shows. Good tunes like *Over The Rainbow* and *White Christmas* and not so silly love songs. The McCartney family piano came from North End Music Stores, known to all as NEMS. At one stage, Jim hoped Paul would join the Liverpool Cathedral Choir but, having failed the audition, he sang with the St. Barnabas Choir.

Quite early on, Paul learned the power of a lyric and a melody to move people and appreciated the virtues of simplicity and sentiment. He attended his first pop concert at the age of twelve, when he saw the British drummer and band leader Eric Delaney at Liverpool Empire. Eric was a showman who soloed on *Skin Deep* and jumped on his drumkit for the grand finale. A couple of years later in 1956, he went to the Empire again to see Lonnie Donegan and his skiffle group. The effect of Donegan's performance on schoolkids everywhere was profound. Donegan had the mad, frantic quality of a rock 'n' roller, even if the musical backing was acoustic, not electric. Lonnie's power to move audiences and his star quality impressed Paul and led him to clamour for a guitar.

Paul knew he couldn't sing and play the trumpet at the same time. The trumpet was also hard on the lips and difficult to master. A guitar would give him the right sound for the exciting new forms of popular music breaking over the nation's ears.

Jim was now attempting to bring up the family alone with not much money coming in, but he managed to buy Paul a guitar for fifteen pounds. He sat down at the piano with his son and showed him some chords. It was then discovered that although Paul was normally right handed, he needed to restring his guitar for left handed playing. Once he had sorted out a comfortable playing stance, the guitar became an obsession. And he was now equipped to join the great rock and skiffle boom.

Skiffle was introduced to Britain by Lonnie Donegan, while he was a banjo player with Chris Barber's jazz band. The skiffle group was part of the Barber set up, performing the stomping home made music of the 1920s that poor Americans played at parties to raise the rent money. Anything could be used to bang out a tune and a rhythm. With a repertoire of easily played, immensely catchy tunes, skiffle came as a ready-made package to excite any bunch of school friends growing out of stamp collecting and building wireless sets.

Donegan hit the charts with *Rock Island Line* in 1956. Within months skiffle mania swept the country. Every school, almost every classroom, had its own skiffle group. The author belonged to one in 1957 called: The Catford Skiffle Kings, playing the washboard with thimbles. The rest of the boys were on home made acoustic guitars, and a tea chest bass complete with broomhandle and string. Many were the blisters, shouting matches and fights as schoolboys attempted to undergo the disciplines of such mysterious rites as 'rehearsals', or as they were usually called: 'practice sessions.' 'Are you coming round our house for a practice?', was the cry when the schoolbell rang. Thus, skiffle provided an army of teenage musicians, all busily learning to be masters of the washboard and guitar, and gaining their first experience as public performers at the local youth club.

It was a marvellous time. The petty crime rate dropped. Guitar makers didn't know

what hit them. But an even more powerful force was beaming across the Atlantic. Although *Rock Island Line* was a hit in America, most Americans had never heard of skiffle. It had long since been forgotten and had been unearthed by British record collectors. What concerned the new generation from New York to New Orleans was the explosive impact of rock 'n' roll.

The same musicologists who rediscovered skiffle announced that the new phenomenon was a commercialised form of black rhythm 'n' blues. But it wasn't quite as simple as that. Rock 'n' roll had a heavy off beat and 12-bar blues structure but was altogether faster, louder and more flamboyant. It wasn't aimed at Black American industrial workers but young whites at High School. It spawned a whole new breed of heroes whose fame spread around the world.... Little Richard, Elvis Presley, Bill Haley, Fats Domino, Gene Vincent, Buddy Holly, The Everly Brothers, Jerry Lee Lewis, Carl Perkins, Eddie Cochran and Chuck Berry.

Their records, imaginative, electrifying, raw and rebellious, transformed popular music and started a movement that would last thirty years and flourish in many guises. And the school kids who were first exposed to its influence converted their own enthusiasm as fans into active participation that led to an even greater rock boom in later years.

At first, BBC radio failed to play the new music pouring into Britain's juke boxes and record shops. They simply didn't have the programming to cope with the onslaught. They were still thinking in terms of 'a recital of gramophone records' and pop music was the province of big bands and ballad singers. But rock 'n' roll was big news. The Daily Mirror did much to foster the interests of the music and served its young, working class readers well, even sponsoring the first visit to Britain by Bill Haley and the Comets. And there was Radio Luxembourg, the commercial station beaming rock from the Continent with signals that tended to fade just at the most exciting moment of a Gene Vincent hit.

On national radio, the first airing of the mysterious new style came when a vocal group called The Stargazers sang *Shake, Rattle & Roll* with the Cyril Stapleton Showband on the BBC Light Programme. Even this non-authentic version could not conceal from audiences the vigour and excitement of the music. And when John Lennon, Paul McCartney, George Harrison and Ringo Starr heard *Heartbreak Hotel* by Elvis Presley, it was a divine revelation. Even more than *Rock Island Line*, this classic performance by the young lion of rock inspired the nascent Beatles into action.

Before Paul had met Lennon, he was developing his skill in the bedroom in front of the mirror, immitating his heroes like Little Richard and Eddie Cochran. He learned to scream and shout and make it sound soulful, with the high whoops and preaching tones that would later become a Beatles trademark. Music making is meant to be a shared experience. It requires you to show off, yet be part of a team. Paul began to learn the required skills early on. He was taken to a Butlin's holiday camp at Filey in Wales when he was fourteen. All such camps relied on talent shows as an important part of their regular entertainments for visitors and a McCartney relative was one of the famous 'Redcoats', whose job it was to get everyone involved. As a result of prompting from the Redcoat, both Paul and Michael went up on stage to have a go at entertaining the mums and dads. Michael had broken his arm and wore it in a sling, but they had brought their guitars to the camp and were determined to show what they could do. We can imagine the laughter and cheers as the two boys earnestly sang *Bye Bye Love*, The Everly Brothers' latest and *Long Tall Sally*, that most shocking exhibition by Little Richard.

Paul's 'Little Richard' act was one of several that delighted his classmates and it served him in good stead that day he went to the Woolton village fete with his friend, Ivan Vaughan. Ivan had told him about this chap John Lennon whose band, The Quarry Men, would be playing.

John, too, had been turned on to music by Donegan hits like *Cumberland Gap* and *Rock Island Line*. But he found rock 'n' roll much more exciting and wanted to sing *Blue Suede Shoes* like Elvis, even when they entered skiffle contests. The Quarry Men advertised themselves as capable of playing all kinds of music, from rock and skiffle to country &

western.

John had been to Quarry Bank High School, which he joined in 1952 and where he quickly won a reputation as a rebel, trouble maker and class clown. His two great friends were Pete Shotton and Ivan Vaughan and, as 1956 dawned, they all became drawn to pop music to provide a focus for somewhat motiveless lives.

Lennon had no musical training but learned to play the harmonica when he was about ten. The impact of *Rock Around The Clock*, played by Bill Haley & The Comets in the movie *Blackboard Jungle,* and Elvis Presley's *Heartbreak Hotel* galvanised John into thinking more seriously about music. John's mother, Julia, bought him his first guitar for ten pounds and she taught him some banjo chords. It wasn't long before John had formed a group with his mates from school which played at parties and weddings, dressed as Teddy Boys.

With such groups constantly fighting among themselves, there was a discernible tendency to weed out the no-hopers among the amateur musicians and to replace them with boys who took it more seriously. Thus began the long process that would result in a school skiffle group becoming a world beating band.

Lennon was born on October 9, 1940, the son of Julia and Freddy Lennon. The latter had run off to sea and Julia handed over the baby to the care of her sister Mimi. John grew up in the suburb of Woolton and went to Dovedale Primary before joining Quarry Bank.

John was always a leader, whether in mischief or music, and his band may have been formed for laughs but surely played with all the passion at its command. It was on July 6, 1957 that The Quarry Men were booked to play at the garden fete in Woolton and here Paul saw John for the first time, playing the old favourites like *Cumberland Gap.*

Later the pair were introduced to each other at the nearby church hall, where the Quarry Men were due to play again later that evening. The monumental friendship began with the revelation that Paul could tune his own guitar and could therefore assist John in this difficult task. And while John tended to forget the words to the rock 'n' roll classics, Paul knew them all off by

heart and would write them out for John, if he so desired. John had tended to cover up his deficiencies by making up his own lyrics and enjoying his love of word play in the process.

The bond of friendship was finally sealed when Paul gave his famous Little Richard impersonation. About a week after Paul had shown John the words to *Twenty Flight Rock* whilst trying to avoid Lennon's somewhat beery breath, he got a message that John wanted him to join the Quarry Men. Paul hadn't bothered to join any of his own school groups so he was free to team up with Lennon. A vacancy occurred in the Quarry Men when John broke a washboard over Pete Shotton's head and the latter retired from the scene. Remembered John years later: 'That was the day – when I met Paul, that it started moving.'

The band with Paul and John played a gig at a local Conservative Club and quite soon Paul began to influence the way the group was run. They got themselves uniforms and Paul questioned the need for their manager Nigel Whalley to receive the same money as the rest of the group from gigs. Paul also attempted to improve the musical standards, trying to coax better performances from the drummer Colin Hanton, which led to rumblings of resentment.

But the new, serious approach to the band, with Paul's added expertise as a rock 'n' roller, meant that the group could command better bookings and more money. Towards the end of the year they were invited to play at a new jazz club opened by Alan Synter, a doctor's son, in Matthew Street, Liverpool. Situated in a cellar under some warehouses, it was called The Cavern.

After leaving school, John, who had intended running away to sea, was sent to Liverpool art college. The Quarry Men continued, with George Harrison a young friend of Paul's added on guitar. It was around this time that Paul and John started to write their own songs. For a short while they changed the name of the group to Johnny and the Moondogs, but they did hardly any work at all during 1958 as skiffle died out and the pop scene underwent one of its transformations.

The following year they reformed as The Silver Beatles with Stuart Sutcliffe, an art

student friend of John's on bass guitar. The band went on a tour of Scotland organised by Larry Parnes, the pop star manager, who used them as a backing group. In 1960, the group made its first trip to Hamburg, the German seaport that closely resembled Liverpool. They were booked by German promoter Bruno Koschmider who knew that the English were second best to the Americans in supplying authentic rock 'n' roll for his clubs.

When Paul first teamed up with Lennon he played guitar and spent many hours with John at home, teaching the latter all the chords he knew. He blew his opportunity to be the band's lead guitarist when he messed up a solo at that first performance at the Broadway Conservative Club. He was relegated to rhythm guitar until they got to Hamburg, where he began playing a more powerful electric guitar. When this fell apart from the battering it took at the nightly performances, Paul switched to piano to play numbers by Ray Charles and Jerry Lee Lewis. When the bassist, Stu Sutcliffe left the group, he loaned Paul his bass. He had to play it upside down to suit his fingering and with piano strings because of the shortage of bass strings. Eventually, he saved up enough money to buy his first Hofner violin shaped bass guitar, which produced a much better sound and became forever identified with McCartney.

The Quarry Men name was dropped in 1959 because it was nolonger relevant with Paul and new boy George, both attending the Institute, and John at Art College. The year was spent in desultory fashion calling themselves silly names and playing at parties for nothing, and still hopefully entering talent contests.

George, the new guitar player, was born on February 25, 1943 in Wavertree, Liverpool to Harold and Louise Harrison. Harold was a bus driver and George was their third son. He went to Dovedale Primary School but never met John Lennon while he was there as he was two and a half years younger and three classes behind. Paul was only one year ahead, however, when George joined the Liverpool Institute in 1954. When he was fourteen, he started taking an interest in playing the guitar and he too fell under the spell of Lonnie Donegan. His mother

bought him a guitar for three pounds and encouraged him to learn to play, even though the strings caused him great agony. Eventually, he got a thirty pound electric guitar which proved much more rewarding to play.

His first group was called The Rebels, which played its debut at the Speke British Legion. In the meantime, he had become close friends with Paul, travelling to school on the bus and talking about guitars. They spent hours playing together, well before Paul had met John. When Paul joined The Quarry Men, he invited George along to see them play and John called up the younger boy to play *Raunchy*, a rock instrumental at which George excelled. From then on, Harrison was part of the group armed, despite his youth, with a good deal of hard won musical experience.

The band and music took up most of the time that was spent either eyeing girls or experimenting with drink. There was not a lot of devotion to academic study, although Paul took a couple of 'O' level exams, passing one. He took another six subjects and it was hoped that he would go to a teacher training college but Paul's teachers and his father had reckoned without the disruptive influence of John Lennon. Paul easily charmed people into believing he was working hard when he was actually 'sagging off' school to practice music with John.

It was during such sessions that John and Paul began to write songs. One of the first was by Paul called, *I Lost My Little Girl*, which he played to John for his comments and approval. Lennon, the man who loved to make up words when he forgot the official lyrics, found that full time song writing was fun. And there began that spirit of competition between the two friends, both trying to outdo each other's latest song. Sometimes they wrote together, or else the songs were strictly Lennon or McCartney products.

Paul started writing lyrics using his guitar to work out the chord sequence. *I Lost My Little Girl* was based on the three chords of G, G7 and C. Sometimes Paul used the piano at home to work out a number and at the age of sixteen he wrote a song that would become one of his most famous and popular, the whimsical, but witty, *When I'm Sixty-Four*. He thought it might be useful for a musical comedy, if not for Paul McCartney, trainee teacher of the future. As he set to work, he either wrote the song as a poem which he later set to music, like *All My Loving*, or the music came in a moment of inspiration and the words were conjured later. One of his finest compositions, *Yesterday*, came to him after waking from a dream, and the extraordinary working title for the tune, held to be one of the most beautiful in pop music, was *Scrambled Egg*. Paul was rightly proud of the melody which was completely original and perfectly formed.

It was the song writing race between John and Paul which would supply The Beatles with the great mass of material that so startled a public used to British groups as little more than pale shadows of the Americans, covering the latest imported hits.

With John enjoying the freedom of the art college, it wasn't long before Paul and George would be lured from school. George left in 1959 and started doing a day job as an apprentice electrician. Paul was in the Sixth Form, preparing for English and Art 'A' levels. But they spent most of their time at one of their parents' home rehearsing. Jim McCartney encouraged the band as he could hear them getting better, and they certainly were a lot louder and harder.

The band didn't get much encouragement in its early days. One of their biggest disappointments was when they took part in a Carroll Levis Discovery show in Manchester. They had called themselves Johnny And The Moondogs, especially for the show, and went down quite well on their first spot. But they could not stay for the all important final spot, where the audience applause would judge the winners. They had to take the last train home to Liverpool – as decided losers.

But at least 1959 wasn't a dead loss. It was the year John Lennon dreamed up the most enduring name for the group. Buddy Holly And The Crickets were at the forefront of the latest wave of rock 'n' roll and John and Paul were great fans of their music and name. It was John who suggested they find an alternative insect.... not Crickets, but Beatles. And scribbling down the name, it seemed clever and amusing to alter Beetles to BEATles. The word had a wonderful symmetry, quaint, yet strong. And its pluralistic nature seemed to invite people to join in,

whatever strange activities Beatles got up to. But there were protests that the name was too short and simple. For the rest of 1959, they were The Silver Beatles.

They auditioned for Larry Parnes, who gave them their first professional engagement with the two week tour of Scotland. The line up included John, Paul, George, Stuart Sutcliffe on bass and Johnny Hutch on drums, and their job was to back Parnes' singer, Johnny Gentle. When they went out on the road, Hutch was replaced by another drummer, Tommy Moore. After the trip to Scotland, Parnes offered them no more work and they were back in Liverpool playing for anybody, including a stripper, and anywhere, including once again, The Cavern.

In August 1960, a new drummer Pete Best, whose mother had opened and run the Casbah Club, was invited by Paul to join the Silver Beatles. He had first met them when The Quarry Men played at the opening night of the Casbah, situated in the cellar of Mrs. Best's house. The new Silver Beatles had got a gig in Hamburg and needed a good drummer to go with them.

One of Liverpool's great characters was a man called Allan Williams, who ran a club called The Jackaranda. He had helped the Silver Beatles get onto Larry Parnes's Scottish tour and their German dates. Pete Best went for his audition with the group at Allan's club and played with more convincing power than any of his predecessors. He was also much better looking.

The trip to Germany was a great adventure and there were some parental objections. Paul's father was upset at the thought of his son rushing off abroad, before the exam results had come in, which would determine whether he could go to the teacher training college. Eventually, Allan Williams came round to persuade him to let Paul go. The party set off by road in an old van and crossed by ferry to the Continent, heading for Hamburg without any work permits.

The band were booked to play at the Indra Club for eight weeks, playing between four to six hours a night, including weekends. It was the kind of gruelling hard work that would forever strip away their happy amateur status and turn them into seasoned pros as they blasted out their favourites by Carl Perkins and Chuck Berry. Later, they

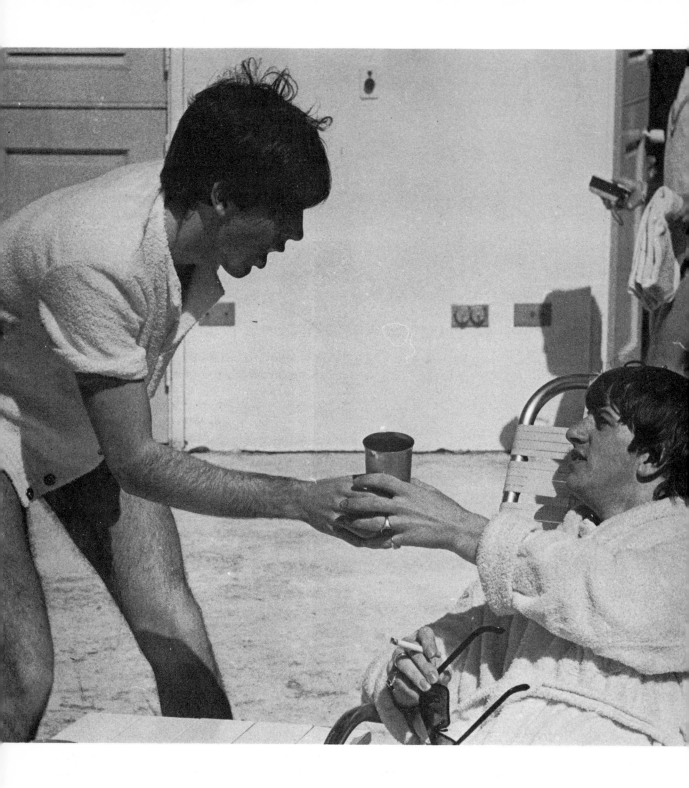

moved on to the Kaiserkeller, where they existed on pils, beer and chips for what seemed like an eternity. At least the daylight hours could be spent writing more songs.

The saga of their German days included the love affair between Stu Sutcliffe and Astrid Kirchner. The German girl befriended the group and helped change their appearance from Merseyside Teds to German student intellectuals, with new clothes and hair styles.

It was in Hamburg that The Beatles became aware of the drumming of Ringo Starr, then with Rory Storm, another Liverpool band playing the Hamburg clubs. Ringo watched their hard stomping set with great interest. He could hardly guess how their futures would be bound up.

When they moved from the Kaiserkeller to the larger Top Ten Club, it was revealed to the authorities that George Harrison was only seventeen and too young to be working in a night club. He was ordered to leave the country, and much to his despair had to go home alone by train. A day later, Pete Best and Paul McCartney were both arrested by the police and accused of starting a fire. They had returned to their old lodgings to rescue their belongings. Paul had lit a match to see where they were going in the darkened premises and accidentally set fire to some of the drapes. They were released and departed, and then John was sent home as well, followed by Stu. It seemed like the end of The Beatles, when they arrived back at Christmas 1960 with no money and no prospects. Paul eventually got himself a job with the Speedy Prompt Delivery company, helping to deliver parcels. When this job fell through, he went onto winding electrical coils and making tea for seven pounds a week. He stuck it out for a couple of months, The Beatles always at the foremost in his thoughts, even though the band hardly spoke to each other after the Hamburg disaster. They played their first return booking in Liverpool back at the Casbah teenage club, where they surprised local fans with their new found vigour and rocking skill.

Although it seemed as if they had blown their big chance of earning fame and money abroad, 1961 would see a renewed drive for success. They played peculiar gigs, like the legendary trip to Aldershot, their first performance down south. After Beatlemania broke a couple of years later, Londoners in particular were amused to learn how The Beatles had come so close to them in their formative years and played to a crowd of about eighteen people.

More important to the group as a turning point, was the dance they played at Litherland Town Hall on December 27, 1960 when local girls began screaming and demanding autographs. They thought the strange looking group, billed as direct from Hamburg, must be German. There was no doubt in those first weeks of the New Year that Pete Best was coming in for a lot of the attention from fans and doubtless Paul was not exactly pleased to be upstaged in the good looks department, either by Stu or Pete. There were squabbles, even fights, but most of them were put down to the exhaustion and strain of working long hours in exhausting conditions.

The band had, at last, found a permanent home in Liverpool at The Cavern Club, the same cellar that The Quarry Men had played a few years earlier. With skiffle long dead, and the Trad boom waning, the jazz club needed to find more popular attractions and was forced to relax its jazz-only policy. With promptings from Beatle supporters like Pete Best's mum and deejay Bob Wooler, the group were hired for new lunch-time sessions, designed to lure in the city's office workers. They began the historic residency in January 1961, after an initial booking on a Tuesday evening, on a guest spot with the regular band, The Blue Genes, who they blew off stage. When they began their regular lunch time sessions, the queues stretched all the way down Matthew Street, as young girls flocked to see the exciting new local band, with Bob Wooler as compere and deejay.

The Beatles' parents went to see their boys at work, some shocked, some delighted. It was impossible to deny the impact the group were having on audiences in the hot, steaming, airless atmosphere, where the band played its bizarre mixture of rock, pop and standards. The Beatles were always determined to be different right from the beginning, and Paul would sing *Till There Was You*, a beautiful ballad that contrasted nicely with *Roll Over Beethoven*.

When Paul sang *Long Tall Sally*, it had a riotous effect on the fans, and the excitement of being a performer, screamed at by the boys and girls and constantly asked for his autograph had to be better than winding coils or delivering parcels. If Paul picked on Stu or Pete Best during the band's periodic teenage rows, it was usually because he wanted to go on improving the band's sound and did not approve of Stu's weak bass playing. When The Beatles went back to Hamburg in April, to play once more at the Top Ten Club, developments would go Paul's way.

They were met in Germany by Astrid and her intellectual friends, the existentialists or 'exis' as they were nicknamed, and who had adopted The Beatles as their own. The time had come for the group to make their first proper recordings, and they were called upon to back Tony Sheridan, under the auspices of German band leader Bert Kaempfert. At the same time, Stu left the group, no longer to be the butt of John and Paul's jibes, but to become once more an art student, and to settle down to marry Astrid and live in Hamburg. It was a brave move that impressed John who, on his return to Liverpool, would engage in mad correspondence with his old friend. There was one positive aspect of this move as far as the group was concerned. The way was now clear for Paul to become the bass player, the role he had long coveted.

By summer, the number of good bands in Liverpool like The Beatles and Gerry and the Pacemakers, was sufficient to warrant a specialist music newspaper to cover their activities. One of John's friends, Bill Harry, decided to start one, called Mersey Beat. It's first edition carried an amusing story about the birth of The Beatles – written by John. Merseybeat charted the rise in popularity of the group destined to spearhead a social revolution.

Recalls Bill Harry, now a PR for RAK Records: 'I was at art college in the Fifties, during the time of the skiffle bands, with John Lennon and Stu Sutcliffe. Attached to the art college is the Liverpool Institute where Paul was studying. We used to have art college dances and I was on the students' union committee with Stuart Sutcliffe. We always referred to the band as 'John's

Group.' They weren't even called The Beatles then. They used to come in and rehearse in what we called The Life Room, where they drew the nude models. They were huge rooms with skylights.

'I remember in one corner playing the kazoo with my band, and Paul and John in the other corner, doing their rehearsals.'

Bill booked John and Paul for the art college dances, and at the committee meetings he and Stuart proposed they use SU funds to buy the nascent Beatles equipment. Dances were held in the basement canteen and on Saturday night, the gloom gave a Cavernlike atmosphere, even before The Cavern had opened.

Every year, Liverpool witnessed the spectacle of Rag Day, when the university students had floats riding through the city, collecting for local charities. The art college joined in and everyone dressed up. Bill remembers talking to Paul on the art college steps, dressed up as a woman. 'He had a scarf over his head and a frock.'

Bill was so intrigued by the band, he went to all their early gigs, including those at the legendary Jackaranda, run by Allan Williams. It was the club where Pete Best auditioned for the group in early 1960. Says Bill: 'At The Jackaranda, we used to sit around all day with a cup of coffee. The toast used to cost fourpence and if you paid fivepence you got jam on it. The Beatles got gigs there when the regular West Indian steel band wasn't there. It was in a tiny brick walled cellar. They used to tie the mikes to broom handles because they couldn't afford any mike stands.'

Bill Harry became a great champion of The Beatles, to the extent of pestering George Harrison into writing his first song (named in response to Bill's constant cries of "Why don't you write like John and Paul?" *Don't Bother Me*). He set up Merseybeat to foster The Beatles as well as all the other Merseyside groups, and to this day retains the secret smile of a man who remembers when nobody outside of Liverpool could be cajoled into taking an interest.

Although he first became friends with John, he had a great liking and respect for Paul. 'Paul was an easy person to get on with. Pete Best was very hard and difficult to talk to. He was introverted and you couldn't hold much of a conversation. You'd have to do all the talking. That was part of his appeal. It was a James Dean thing. In those days everybody wanted to be like James Dean – mean, moody and magnificent. Paul had what they call 'middle class values' and that was due to his father Jim who was a lovely man. Jim respected people's feelings and was sensitive to people. He taught Paul always to be courteous and not to be rude and to help people out. Paul would have made a great PR man. I always thought of him as The Beatles PR.'

'I always found Paul very caring towards people. I can't understand the villification he's received in the media over the years. He was cast as the baddie when The Beatles broke up without anyone really understanding. It was the only way he could do things at that time. He was advised to do that and he had no other choice. And then of course, for some reason, people resented Linda. He made his choice, got married and had a happy family. Other people seem to resent this, as if they have a right to be part of his life. They would have preferred the fairy tale romance with Jane Asher to have continued, and they were disappointed when it didn't.'

Bill remembers a night when in the hurly burly of trying to escape from a Beatles concert after the show, he left all his money and clothes in the back of Paul's car. He and his wife, Virginia, were stranded in Manchester at midnight. The next day Paul's dad came and delivered all Bill's stuff, explaining that Paul had circled the theatre trying to find the errant Merseybeaters.

'Paul was always the diplomat, always very helpful and would go out of his way to talk to people. He used to take Virginia home. She lived six miles out of town and if the last bus had gone, he'd have to walk all the way home. Paul gave me loads of pictures of them in Hamburg for us to use in Merseybeat and he used to write me letters wherever they went. Paul and John went on a trip to Paris to see Johnny Halliday and Paul wrote me a very funny letter. His writing was very like John's; full of humour and wit. So I printed the letters as articles. He wrote about how they went down in Hamburg. He was witty and didn't do as much nonsense stuff as John. I often wondered in later years why he never wrote again because he's never done much except for the odd introduction to books. Just a bland paragraph or two.'

'Paul has a great sense of humour and he's a really nice person, polite and well mannered and with a marvellous memory for people. He can meet people and instantly recall who they are and what they do. He used to have a girlfriend then called Dot and I used to see him around with her. But he had to keep her in the background later on, once they started getting known in the area. I remember at the Aintree Institute, the girlfriends had to sit in the balcony, out of the way of the screaming girls, in front of the stage. If the fans found the girlfriends, they would have beaten them up! The girls were terribly jealous. Dot got married and is living in Canada now.'

Chapter Three

FROM THEM TO US

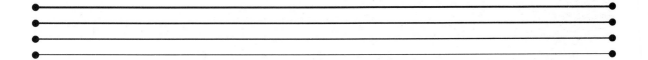

'Once upon a time there were three little boys called John, George and Paul, by name christened. They decided to get together because they were the getting together type.'

That was John Lennon's way of introducing The Beatles to the world, in his article in Merseybeat's first issue, in July 1961. The full title on the piece was 'Being A Short Diversion On The Dubious Origins of Beatles: Translated From The John Lennon.' It was a first taste of Beatles humour, although the headline was actually written by the editor, Bill Harry. Later, much was made of how the magazine in its enthusiasm had spelt 'Paul McArtrey' in a picture caption when the group topped their popularity poll.

'Everyone goes on about how in Merseybeat we couldn't even spell his name right. What happened was I had been working on the magazine for a year before it actually came out. I had the idea in 1960 and started to find a printer and all the rest of it. I had asked John to write about the history of The Beatles, because I was determined to put them into every issue. So John wrote the piece which I called: ''The Dubious Origins'' etc. He wrote about each member and HE wrote ''Paul McArtrey.'' That's how he spelt it! And I used that in a couple of other issues, assuming John's spelling was correct. We had a gossip column in which we'd say: ''Howie Casie says Paul is the best singer in Liverpool.'' Or we'd say, ''Paul is better than Cliff Richard.'''

One of the reasons Bill was so impressed by The Beatles was their capacity to write their own material, and put them head and shoulders above all the other local bands.

'By that time, John and Paul had already written eighty original songs. This is where their strength lay. There were a lot of other great groups on the scene: King Size Taylor, Faron's Flamingos, Rory Storm, Derry Wilkie & The Pressmen and The Big Three. But The Beatles wrote their own songs and the others didn't.

'They didn't sit down and write together. They wrote individually and came together to suggest ideas. It wasn't like Rodgers & Hart. John wrote songs. Paul wrote songs and their fans could always tell which was which. They just got together to advise each other; a middle eight here; a few lines there. But every one was ''Lennon & McCartney''. That's how they acknowledged it.'

As The Beatles' fame percolated beyond Liverpool, there was a great wave of pride throughout the city. Pubs displayed pictures of the group. The Cavern Club became a shrine.

The first pop fans in the country at large heard of The Beatles when *Love Me Do* was slipped into jukeboxes and was played alongside the other rhythm and blues hits of the day. The Beatles sounded .... different. This wasn't the usual British attempt at frantic, yammering rock 'n' roll with a Cockney accent. Somehow, the Liverpool accent was better suited to the blues. It had an authentic ring and the nasal twang wasn't far removed from New York's drawl.

Love Me Do left pop fans wanting to hear more about this strange new group and the rumours spreading around the country only fed curiosity. Friends told each other that the group had been going for years, that they wrote all their own songs, and were going down a storm in their own town. For the first time, Londoners, in particular, felt left out yet fascinated to know there was life beyond Potters Bar.

Soon the national newspapers began to pick up on the phenomenon after *Love Me Do* got to Number Seventeen in the chart. The record made Number One in America when it was re-issued there in 1964. From here on The Beatles were hardly out of the papers somewhere in the world on a daily basis for the next six years.

And it had all been set in motion by Brian Epstein's persistence and faith in the group he had finally signed to management. Brian Samuel Epstein was born to Harry and Malka (known as Queenie) on September 19, 1934. His father owned a furniture store founded by Brian's grandfather Isaac, a Lithuanian immigrant. Brian was supposed to go into the family business but did badly at school and was expelled from Liverpool College at the age of ten. During his teenage years, his main interests were in acting and painting and he eventually announced he wanted to leave Wrekin College in Shropshire to go to London to be a dress designer. This caused alarm and consternation and his request was turned down by his fearful parents. At the age of sixteen, in 1950, he went to work at the family store in Walton, Liverpool.

In 1953, he was conscripted into the Army to do his National Service and anybody less suited to the army would be hard to find. He was sensitive and lonely and his life style just clashed with rules and regulations. He dressed so smartly he was once accused of impersonating an officer.

He was discharged as unfit for military service and returned to the furniture store, with some relief, where he ran the record department. He grew bored with this after a while and went to London to enroll at the Royal Academy of Dramatic Art. He still dreamed of being a famous actor. But backstage drinks at the Liverpool Playhouse was one thing; the competition on the London acting scene was far less pleasant and sociable. As he admitted in his biography, *A Cellarful Of Noise*, 'I grew to loathe the place and the other students.'

In 1957, at the age of twenty-three, he was put in charge of the record department at the new family store in the heart of Liverpool. He set to work with a will and established a system of stocking so that any customer could get the record of their choice. It was when Raymond Jones went on his quest for The Beatles' *My Bonnie*, that Brian felt his system was being challenged and became determined to track down the unknown group. He didn't know it but he had already seen The Beatles – the youths who came around his store chatting up the salesgirls.

Brian discovered the group were playing locally at The Cavern and went along feeling out of place and embarrassed. But when he saw the band performing their rough and ready act, full of jokes and horseplay on stage, he was captivated.

He approached them afterwards, his nervousness heightened by his susceptibility to male magnetism. To his surprise, he found the group regarded him as a local celebrity and was made welcome by John, Paul, George and Pete Best. They played him *My Bonnie* in an alcove in the club and he felt he wanted to help them reach a wider public, even beyond the realms of the North End Music Store.

After a series of inconclusive meetings, he eventually asked them if they would like him to manage their affairs. The group were enjoying themselves but they hadn't got much further after five years of fooling around. John Lennon said 'yes' and the rest of the group agreed. From then on, Epstein flung himself into the job of promoting The Beatles. At first, they hit the stone wall of corporate indifference. Trying to get a record contact in London was a tough job and Brian grew fearful the boys would loose faith in him.

Epstein raised their local gig money and got them a record test. Then came the famous put down from Dick Rowe, head of A&R at Decca. 'We don't like your boys' sound. Groups of guitarists are on the way out.' Brian exploded and said one day The Beatles would be bigger than Elvis Presley and Decca were out of their minds. He was right on both counts, but he was told bluntly: 'You have a good record business in Liverpool. Stick to that.'

The Beatles were still writing their brilliant songs scribbled on the backs of envelopes but it seemed the rest of the world

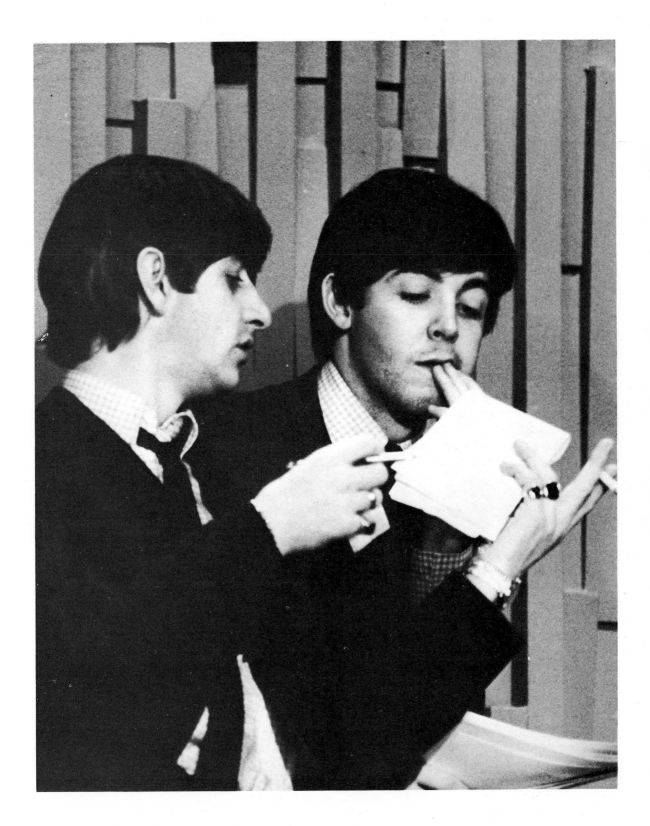

would never know about them. In the summer of 1962, after the group had made their third trip to Hamburg, Brian met producer George Martin. He had first taken him demo tapes to the HMV Record Store in Oxford Street and had them turned into a record. The technician making them told music publisher Syd Coleman that the songs were good. He in turn tipped off Martin, who was the first record company man to take an intelligent interest in the music. An audition was arranged for June and the group were overjoyed. In October 1962, *Love Me Do*, the first George Martin production of a Lennon & McCartney song was released on Parlophone. At the same time, Epstein had to perform one of his first tough managerial duties, and sack the drummer Pete Best in favour of Ringo Starr, just before the group's first EMI recording session in September.

Epstein had to learn to cope with the fantastic rush of success that followed. *Please Please Me* was a Number One smash in January 1963. There were tours, three within a few months, riots and a trip abroad to Sweden. Within a year of *Love Me Do* being a hit, they were booked to play on the prestigious TV show *Sunday Night At The London Palladium*, and in front of the Queen Mother, Princess Margaret and Lord Snowdon at the Royal Variety Show.

The four lads from Liverpool had become the darlings of showbusiness and royalty, and the Lennon & McCartney team worked overtime, producing hits from *From Me To You* and *She Loves You*, not to mention their debut album *Please Please Me*. When their *With The Beatles* album was released in November 1963, the advance orders were for 250,000 copies, the highest in pop history. The Beatles were breaking records and setting precedents and nothing could stop them.

In December that year, they had seven records including singles and EPs in the Top Twenty and their fan club membership topped 80,000. The Times music critic called them the outstanding English composers of the year, and every witticism to come from The Beatles was eagerly quoted, like John Lennon's remark at the Royal Variety Performance, on November 15, 1963: 'Those in the cheaper seats clap. The rest of you rattle your jewellery.'

The Beatles' success completely reshaped the British pop scene, giving home artists a new confidence. Cliff Richard and The Shadows had hits, but this was ridiculous. And there was a flood of Liverpool talent who became associated with The Beatles through Brian Epstein's managements, singers like Gerry & The Pacemakers, Cilla Black and Billy J. Kramer. People talked excitedly about *The Mersey Sound* and A&R men trekked north to find new groups to sign. The Beatles even wrote hits for other artists, like *Love Of The Loved* by Cilla, *Hello Little Girl* by The Fourmost, and *Bad To Me*, by Billy J. Kramer.

On June 18, 1963, Paul celebrated his 21st birthday and he was ceremonially 'bumped' on the pavement outside EMI studios, where a large crowd of onlookers gathered. Later he held a birthday party at his Aunt Jinny's home which became decidedly noisy. By now, Paul was beginning to grow accustomed to hero worship and the life style of a pop star. He drove a snazzy Ford Cortina and took a holiday in Greece. He was besieged by girls and was hailed as the most beautiful of The Beatles. When it came to dress and looks he tended to side with Brian Epstein. The famous collarless Beatle jacket always looked better on him than the rest of the group.

Bill Harry didn't get invited to Paul's twenty-first birthday party. 'Brian Epstein didn't want any press men there. It was in case something happened, which it did. Billy J. Kramer gave me the details. John beat up Bob Wooler, the Cavern DJ and Bob was very badly hurt.' Bob was the ex-railway clerk who had become involved in music and helped The Beatles get the famed gig at Litherland Town Hall. He had also written enthusiastically about the group in Merseybeat, saying, 'Such are the fantastic Beatles. I don't think anything like them will happen again.'

After the punch up, John came up to some girls in the garden. Says Bill: 'He grabbed one by the tit and squeezed her. John was very drunk. She pushed him away and started insulting him, and he swung at her. Billy J. Kramer and Billy Hatton of The Fourmost grabbed him and held him down. Cynthia came out to get him home and there were floods of tears. You can imagine what would have happened had the press been there. Paul never misbehaved. He could hold his drink. The party was held at his Aunty's house. He was always one for his family life. It was bred into him. When they made the 'James Paul McCartney' TV show, they had a scene where they recreated the pub atmosphere Paul liked.

His family was sitting around a table having some drinks. The girl came to deliver the glasses and the cameras were on them. She stood there – waiting to be paid. Paul hadn't realised he would have to pay her and hadn't brought any money. Pop stars *never* carry any money. Then he felt something on his knee. It was his father, with a five pound note under the table. He put it in Paul's hand so he could pay the waitress.

'In the early days, right up to 1966, The Beatles only got fifty pounds a week in cash each to carry around with them. And since then, all his life, Paul has been trying to keep a sense of proportion and reality with his children and his marriage and not to get into the mad, mad world of the millionaire jet set.' Bill points to the children of Hollywood stars who have either committed suicide, had drugs overdoses or mental problems. 'Paul tried to keep a sense of balance and bring up his children like his father would have done.'

'Even so, it has been difficult because he cannot get away from the fact he is who he is. He's made a braver attempt than anyone else. He got married and stayed a family man. With the others, it was sort of different, wasn't it? It was appropriate the first musical score he wrote was for *The Family Way.*

Paul was described as 'The Ultimate Mr. Nice Guy' in Fan magazine, from the beginning. He tried to soften the blunt, abrasive approach of John and George. But he was no angel and often grew sick of the 'Mr. Keeny' role. Even as a kid he had resented being sneered at by the rougher kids on the estate because he went to the Institute. He was just as capable of thieving cigarettes, and chasing after money, women and clothes, the obsessions of most growing lads. What he most wanted out of life was one hundred pounds a house, a guitar and a car. It didn't seem much to ask, but then it seemed like baying for the moon.

Just three years after his twenty-first birthday party, Paul was able to buy a house, a large detached three storey dwelling, in London's St. John's Wood for forty thousand pounds. It was not far from EMI Studios where so much Beatle – and McCartney – music was created.

Chapter Four
BEAUCOUP OF BLUES

In early 1964, The Beatles began their conquest of America. Perhaps their success could be measured by the fact each member of the group became the kind of celebrity every diplomat's daughter wanted to meet. Nobody was higher on the dating list than Paul.

Young, rich, good looking and talented, Paul epitomised the Sixties' obsession with youth and glamour. Fan mail poured in by the truckload until it filled a whole warehouse in New York alone. Back in Britain, The Beatles had finally relinquished their Liverpool roots and moved down to London, where John and Cynthia set up home. Paul was still unmarried, but his regular girlfriend, the beautiful actress Jane Asher, was shortly to become Mrs. McCartney – or so everyone believed.

Paul was pursued by reporters who wanted to know when he was finally going to take the plunge. He told them: 'I've got no plans. But everybody keeps saying I have. Maybe they know better. They say I'm married and divorced and have fifty kids, so you might as well too.'

In fact, Paul was plagued by paternity suits from Liverpool and Germany and Beatle lawyers were set to work to deflect them. It was all part of the increasing strain of being a Beatle. Interest in all their activities was reaching fever pitch. The group had become rock music's royal family, an inspiration to countless aspiring artists and a challenge to established ones. In London, they were courted by the newly risen stars of a rapidly expanding rock culture. They turned on to Bob Dylan, became friends with The Rolling Stones and sallied forth to

midnight parties with the drinkers, swingers and fellow rockers. In a private, protected Beatle world, they were medieval princes, allowed to enjoy themselves in riotous fashion, without the might of the State thundering down.

Their public triumphs included *I Want To Hold Your Hand* hitting the American singles chart, and their February arrival at Kennedy Airport, when over ten thousand fans were attracted by a mixture of curiosity, fan fever and pubicity. When they appeared on the Ed Sullivan TV show, fifty thousand people applied for the seven hundred studio tickets available. They played their first concert at Washington's Coliseum attracting an audience of twenty thousand, an event followed by the notorious party at the British Embassy when the group were mobbed and jostled by the upper crust guests.

During March, they started work back in England on their first feature film, *A Hard Day's Night* and for the rest of the year the group were busy touring Europe, Hong Kong and Australia, where over three hundred thousand turned out to greet them at Adelaide. Even the British Prime Minister, Harold Wilson, a Liverpudlian himself, was swept away with enthusiasm and hailed the group as the nation's 'best exports'. And when *A Hard Day's Night* was given its premier in London's West End, the film critics were ecstatic, hailing Ringo Starr's performance as the best thing in silent comedy since Chaplin. Ringo actually fell ill during the year and was temporarily replaced by Jimmy Nichol.

In August 1964, the band went on its first full length American tour and broke records

John Ratby puts the finishing touches to a portrait of Paul for exhibition at the Royal Academy.

37

in all departments, while *I Feel Fine* was a Number One single at home in the autumn and the *Beatles For Sale* LP was a Christmas smash. In between, the Lennon and McCartney song writing team was still churning out hits for others with *A World Without Love* being courteously donated to Peter And Gordon. At least it was kept in the family. Peter Asher was Jane's brother. The Beatles weren't just handing out hits. By their example they were encouraging American record companies, publishers and media to take British pop music seriously for the first time, and that interest helped a succession of artists for the next twenty years make the trip across the Atlantic to recognition, acceptance and fame.

All the touring meant that Jane and Paul were often parted. They had met in May 1963, back stage at the Royal Albert Hall in London, after a concert. Later that year, Paul began to live with Jane and her parents when visiting London, until he bought his house in St. John's Wood. The rumours were so persistent that they were about to be married, that Brian Epstein made a firm denial in *Merseybeat* and Paul denied it while at a *Ready, Steady, Go* TV Show. A year later, however, Jane was confidently confirming wedding plans, and they were still going out together and going on holiday to Switzerland. By 1966, however, Paul was once again denying, in interviews, that he was considering marriage. Then a year later in 1967, while on holiday on his farm in Scotland, he confirmed their plans to marry and then, on Christmas Day 1967, they announced their engagement. A few months later in February 1968, Jane went with the rest of The Beatles to Rishikesh, India to meditate with the Maharishi, and she accompanied Paul to his brother Mike's wedding in Wales. But although she was getting nearer to the altar, Paul in the meantime had met and fallen in love with another.

Jane finally broke the suspense and told the world that the engagement was off when she appeared on the Simon Dee chat show on BBC TV in July 1968.

It was in 1967 that Paul first met American photographer Linda Eastman at the Bag O'Nails Club, a cheerful haunt of musicians in London's Kingley Street where Jimi Hendrix sometimes played. The next time they met was in America at a press conference for Apple. Linda slipped Paul her telephone number and he called her that night. It was the beginning of an association that would have a tremendous influence on Paul's career, and the future of The Beatles.

The intervening years saw an astonishing saga unfold around the group. It seemed that all the worst possible predictions that could be made about a much loved and super successful group, came true with unrelenting finality.

At first they enjoyed it all with undisguised pleasure. Then the ceaseless demands and easy conquests bred in them mistrust, which affected them all in different ways, but led to their ultimate demise. Their need to grow and expand and take advantage of sudden wealth and fame in a creative way was stymied by inexperience and lack of the right kind of education. The Beatles were sharp, witty and human. But they hadn't been to the kind of schools that prepare you for power and wealth. It was only after they had learned from bitter experience how they could be milked and robbed and generally taken advantage of, that The Beatles individually learned to be businessmen, to hold on to their hard won riches and put them to work.

First came the disasters. During the summer of 1967, the British pop music community had been converted *en masse* to the hippie credo emanating from America's West Coast. The smell of incense and pot wafted, where once the fumes of whiskey and beer prevailed. Kaftans, beads and bells were paraded along the Kings Road (to the scorn of passing lorry drivers), and there was much excited talk of the drug culture, young versus the aged, and the principles of love, peace and music.

For The Beatles, along with their contemporaries, such ideas seemed to fill the empty void of pop music, with its shallow values, where a Number One hit seemed to be the sole goal in life. The Beatles had enough accolades to fill the walls of all their mansions. But what did it all mean? They knew all there was to know about materialism and they didn't scorn it. If nothing else, it offered protection but it did not fulfil all their awakening spiritual needs.

The only alternative they knew of was the

Church, but that reeked of cold draughty halls, the echoing voices of the righteous and the dull thud of musty hymn books, more ancient than modern. Their spiritual vacuum would be filled by a much more exciting and seemingly relevant moral stimulus. Along with the Californian cults for astrology, numerology and magic, the art of transcendental meditation had become hugely popular, giving depth to empty, shallow lives. Film actors and pop stars flocked to study with the leader of the cult, the Maharishi Mahesh Yogi, already familiar to Londoners from large advertisements on the tube stations. George Harrison, with his interest in the sitar and music of Ravi Shankar, was at the forefront of the Liverpudlians' investigation of matters Eastern but all the Beatles went to a lecture by the Maharishi at the London Hilton. Later, the great mystic invited the group to his lectures at, of all places, the University College, Bangor, in North Wales.

It was all part of the evolution of The Beatles. The public at large had come to love the four moptops in the collarless jackets. The new Beatles with longer hair, moustaches and clothes that looked as if they had been rifled from the theatrical trunk of some Victorian concert party, were much harder to take. But the leap into the hippie era was marked by one of their greatest artistic triumphs, the writing and production of *Sgt. Pepper's Lonely Hearts Club Band*, released at the height of an unreal, but singularly pleasant, summer.

The old group had by now stopped playing 'live', with their last concert in Britain at Wembley and their last ever concert at the end of their US tour in San Francisco, on August 29, 1966. From then on, the group had concentrated on studio work and, with the time and money available, experimented with new sounds, techniques and concepts. They advanced pop music by a decade in the process. Early clues to their new direction had been detected on such tracks as *Tomorrow Never Knows* on the *Revolver* album, released the previous year. Then came such astonishing works as *Strawberry Fields Forever* coupled with *Penny Lane* and released in February 1967.

Together with producer George Martin, The Beatles climaxed their experiments with *Sgt. Pepper*, recorded at Abbey Road during the early months of '67. Their changing music, life styles and attitudes, and more importantly their decision not to tour meant their manager was becoming redundant. Epstein was tormented by the fear of losing his grip on the boys he had discovered in a cellar and had elevated to godlike status. At the same time, he had the sensitivity to understand he couldn't interfere. The boys were growing up and he couldn't stand in their way.

He busied himself with the Saville, in London's Shaftesbury Avenue (now a cinema), and turned it into one of the first prestigious rock music venues. If he couldn't make it as an actor, at least he had the satisfaction of seeing his name painted in gold lettering over the door of a theatre.

Here were staged some exhilerating concerts. The Who, Jimi Hendrix, Cream and The Bee Gees were just some of the bands who played there. It was during the break between two shows by the Jimi Hendrix Experience, that the shock news of Brian's death was announced. 'Brian who?', screamed one girl on the steps of the theatre on discovering her show was cancelled.

Brian had not fought against the new influences at work on The Beatles. He desperately wanted to be accepted as one of them and he too had experimented with LSD and taken an interest in Indian religion. But when the group made their pilgrimage to Wales by train without him, Brian went to his Sussex home feeling immensely depressed. Emotional, easily slighted, he felt let down at the number of friends who failed to join him, for various reasons, over the Bank Holiday Weekend. On August 25, after dinner, he drove back to his London home where he took an overdose of sleeping tablets and was found dead in bed, two days later. It was Paul who had the task of breaking the news to the other Beatles, just celebrating their new membership of the International Meditation Society.

It was believed that Brian had committed suicide. But at the inquest a verdict of accidental death was recorded. Immediately, Beatle affairs were taken over by Brian's younger brother Clive. But it wasn't long before the old NEMS operation, with its roster of Liverpool stars, collapsed. The Beatles had other plans. From now on they would run their own affairs – or so they hoped.

Brian's death sent a shock wave through the entire music business and The Beatles, for once, were at a loss for words. The calming influence of the meditation course seemed to bolster them against the hard clamour for comment and tribute.

Were The Beatles finished? If only to bury that suggestion they plunged themselves into work and feverish activity. It would culminate in the setting up of the extraordinary Apple organisation, and The Beatles' first self-produced film, *The Magical Mystery Tour*.

Paul quickly emerged as the Beatle most determined to carry on. He called a conference at his London home in early September to discuss future plans with the other three, and he told reporters that as far as he was concerned nobody else could replace Brian as their manager. They wanted to manage themselves.

The stream of daily events that dogged The Beatles was both confusing and upsetting. The public had largely supported the group when they were awarded their M.B.E. medals by the Queen back in the summer of 1965, despite the howls of protest from retired colonels. They had been amused by their dabblings with mysticism and were impressed by the constantly rising quality of the music, and seemingly endless supply of imaginative, cleverly wrought songs.

But Epstein's death cast a long shadow and an increased level of intolerance was detected. Adulation was in danger of becoming alienation, as first the group admitted their experiments with drugs and then John and Yoko Ono began their much misunderstood manipulation of the media in the cause of peace.

Said John Lennon: 'After Brian died, we collapsed. Paul took over and supposedly led us. But what is leading us, when we went round in circles?'

Paul had a lot to contend with as he tried to be 'the keeny' and become the old group's motivating force. There was George Harrison's resentment at being overshadowed as a songwriter and understandable dislike of being told how to play his guitar. There was John's growing cynicism about The Beatles and instinctive dislike of being ousted as leader of the gang. There was his growing love and dependence on Yoko Ono. There was the battle over the financial control of The Beatles, John favouring New York accountant Allan Klein whereas Paul much preferred his prospective father-in-law, Lee Eastman. AND there was The Beatles' first flop – *The Magical Mystery Tour*, which had been Paul's brainchild.

The film was conceived during a flight across the Atlantic. Paul recalled the English tradition of mystery coach tours. Wouldn't it be great, he reasoned, to hire a coach, actors and film crew and pack them off with The Beatles down to The West Country?

They wandered aimlessly about the countryside filming surrealistic scenes set to some interesting new songs. In effect, it was the first promotion video, well ahead of its time. But it went down badly with critics and public when it was shown on small black and white TV screens as a Beatles' Christmas treat. Prople wanted a follow up to *Help!*, not a dose of surrealism. People can be very boring at times. The film wasn't half as bad as everyone made out but nevertheless it was a disappointment, and The Beatles weren't used to flops. There were cries of 'witless rubbish' where earlier there had been glowing praise for *Sgt. Pepper*. The summer of love and peace was turning into a winter of discontent. But the group, under Paul's impetus was not going to give up, or throw away all their gains and victories. There was a new challenge looming.

The first steps were being taken to set up a creative empire controlled by the artists and not the grey men in suits, the villains of rock 'n' roll's dream world. Paul announced the new venture which would be called Apple – a fresh, crisp name which Paul had conceived and would become one of the world's most famous logos – or company trademarks.

Said McCartney: 'We want to help other people, but without doing it like a charity and without seeming like patrons of the arts. We always had to go to the big man on our knees, touch our forelocks and say, "Please can we do so and so?" We want to set up a good organisation.... not one that doesn't care.' Paul might have been thinking of the days when the group made five

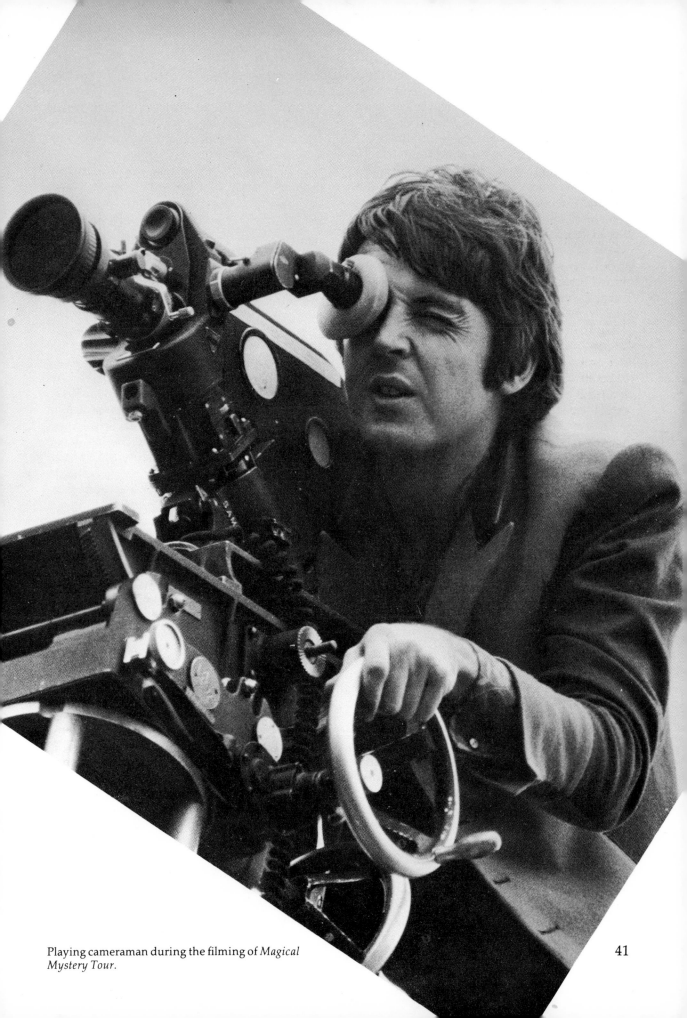

Playing cameraman during the filming of *Magical Mystery Tour*.

promotion films for some of their greatest hits at Twickenham Studios for under £700 and EMI complained about the bill!

The Apple Boutique, with clothes designed by an aptly named team from Holland, the Fool, was the first manifestation of artistically controlled business activity and opened in London in December 1967. Then The Beatles Ltd, which had been set up in June 1963, changed its name to Apple Corps Ltd in February 1968. Its divisions included Apple Electronics, Films, Music Publishing and Records. Apple Records were distributed by Capital in America and EMI in Britain. Apple Corps had a built-in pun that would later turn sour, and rotten.

With offices at 95 Wigmore Street, the new company set to work, carrying with it the dreams and aspirations of all four Beatles and a generation of fans and artists. It wasn't their fault when the dream became a target for scroungers, fanatics and con merchants who walked out of the building with TV sets under their arms and even stripped the lead off the roof. The biggest theft was The Beatles' innocence.

Perhaps the first tactical mistake had been Paul's idea for a poster that would act as a beacon to all in search of a free handout. It pictured a busker with the caption 'This man has talent!' It went on to explain that he had sent a tape to Apple and other aspiring talents were advised to do the same. The punch line read: 'This man now owns a Bentley!' The posters went up all over London and appeared as advertisements in the music press. The result was a deluge of hundreds of tapes. It was a well meant, harmless exercise in keeping with the spirit of the group.

But later every crank, Hell's Angel, or representative of some oppressed minority was marching into Apple demanding money or favours as a right and, as is the way with all scroungers, became threatening and abusive. The reasons behind the businessman's anonymous suits and security screen of secretaries and jobsworths became all too apparent.

Apple did begin to function well, despite all the eccentricities. They had the money to back their hunches and an eager audience waiting to see what they had to offer. They broke some fine new talent, among them

James Taylor and Mary Hopkin, the Welsh girl singer. Twiggy, the famed model, had seen Mary on TV's *Opportunity Knocks* and recommended her to McCartney. Paul signed her to Apple and wrote her first smash hit, *Those Were The Days*.

Paul had also written the amazingly powerful new Beatles' anthem *Hey Jude*, which was played almost non-stop on the radio, and became Apple's first smash Number One hit. Together with some controversial signings – The Black Dyke Mills Brass Band and the Modern Jazz Quartet – it seemed Apple were doing everything they set out to achieve. The various Beatles dutifully went into the office each day to supervise and even backed away from their involvement with the Maharishi. They left his headquarters in Rikikesh, India in April 1968, and Paul and Jane Asher for their part declared they had had enough. Towards the end of the year a Christmas party was held at the new Apple office in Savile Row – and John and Yoko dressed up in Santa Clause suits to distribute presents to the staff's children.

Despite the success of Apple, and the united front The Beatles still presented to the world, there were deep fissures and alarming cracks beneath the surface. By now the marriage of John and Cynthia Lennon was over and John had spent most of the year openly in the company of Yoko. They held an art exhibition in London, one of the first of a series of surrealistic events that, together with Yoko's hideous singing, would enrage and baffle the populace. And word began to filter through that money was pouring through Apple at an alarming rate. John publicly pronounced it was going broke. One of his first drastic steps was to order the closure of the Apple Boutique which had become tatty and nasty, and on his instructions, all the clothes were given away resulting in a mad, sad scramble.

George Harrison demonstrated his frustration by ordering the removal of a partition which had incurred his wrath in the Apple office, and broke it down with a sledge hammer. Ringo was so upset by his decreasing role within The Beatles, which could not be alleviated by small film parts, that he threatened to quit the group. To counteract this negative attitude and to restore enthusiasm, Paul set up plans for the first live concerts in three years. But a rift had grown between John and Paul, made harder to bear by John's involvement with the strange, unfamiliar Yoko. When Paul wanted to make The Beatles out to play in small, cosy gigs, just like the good old days, John told him succinctly that he was 'daft.' The air of bitterness and mistrust was captured on film. With the sort of bad timing The Beatles had always managed to avoid in the past, they had started to make a documentary about themselves, which became *Let It Be*, early in 1969. The end was nigh.

Lennon & McCartney had become John & Yoko and Paul & Linda. The excess of flies in the ointment included the manager figure they said they never wanted, the much feared Allan Klein who had long boasted of his ambition to take over the most famous pop group in the world. Perhaps out of fear, bravado or misplaced trust, John had let him in and he was appointed The Beatles' 'adviser' (a phrase made sinister by the language of the Vietnam war) in February 1969. The schism between McCartney and Klein would lead to the dismemberment of the group. It was John who first announced that he wanted to quit but it was Paul who took the plunge with a pre-emptive strike. Four years later, there were those who sided with Paul or John over the issue. For Paul, it was the last thing he wanted. But if he couldn't exercise his judgement over the group, then he certainly wasn't going to stick around and become a part of the new Klein empire. The plot thickened.

A chilly scene from *Help!*

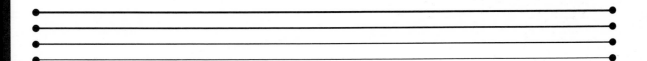

When Paul wrote *Get Back*, although ostensibly about Jo Jo who left his home in Tucson, Arizona, for some California grass, the song was seen as a cry from the heart to revive the spirit of the old group and get back to their Beatle roots. The group had not played 'live' for years and it seemed a good idea to dispel the notion they were just a peg for George Martin's studio experiments.

Paul wanted to show the group at work in a film that would be part of a multi-media project including a book and an album. Work started at Twickenham Studio in January 1969, but despite all Paul's efforts, he could not motivate his partners. John in particular seemed to have lost interest. But there was one historic outcome of it all when the group played *Get Back* in front of the cameras, and a small knot of bemused spectators, on the roof of the Apple building in Savile Row. It turned out to be the band's final public performance, although few then believed such a stunt could possibly be the mighty Beatles' farewell.

After the disaster of the filmed recording sessions, the project was shelved, although many of the unused songs from the *Get Back* and *Let It Be* sessions turned up on bootleg albums. While this was going on, Allan Klein had arrived in London with his ABKCO company planning on taking over The Beatles. He already managed The Rolling Stones and now his ambition of winning over the world's number one band was within his grasp.

A meeting was arranged between The Beatles, Klein and John Eastman. As a result, Klein became the manager, after promising to raise the group's royalties, which he managed to achieve. But McCartney refused to sign with Klein. He had wanted the Eastman family to take over Beatle business; John Lennon and the other Beatles preferred Klein's offer. Thus, three Beatles were in one camp, with Klein in charge of Apple and pruning the operation with ruthless efficiency, whilst Paul was out on his own, his affairs handled by Lee and John Eastman.

It was a fraught situation that did not help the deteriorating relationships within the group. The Beatles now looked careworn, with straggly beards and slovenly clothes. Brian would have been horrified. And the group's lurch towards disintegration took place against a background of increased police activity against the stars of rock and the 'alternative society' who were easy prey compared to the tougher nuts of organised crime. Pop stars, it was felt, were creating a bad example and had to be taught a lesson. George Harrison's home was raided and George and Pattie arrested, charged with possessing marijuana. Even The Beatles' roof top concert on January 30, which had after all been staged to fulfil a promise to the public, was stopped by the police.

Like the crescendo at the end of *A Day In The Life*, The Beatles' lives seemed to be reaching a high pitched note of hysteria. In the gloomy winter months of early 1969, it seemed it must all end with a crack of doom. The press seethed with stories about the antics of John and Yoko and it seemed to the public that their old Beatle heroes were either becoming unhinged or were the victims of a conspiracy. Perhaps a little of both was true. Certainly in the smoke filled board rooms, battle raged for control of a rich empire. The old Brian Epstein company NEMS was taken over by the Triumph Investment Trust; Northern Songs, which published the works of Lennon & McCartney, was taken over by Sir Lew Grade's ATV, all of which caused much chagrin among the boys who had set up Apple in the hopes of avoiding the clutches of the City tycoons.

With *Let It Be* apparently a wasted effort, Paul decided to plunge into musical activities with other artists, producing more records by Mary Hopkin including: *Post Card* and *Goodbye* and joining in on bass and drums with Steve Miller on a recording session at Air Studios.

Paul's musicianship is a mixture of intuitive brilliance and hard won experience. Curiously enough, it took several years after the initial shock of The Beatles' collective impact subsided before Paul's wide ranging ability began to be properly appreciated. His stature as a pop idol obscured his steadily maturing talents.

But quite early on, other musicians recognised and developed a healthy respect for his technical expertise and certain indefinable qualities. They could hear the driving swing of the bass playing on so many Beatle records, the harmonies, feel for melody, and unerring choice of a phrase. 'I wish I could write a song like Paul McCartney' was the title of a single released by a fellow composer.

One of the first to call on Paul for direct help rather than prayers, was the Bonzo Dog Doo Dah Band. They were sufficiently unabashed to ask him to produce a Bonzo single. A group of ex-art students who had taken their anarchistic and hilarious stage act from colleges to the wider stage of rock, the Bonzos were notorious for rows and internal dissent.

They had been working on a song called, *I'm The Urban Spaceman* and recalls their sax player Roger Spear: 'The recording was at a stage. We sensed there was something there, but it was a case of Bonzos fighting Bonzos. If anyone made a suggestion they would be shouted down. We really needed someone we would all respect to produce us, and Paul was asked if he could come down and help us out. We had met him before

when we appeared in a scene in the *Magical Mystery Tour*. (Originally, The Beatles wanted the New Vaudeville Band but Mike McGear, who was then in The Scaffold and had worked with us, said, "Oh, there is a much better band – The Bonzos."

'So we had appeared in a scene filmed in Raymond's Revue Bar in Soho. We were all surprised when Paul actually came down to help us re-record the song. It was at Chappell's studio in Bond Street. At first I thought it was some geezer who had come in to mend the radiators.' He didn't know what he was doing. He could talk to the engineer and explain what he wanted without knowing how it was done. He'd say: 'I want a bit of so-and-so here,' and somehow he would get the effect he wanted. Immediately he came in on the session, he brought a touch of genius.

'Our bass player was an American, Joel Druckman. And he was struggling. Everyone was tearing their hair out. It had then got to the stage where the engineer was asleep and the roadies were eating bags of chips. Suddenly, Paul rushed out of the control room and shouted: "It goes like this!" and snatched the bass out of his hand and showed him what to play. He started to play and this great sound came out. Immediately the engineer woke up, and of course that was it. A hit.'

'But Paul said, "I'm not doing it for you." He showed the bass player what to do but he wouldn't play the bass line on the record. In the end he did play some ukelele. He thrashed at it along with Neil Innes and Viv Stanshall, out in the corridor, and you can hear it plinking in the background.'

'He had this magic feel for a hit. And there was no argument. Paul said you did something and everybody did it. But he insisted that we didn't use his name. He didn't want anybody to think the Bonzos had a hit on the back of The Beatles. So he used a pseudonym.' The production was thus credited to one 'Apollo C. Vermouth.' But the name wasn't invented by Paul. Says Roger: 'Our bass player had brought all these silly names with him over from America and one of them was Apollo C. Vermouth. Of course, it was cleverly leaked to the press that it was really Paul McCartney. He was only with us for a day but it was extraordinary what he

Paul goes down a storm at Mary Hopkin's old school.

achieved.' *I'm The Urban Spaceman* got to Number Four in the charts in 1968.

By now, Paul had separated from Jane Asher. The beautiful actress had her own career to follow and would never be able to devote herself entirely to Paul who needed a wife who would be keen on traditional family life.

Rumours had been spreading from America that new love Linda and Paul were about to be married, which were hotly denied, at least by the fan clubs who still entertained hopes that Paul would marry Jane. But the American photographer who had a six year-old daughter, Heather, by her previous marriage, was constantly by Paul's side, visiting Ringo on the set of *The Magic Christian*, the movie he was in the throes of making with Peter Sellers. Then a few days later, on March 11, it was officially announced that the wedding would take place the following day! Linda went to the Register Office in Marylebone to make the arrangements while Paul dashed into a local jeweller's shop – which was closed – and managed to convince the proprietor he should open up and sell him a wedding ring – for twelve pounds. The wedding took place the next day, on March 12, 1969, with Paul's brother Michael as the best man and with Heather as the bridesmaid. After the ceremony at the Register office, the couple went to a church in St. John's Wood to receive a blessing and then held their reception at the Ritz Hotel in Piccadilly. A few days later, the new family flew off to New York for their honeymoon then returned to London to set up home in St. John's Wood.

If this caused a stir among Beatle watchers and tears among Paul's fans, then it was a bombshell when on March 20 John Lennon and Yoko Ono flew from Paris to Gibraltar for a quiet wedding. The news was described by the American Beatles' fan club as 'shocking'. But the real shocks came a few days later when John and Yoko turned their 'quiet wedding' into an international circus with their 'Bed In' at the Amsterdam Hilton. They next unleashed 'bag-ism' with John and Yoko sitting inside a bag in a hotel in Vienna, to promote their film *Rape*. John changed his second name from 'Winston' to 'Ono' (once again making use of the Apple office roof for the ceremony) and then went to Montreal to hold a seven day 'Bed In' for peace, where John wrote and recorded *Give Peace A Chance*. All this activity allowed Paul and Linda to enjoy their first few weeks together in some privacy, as all the world's media homed in on John and Yoko.

More importantly, *Give Peace A Chance* was credited to The Plastic Ono Band, the first independent Beatle single release. It came just after the release of *The Ballad Of John And Yoko*, which was recorded by John and Paul and got to Number One under The Beatles' banner.

This seemed to hint that John was ready for a breakaway move. If he could make records on his own, then he need worry no further about prolonging the agony of The Beatles, soured by boardroom battles and the conflicting interests of the four members. But there would be one last fling and one that, as it turned out, was to be one of the group's best combined efforts for a long time. Paul got in touch with George Martin and the old team once again went back to the EMI studios and work began on the *Abbey Road* album. The bad feeling caused by the *Get Back* sessions was smoothed over and the results were good, with Paul contributing the rather maniacal *Maxwell's Silver Hammer*, *Oh Darling* and a fine selection of songs on side two that included: *Carry That Weight* and *You Never Give Me Your Money*.

The July and August session for *Abbey Road* when they were released, came as a great relief after the strain imposed on listener's patience and goodwill by such albums as John and Yoko's *Unfinished Music No.2: Life With The Lions*, and George's experiments with electronics. Until *Abbey Road*, it was feared The Beatles had lost their ability to write and sing – along with their sanity. The album cover showed all four Beatles on the Zebra crossing in Abbey Road. It seemed the team were reunited, with John resplendent in flowing hair and white suit, resolutely at the helm, and Paul bringing up the rearguard, clean shaven, in a smart suit, albeit, with his shoes and socks inexplicably missing. You could almost hear the sighs of relief.

But looking again at Lennon leading The Beatles, here was a figure, whose hands in pockets and hunched shoulders signified a man detached and aloof, seeking perhaps to walk away rather than lead forward. And indeed, John's contributions to *Abbey Road* with *Polythene Pam* had been less notable even than George's, who came up with two classics, *Something* and *Here Comes The Sun*.

John had insisted on having Yoko in the studio, in bed, following their recent car crash in Scotland, and this could not have pleased the rest of the group. Then in September, at a meeting called to discuss Beatle affairs, John told the others he wanted to quit and said: 'I want a divorce – just like I had from Cynthia.' On September 13 he and Yoko, together with The Plastic Ono Band, featuring Eric Clapton on guitar, had flown to Toronto to play at the Rock 'n' Roll Revival Show. He had told Eric of his decision to quit The Beatles *en route*, and the concert gave him the courage to make the break. But his decision was kept secret, mainly to assist Allan Klein in contract negotiations.

Paul's temper could not have been improved during this time by the extraordinary and ridiculous rumours that were being circulated in America to the effect that he was dead, based simply on his brief retreat for some peace and quiet up in Scotland, and a few 'signs' supposedly uncovered by a Detroit disc jockey, like Paul's barefoot appearance on the *Abbey Road* album cover. Paul had to spend some time denying the rumours, but eventually American national newspapers put an end to the scare by printing the proof positive that Paul was alive and well. Indeed he had started work on his first solo album. And at the height of the rumour mongering, Paul and Linda had been celebrating the birth of their first child, Mary, born on August 28.

For the rest of 1969, after John had announced his intention to quit, the world's most famous songwriting team hardly spoke to each other. Lennon, much excited by his first 'live' appearance away from the group when in Canada, repeated the exercise with an unexpected appearance at the Lyceum Ballroom in London with The Plastic Ono Band.

Although John, perhaps by now, considered The Beatles to be past history, there lurked a skeleton in the cupboard, the tapes of the *Get Back* and *Let It Be* sessions. Allan Klein was determined that something should be made of them. After all, why let the bootleggers have all the fun and profit?

Klein invited famed American producer Phil Spector to come to London to prepare the tapes for an album. First he produced John Lennon's *Instant Karma* single which proved an instant hit, and then he got to work on the tapes. Although he had kept John's single simple, he undoubtedly yearned for a chance to make production job that harked back to the famed 'Wall of Sound' approach that had made his name ten years earlier with the Crystals and Ronettes. The one track that he felt deserved this treatment was Paul's beautiful song, *The Long And Winding Road*. He overlaid the track with an orchestra and choir and although the brass answering phrases sounded quite effective, the choir and strings sounded altogether too sentimental and trite, and tended to make a mockery of Paul's performance. Both he and George Martin tried to prevent the single being released in that form, and Paul declared himself shocked and angry at the Spector production. When he failed to stop the release, he decided that he would leave the group. And there was no chance he would keep the split a secret.

He had tried to keep The Beatles going and with *Abbey Road* had attempted to bring back some sanity to their music. But now he felt thwarted, snubbed and betrayed. He would quit the group and at the same time release his own solo album, recorded alone in Scotland, before the next Beatles' album and simultaneously Ringo Starr's first solo album were released.

Ringo went to see Paul at St. John's Wood to try to mollify McCartney and get him to delay the release of *McCartney*. But Paul had cracked. He was tired of being Mr. Nice Guy and the organiser. Nobody wanted to do things his way so he'd pull the rug from under all of them and go it alone.

Eventually, the release dates of the three albums were sorted out and *Let It Be* was delayed until after the release of *McCartney*. The *Let It Be* single was a huge hit in March in both Britain and America but when the film was premiered in May, none of The Beatles turned up to see it. Paul was too busy forming his own McCartney Productions Ltd. With the release of *McCartney* on April 17, the national press had finally broken the news to the world – Paul McCartney was no longer a Beatle.

There was a flood of denials from Apple, from the fan clubs and even George Harrison was quoted as saying he thought the split was only temporary. But Paul had burned his boats.

He agreed that the band had broken up months before his announcement. 'First Ringo left when we were doing the White Album because he said he didn't think it was any fun playing with us any more. Then George left when we were making *Abbey Road* because he didn't think he had enough say in our records. After a couple of days he came back. 'Paul recalled how in the Autumn of 1969 he had tried to get the band playing good music again by acting like a real group and going out to play night stands in unlikely places, 100-seater village halls.

'So one day when we had a meeting, I told the others about my idea, and asked them what they thought of it. John said, "I think you're daft." I mean he is John Lennon and I'm a bit scared of all that rapier wit we hear about. And he just said, "I think you're daft. I'm leaving The Beatles. I want a divorce."'

Paul had made a pre-emptive strike by leaving and it seemed like the public were behind him, despite the growing fury of the Beatle camp. *McCartney* went to Number One in the American album charts for three weeks and sold a million copies in three weeks. The next move was for Paul to get his lawyers to propose The Beatles' partnership to be dissolved. He then decided to sue Allan Klein but could not do so without sueing Apple and the other three ex-Beatles. The year ended with John Lennon accusing Paul of having caused the break up by attempting to dominate the group, while Paul in turn filed a suit against The Beatles & Co. to legally end the partnership.

The bitterness was very sad, especially for their old friends and fans from the Liverpool days. Says Bill Harry: 'It was a very difficult time for them all. They had lived in each other's pockets for so many years. They had been closer than family. They were put in a glass cage and very few people ever had been in a collective gold fish bowl before. The Sixties saw the arrival of mass media. TV came into its own. Elvis had been a single performer. No group had ever received so much world attention.

'Everything they did was observed by somebody or other. They were so close it was tighter than a marriage. Suddenly, there was this parting and it was very bitter. John wrote *How Do You Sleep?* and accused Paul of having a go at him in his lyrics. But you can't find any reference to John in Paul's song. John was paranoid about Paul. He kept saying he was talking about him in his songs. But try and find these references!'

Bill Harry is convinced that much of the blame for the break up and bad feeling rested on the shoulders of those who sought to profit from them. 'Allan Klein had a hand in *How Do You Sleep?*. I'm sure he wrote part of it. I wouldn't be surprised if he hadn't encouraged all the anti-Paul feeling among the others. They were going to form a group without Paul. They were getting rid of Paul and bringing in Klaus Voorman to play bass. They would continue as a quartet under the name The Ladders. Paul was very upset about it.

'Allan Klein manipulated them all. When Paul was still in The Beatles he had done his *McCartney* album. When it was due for release, Allan Klein decided The Beatles' new album should come out at the same time as Paul's. It was terrible planning. No sensible manager would do that. That's when they sent Ringo round to his house to tell him to delay release. He was so upset that, although he liked Ringo very much, he had words with him and threw him out.'

'Klein had done a lot to put Paul's back up. He had sacked all their friends. And he had manipulated John. He wanted The Beatles even when Brian Epstein was still handling them. He was waiting for his opportunity. When John made a statement to a journalist (Ray Coleman) about the financial state of Apple, Allan Klein read it and came over to London to meet John and Yoko alone at the Dorchester Hotel.

'John was very impressionable. He was putty in the hands of so many people. When Allan Klein came along he was very calculating. He knew all the songs, all the music and knew about John's background and the death of his mother. Klein told him how he had been an orphan too and was raised in an orphanage and had to fight his way up from the streets.

'John said, "Right, you are our manager," He sent a note to Sir Joseph Lockwood of EMI saying "Dear Sir Joe, Allan Klein handles all our stuff." But Paul had already made arrangements for the Eastmans to take over their affairs. It was all set up. Then John said "No" and talked the others into backing Klein, which led to the split.'

'And I think Allan Klein drove in the wedge. If anyone was responsible for The Beatles break up it was Allan Klein – not Paul. The Eastmans told Paul he had no choice. He had to have Klein as his manager because the other three had decided in his favour. The only way out would be to take proceedings against them. He knew that Klein hated him and life wouldn't be very happy under his management.'

Bill Harry was shocked at the way his old friend John treated Paul. 'When John was living the life of a recluse in the Dakota building in New York, Paul went over to see him. He called him up on the intercom and John didn't want to know. He said "It's not like Liverpool now. You can't just come calling. Go away." Now that's amazing for John to turn Paul away after all those years. But John was being manipulated by so many people, including all the Yippies, which resulted in that diabolical album *Sometime In New York City*. Instead of leaving him to write his own stuff, they had to interfere. Even Yoko insisted on being on every one of John's B sides. People were afraid of or in awe of John. Yet others were able to manipulate him. He had a strong personality and yet people were able to turn him against Paul.'

Bill thinks it was all Mick Jagger's fault that Klein took hold of The Beatles. 'Mick recommended Klein to John because he managed the Rolling Stones for a while. Then Mick realised the truth and went to Apple to warn John and say, "Don't have anything to do with him." But while he was there Klein came into the room so he didn't say anything. He had recommended him and then felt guilty about it.'

'Allan Klein wanted to get more money for himself so he wanted everybody out, no matter who they were or how long they had been associated with The Beatles. He just needed one excuse and out they went. It's

true people at Apple had gone over the top, but now Klein was sacking all The Beatles' personal friends. They were trying to find John and he wouldn't answer the phone. It was heart-wrenching. All the people who had been with them from Liverpool were being stepped on by some whizzkid from America, as if they were nothing.'

But the rot had begun well before Klein stepped in and the cracks began appearing after the death of Brian Epstein. 'The Beatles were untogether because they had no proper management,' opines Bill Harry. 'They were unclear as to what to do next. So Paul tried to pick them up. When anyone is down or depressed, you have to give them a kick up the arse. You can't do it by saying "Shall we, er, do something?" You've got to have a bit of discipline. Paul was trying to keep them alive as a group and keep the spirit going. He had to be tough to do this. That's why he came up with the idea of the *Magical Mystery Tour*. It was HIS idea. Something to keep them going through a bad patch.'

'He had to show drive and energy because the others were apathetic about everything. If you are in a group, part of them feeling down, you've got to be a bit tough and you have to be a bully. It was only with their interests at heart.'

'But of course, they all started to feel resentful. George Harrison started going on about how they never used his songs and he'd been badly treated. They were surprised at this. Even John was hurt by this because he'd always written special numbers for George.'

There was undoubtedly tension between them but Bill believes that Klein drove a wedge into the crack. 'The facts speak for themselves. Would any manager, handling the greatest group in the world, try to ruin one of the group member's solo albums by releasing a Beatles album at the same time? Knowing how Paul felt? Knowing that Paul resented him?'

In 1972, John Lennon talked in characteristically candid fashion about his version of events and said that after all the Beatle years of success, none of them had much money in the bank. 'Paul and I could probably have floated but we were sinking fast. When Allan Klein heard me say that he came over right away. As soon as he realised that I

knew what was going on he thought to himself, "Now I can get through." Now I have got lots more than I ever had before. Allan got me more real money in the bank than I've ever had before."

John had told Paul he was leaving, without making an announcement. Then six months later, Paul announced HE was quitting. 'I was a fool not to do what Paul did, which was to use it to sell a record. He's a good PR man Paul. I mean he's about the best in the world. We were all hurt that he didn't tell us what he was going to do. We didn't want to put out *Let It Be* and Paul's LP at the same time. It would have killed the sales. There has to be timing. We're not idiots.'

John and George asked Ringo to go and talk to Paul because Ringo had not taken sides in arguments. 'We thought Ringo would be able to talk fairly to Paul. He attacked Ringo and started threatening him.'

John admitted that after the death of Brian Epstein, The Beatles were finished. 'Paul took over and supposedly led us, but we were going round in circles. We got fed up being sidemen for Paul. *Let It Be* was set up by Paul for Paul. That's one of the main reasons The Beatles finished.' As far as John was concerned, the film said: 'We can't get together, we don't play together anymore, leave us alone.'

The following year a receiver was brought in to handle Beatle assets and Allan Klein no longer had control over the group. Then in June 1973 the other three Beatles in turn sued Allan Klein (bitter irony for Paul), alleging fraud and mismanagement. Klein sued all four Beatles for damages and got around five million dollars for his pains. The Beatles were finally dissolved, financially speaking, in 1975.

'I didn't leave The Beatles. The Beatles have left The Beatles but no one wants to be the one to say the party's over,' was Paul's famous remark as the Sixties passed into history, leaving millions around the world feeling exhausted and grateful it was all over. The Seventies would seem calm and rational in comparison, and with the onset of an oil crisis and recession, a deal more practical.

Paul's first hesitant steps into a solo career seemed like they might be blighted by the ill-feeling engendered by the break up. He kept away from the public eye, living in Scotland, far away from the stews of London. His new music seemed ramshackle and lacking in firm direction. The lifting of his Beatle role seemed to set him off balance. The others however produced a great outpouring of ideas. George Harrison indulged in a triple album, and John blasted off with *Cold Turkey*, *Power To The People* and the passionate albums full of songs like *Working Class Hero*, *I Found Out* and *How Do You Sleep?* This last item on *Imagine* was a direct attack on Paul, and an unprecedented public rebuff.

'A pretty face may last a year or two, but pretty soon they'll see what you can do. The sound you make is muzak to my ears,' he sang with quivering scorn. But although George, John and even Ringo scored early successes, it was Paul who built, slowly but surely, a structured, fruitful solo career and most important, he brought to reality the dream that Lennon had dismissed as 'daft' – playing live once more in front of eager audiences.

Paul had vowed he would never become an 'ABKCO Managed Industry' and set to work to create his own business environment. And now he had a loyal ally who would help him day by day – from playing the synthesiser to frying the bacon. Linda McCartney had suffered grievously at the hands of 'fans' in the early days of their marriage, running the gauntlet of abuse on the streets and graffiti on the walls of her home. But she smiled resiliently, only really getting angry when her husband was attacked by critics. She denied that she had set out to 'change him'.

Said Linda after a few years of marriage. 'He hasn't really changed except that he used to club it and chase chicks and now he's very involved in his family. He has a sense of humour but he's a bit moody as well, as a Gemini. I'm calmer and a Libra and the signs are supposed to go well together. Paul brings out the maternal instincts in me and I definitely mother him. Yet he is my strength. I don't blow up as easily as I used to.'

Linda was unhappy when she experienced the resentment people felt towards her, yet learned to accept it as part of the job. 'There was a lot of friction and bitterness over The Beatles break up. John was restless and more into working with Yoko than Paul. So Paul quit. Suddenly he was out of a job. Imagine that. It could have destroyed him.'

Linda suggested the couple live in the country to help Paul unwind from all the years of pressure and tension. They began to herd sheep on their Scots farm and Paul spent time clipping wool. It was a welcome change in lifestyle. He practised his skills as a carpenter. But after working with stone and wood for a while Linda noticed that Paul was getting a faraway look in his eyes. 'He missed personal appearances and companionship. He wanted someone to share his music. So he began to teach me to play.' Linda and Paul began to play music together, just for fun and slowly the idea of forming a group was born. It would be called Wings, and it would be different. No over-the-top launch, no fanfares, just a toe in the water and an eye for the future.

In May 1971 Paul and Linda released the album *Ram* aided by drummer Denny Seiwell. It was produced by the couple and the cover picture showed Paul holding a ram's horns, taken by Mrs. McCartney. On the inside was a rather strange picture of Paul and Linda dressed up to look like John and Yoko, wrapped in bedsheets. Among the tracks were *Ram On*, *Heart Of The Country*, *Monkberry Moon Delight* and *Uncle Albert*Admiral Halsey*. It was.... strange. Denny Seiwell was invited to join the new band and went to Paul's farm in Scotland to wait, while Paul recruited the rest.

His choice for guitarist was Denny Laine, who had come to fame as a member of The Moody Blues. He had impressed Paul with his version of *Go Now*, the group's Number One hit, and Denny and Paul had been drinking mates on the London party scene. Denny had formed his own Electric String Band then fallen on hard times. Paul would give him a career that lasted ten years. His reward for such generosity came in 1984 when Denny complained of his former partner's alleged 'meanness' in a series of national newspaper articles.

Back in 1971 the McCartneys welcomed the two Dennys who rehearsed in a barn. It wasn't soundproof and the noise could be

heard two miles away. Linda explained that Paul needed to work. He wanted to be part of a band and make records, and could not live by sheep alone. *Ram Off* was now the cry and so Wings rushed to the studios and cut *Wild Life* which came out in December that year. Its songs included *Big Bop, Love Is Strange*, and *Wild Life*. Not bad, but the album was not greeted with universal enthusiasm. Indeed it seemed in danger of sinking without trace. The band had made the mistake of not putting their name on the cover. The days where a rumour could sell an album were over. They had taken low-key reticence too far, just as Eric Clapton had done with his Derek & The Dominos disguise. But Paul had plans. He would not be deterred by one flop among friends.

Early in 1972 Henry McCullough was added to the band on guitar and vocals, and in February the group set off a bold, imaginative experiment. It was a tour of colleges of a kind The Beatles could not have done without being torn limb from limb. Their first date at Nottingham University on February 9 was arranged the day before. The band also released a single, the controversial *Give Ireland Back To The Irish*, which had been sparked off by the Bloody Sunday shootings in Northern Ireland.

It was Paul's first heavy political statement and was rushed out as an instant reaction to the events in Ireland. It was banned by the BBC, but despite lack of radio plays, became a Top Ten hit. In response to the official condemnation of his stance, Paul released as his next single *Mary Had A Little Lamb*. At least it looked like a jibe against society which would only accept pap from its pop stars. But said Paul: 'I've a daughter named Mary, and she always pricks up her ears at this tune. I thought I'd record a song for her.'

If there was any confusion in Paul's mind about his direction as a composer, then his resolve to play 'live' was fully confirmed. It was the best move he could make. It gave him the pleasure of being in a band again and the perfect environment to work. The unspoken challenge was to build up Wings until it equalled The Beatles and took a positive part in the, then, thriving rock scene.

The famous college tour was a more practical version of the *Magical Mystery Tour*.

The band set off in cars, stopped off where they felt like it and asked if they could play. They played first at Nottingham University unannounced, with no advance publicity and charged only 50p at the door. After expenses were deducted, they split the money between the band and the two roadies, Ian and Trevor. Social secretaries at the colleges just didn't believe it when the gang turned up. Then Paul had to get out of his car and walk into the office before the secretaries would believe the tale of the advance party of roadies. During the two weeks on the road, Wings visited York, Hull, Scarborough, Newcastle, Leeds, Sheffield, Salford, Birmingham and Swansea. The experience proved to Paul they could work together. Next stop was a full invasion of Europe.

The rest of Britain and America would have to wait until Paul felt ready to face highly critical audiences laced with journalists. They would play 26 concerts in nine countries, starting in France. 'Why no British dates,' asked a reporter. 'Because he doesn't like the British press,' came the response from his entourage.

Explained Paul: 'I'm not coming back. I'm starting all over again and working my way upwards. It's like boxing. You don't fight Cassius Clay on your first time out. A year ago I used to wake up in the morning and think, "I'm a myth. I'm Paul McCartney." And it scared the hell out of me.'

It was extraordinary, but the wealthy, successful and happily married young man felt assailed by paranoid fears. 'I'm frightened by people, by the press and by Allan Klein, who shall remain nameless and who I can't stand,' said Paul. 'People called me a hermit for going off to Scotland with Linda. But it wasn't until she came along that I realised what was happening to me. She made me see I was surrounded by con men and leeches. I didn't need to be mollycoddled.'

Rehearsals for the European trip began in a converted cinema on Fulham Broadway, then owned by the group Emerson, Lake & Palmer. Well known rock photographer Robert Ellis, who later became official Wings' lensman, was invited along to an early rehearsal there by promoter John Morris. An American, he had earlier helped set up North London's Rainbow Theatre as a

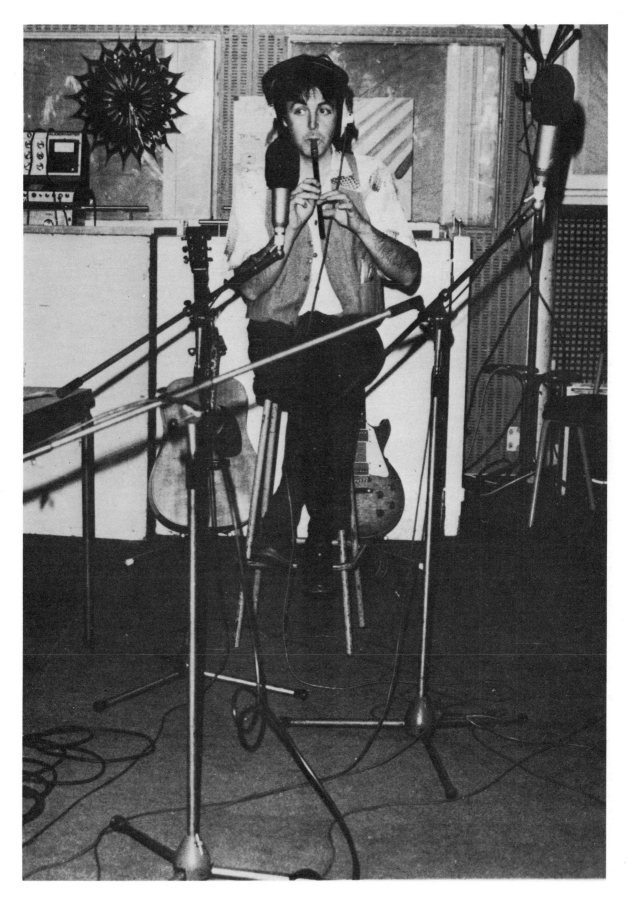

venue. Morris contacted Ellis at a reception for Alice Cooper at Chessington Zoo. He explained he was involved in helping a 'major artist' arrange a European tour and wanted Ellis as tour photographer. When the major artist turned out to be Paul McCartney, Robert fell off his chair.

'I went to the rehearsal hall and the McCartney babies were sitting on rugs laid out in the middle of this empty seating area in the hall, quite oblivious to the God awful racket on stage. This was in 1971, when Stella was just born (on September 13). The band broke for tea and Paul took me to a little cafe round the corner for a talk. Nobody recognised him for a quarter of an hour, until the inevitable happened and somebody asked him if he was really Paul McCartney. Bits of paper got stuck under his nose and we didn't talk much business. But he was very casual and easy going.'

Later they went back to the hall and Robert busied himself setting up borrowed lights to picture the band who had been working practically in the dark. Later he came back with an assistant and Linda, the erstwhile rock photographer, was most impressed. 'Gee Robert, you must be good. I could never afford an assistant!' she laughed.

Paul wanted Robert to come on the tour and was most annoyed when Ellis explained he had already accepted an invitation to visit Japan with ELP. Eventually a compromise was reached and Ellis promised to join Wings in Scandanavia towards the last leg of the trip.

Paul had been busy planning the tour as a huge adventure and was not used to people turning him down. One of his more bizarre ideas was to transport the family around the Continent on an old double decker bus with an open top that had once belonged to Great Yarmouth Corporation. It was kitted out with a kitchen, bunks, stereo and mattresses on the roof for sunbathing.

'They painted it in gay multicolours,' recalled Bob, 'and put "Wings Over Europe" along the sides, together with names and faces painted on the panels. The idea was to have a sight-seeing tour of Europe with all their sleeping accommodation inside. I think it lasted two gigs. It was so inconvenient to travel in this gaily painted bus! The driver religiously followed them around, but nobody used it. It just took too long to get anywhere, so it ended up as a showpiece outside the gigs.'

Wings made their debut in front of two thousand people at a Greek style amphitheatre in Vallon, France, on Monday July 15, 1972. The band played for ninety-five minutes and Paul announced the numbers in French with a Liverpool accent. 'Chantez a bit if you know les mots,' he joked. Although there were problems with the amplifiers, the show was deemed a great success and excitement was at fever pitch. It was Paul's first publicised gig since 1966. The band played material from *RAM* and *Wildlife*, and Denny Laine sang *Say You Don't Mind*. Paul played *My Love* at the piano, giving Linda meaningful looks, and they all had great fun on *Hi, Hi, Hi*.

As the tour progressed, it became apparent that Linda and Denny were thoroughly enjoying themselves creating an old time rock band, with lots of blues and rockers in the repertoire. Recalled Bob Ellis: 'Singles like *Hi, Hi, Hi* and *C Moon* were typical of that first tour and their sort of gimmicky rock approach. But Paul wasn't very happy with that and found it musically unsatisfying, even by the time I joined them towards the end of the tour. He was already thinking beyond that to the next tour and developments within the band.' The problem with the first tour was that it was Paul McCartney & Wings. The individuals were rather swamped by Paul McCartney, ex-Beatle. And Linda was being absolutely slated to hell for inability to play. She was very sore about that and it made them quite defensive. The other members of the band also felt dragged down by Linda's capabilities but they were prepared to go along with her because she made a great effort to keep the spirit going. She was like a manager really. Although she was noted for her interference, she was really an over-seeing spirit who wanted to see that Paul was well taken care of, and the rest of the band as well. And as a result, there was a very good group feeling in those days.'

But, within days of the band hitting the road, there were rumours that Linda was about to quit the band. Paul hit back. 'We like having Linda in the group. She is a great

influence on us. She is no Billy Preston, granted, but I would not like a very technical keyboard player because they tend to want to take over. Linda isn't a Pro, but if people don't like it, they shouldn't come next time. I couldn't care less. How can Linda "Quit the band?" She's only just joined. We love her playing in Wings and its great for us all playing to audiences.'

If some people saw Linda as a manager, then it didn't matter because there were no official managers. Paul had suffered enough from that in the past. There were no titles given to anyone within the McCartney set up, and people came and went depending on how successful they were at their job.

Later on, as McCartney Productions expanded, a manager was appointed, Brian Brolly who came from MCA Records, but the ultimate boss was always Paul who delegated authority as he saw fit.

'What Paul wanted most on those early days was to steer a group to international success without trading too much on his own name,' says Robert Ellis. 'He wanted Wings to be a household name, and he tried in successive bands to delegate the musical work among the members, but it was never terribly successful. It was always McCartney's own music and lyrics that dominated all that Wings did. So he was saddled with it being Paul McCartney & Wings. The various band members who left did so for basically those reasons. On one hand, Paul wanted the members to make a valid contribution to the group entity, but he didn't want to bury his identity too much, and

make anybody indispensible. He used to say he'd missed all the early years of being in a group. The Beatles had gone from nowhere to international stardom in such a short time and had been totally out of control, that he wanted to go over the same ground with Wings and control it every inch of the way to please himself and everybody working in the entourage. He didn't want to relive The Beatles. He wanted to create something new. But he didn't want The New Beatles. He wanted to use his experience and skill to steer the band to international success. He paid no attention to other bands like The Who or Moody Blues. But they paid a lot of attention to him! There were constant streams of band members, management people, and record companies coming to Paul for advice.'

Paul had emerged as a guru figure in the rock fraternity and rock star suffering traumatic conditions in their own groups would turn up to Wings' gigs, at the hotel arrive on the plane, or bus to enter private discussions and beg for help.

But Wings soon developed its own internal problems. Says Robert Ellis: 'The trouble with the first formation was that Denny Seiwell and Henry McCullough were two different people. Apart from one being American and the other Irish, McCullough was an old hand at the session game and had fairly low horizons in terms of what he wanted out of the business. He didn't go for the superstar bit. He didn't go for the jet-setting future McCartney had planned for Wings.'

Chapter Six

BAND ON THE RUN

Hi Hi Hi, released towards the end of 1972, restored Paul's credibility with critics who had poured scorn on previous efforts. It was undoubtedly one of Paul's catchiest tunes in a long while and, coupled with the reggae influenced *C Moon*, made a highly attractive package during a year when there had been no album release. Once again, McCartney was effectively banned by the BBC. This time it was suspected that *Hi Hi Hi* was a drug song. Fears were aroused by Paul's much publicised arrest in Sweden, followed by another 'drugs bust' a month later. As a result of this, he was fined £100 for allegedly growing cannabis on his farm at Cambeltown, and this created problems regarding his being granted an American visa.

Paul was undoubtedly feeling aggrieved and exasperated during this period. He was desperately trying to establish Wings and yet with constant legal wrangles going on in the background, the ghost of The Beatles kept coming back to haunt him.

'Don't ever call me ex-Beatle McCartney again,' he snapped at a reporter in November 1972. 'That was a band I was with. Now I'm not with them. Now I've got another band. We're not bothered about trying to please the people ALL the time. All we want with Wings is to please ourselves with our music. I get irritated by people constantly harping on about the past, about the days when I was with that other band. The Beatles were my old job. We're not friends. We just know each other.'

Wings would suffer at least one more major hiccough before it could even begin to function in a way that would satisfy both Paul and the public. Nineteen seventy-three would prove an exciting year.

In the March the first 'official' Wings tour of Britain was announced, including thirty dates and four shows at London's Odeon, Hammersmith. The tour was a sell out but it didn't stop the critics sniping. Paul complained: 'One guy came to see a soundcheck and reviewed that as the show, saying he didn't think much of Linda's organ playing, when she was in fact playing the piano!' Despite it all, the McCartneys seemed to be thoroughly enjoying themselves and even found time to play at the Hard Rock Cafe in Piccadilly in aid of the Release organisation.

When the band hit the road the reviews hailed: "A triumphant return." But said one reviewer: "The only disappointment was the performance by Linda who hardly justifies her presence in the hardworking group." Responded Linda: 'Whatever the critics say, the people like us. I don't care what they say about me, but I hate it when they underestimate Paul. I could kick them in the face.'

Wrote Chris Charlesworth in the Melody Maker of the May 19th performance at the New Theatre, Oxford: "Paul has at last shaken off the post-Beatles stigma which has hampered his every move in the past three years. Wings proved themselves to be a group to be reckoned with. Paul was shattered at the reception and had to re-appear to admit Wings had played all they knew."

The Daily Mail reported: "They started with a cold, stubborn audience, determined not to give a handclap that hadn't been sweated for. They ended with the audience on its feet, stamping and cheering."

Enthusiasm for the band seemed to be shared by its members, especially the loyal Denny Laine who said after the tour: 'Wings has tremendous potential. We seem to get better all the time. It took us a lot of time to get things going. You know Paul with his reputation could have come back and played all the old Beatles numbers associated with him. It would have been easy. That wasn't him. Wings is Wings, not McCartney revisited.'

Paul explained why he had taken such an unpredictable route after The Beatles: 'When we formed the new band it hadn't played anywhere. I didn't want to go and play Carnegie Hall with this ropey band. So

that's why we piled into the van and took off up the motorway. We had faith it would work out. When we got to Nottingham University we just went in and said: "Hello, we're here and would you like us to play?" And they said: "Yeah, of course. Come back tomorrow lunchtime and we'll have it all set up for you." The first official tour had all the press filling up the front two rows with thir notebooks out. It was really kind of scary.'

In April 1973, Wings released their first album since *Wild Life* called *Red Rose Speedway*, which featured a shiny motorcycle on the cover and Paul with a rose stuffed in his mouth. It included one of Paul's finest new songs in years, *My Love* and was the best produced McCartney product since the Beatle split. It was also the last work by the band with McCullough and Seiwell.

My Love was a huge hit single and was featured on the hour long show built around the composer called 'James Paul McCartney'. It was made by Lord Grade for ATV and shown in America where it got mixed reviews. It showed Paul as an all round entertainer and he didn't quite pull it off. He fared better writing the music for the new James Bond movie *Live And Let Die*, which was scored by George Martin and had a dramatic theme. Paul was even invited to write a new theme for the TV series *Crossroads*, and although it was tagged onto the later Wings album *Venus And Mars*, it was subsequently dropped from the TV show. The hiccough came when McCullough quit Wings in July and then just before the band were due to fly to Lagos in Nigeria to record a new album, drummer Denny Seiwell dropped out. He rang up Paul and said: 'Hey man, I can't make the trip,' five minutes before they were due to fly out. Commented Linda later: 'We spent two years getting Wings together and after all that work we got personality problems. We only wanted to go to Lagos because it was sunny. We got a list of studios in three sunny places – Lagos, Rio and Mexico City.'

But she denied that there had been a big row when Henry had quit. 'It was because of a silly little musical thing on Denny's song. Denny had a song and Henry was asked to play this little bit – and he didn't. Then he just rang up and said, "I'm quitting." We haven't seen him since. When we threw the band together to get working on stage, we didn't really know Henry and he didn't know us. We had Seiwell, Laine, Paul and myself and thought we'd like a lead guitar player to take some of the weight off. Somebody mentioned Henry and he came to one rehearsal. It worked out great on the road. But it was a real surprise when Seiwell left.'

Although Linda and Paul tried to play down the sudden departures of two Wingsmen, says Bob Ellis: 'They felt very badly let down. But McCartney already felt dissatisfied with the group format and it was clear to everybody he was going to change it. So it didn't surprise me when they went to Nigeria without the other two. The tension generated before the recording of *Band On The Run* pulled them very much together.

'The relationship between McCartney and Denny Laine improved dramatically at that time. Up until then it had been Paul and Linda versus the rest and Denny was trying to be the peace maker. But it didn't come to anything more than natural wastage of band members. So they went on their own and produced their finest album! They did it under adverse conditions which produced urgency in their music which makes that a stand out album.'

One of the strengths of the album was the powerful drumming which gave the band considerably more drive. And the replacement drummer for Denny Seiwell was Paul McCartney. His skill as a percussionist came as a surprise to many, even those who already noted his talents as bassist and keyboard player. Said Bob Ellis: 'He loves playing drums and the first thing he does as a rehearsal is sit down at the drums, everytime. He never picks the guitar up first. It's always the drums which he will play for up to half an hour before touching a guitar or sitting at a piano. The only instruments he can't play are reed and brass. He can't play a trumpet to save his life, which he's very sad about. He loves fooling around with them, but he has to get horn players in.'

Paul wrote most of the material for *Band On The Run* in Africa, and it was recorded at the ARC Studio and EMI Studio in Lagos, with brass added later in London. It included powerful new songs *Band On The Run*, *Jet* and *Let Me Roll It*, which would

become an integral part of future tours. As previous albums had been so disappointing, it took some while before critics and public woke up to the significant improvement in Wings output and sales were slow when it was first released in November 1973. Songs like *Bluebird* began to penetrate the consciousness, and by the end of 1974 it had sold over five million copies in America alone and had become one of EMI's top selling albums of all time. *Band On The Run* showed that Paul had regained control over his output and shaken off the image of ramshackled amateurism that had dogged his solo career thus far.

With Allan Klein sueing all the ex-Beatles, including Paul, for damages during the summer of '73, perhaps it wasn't surprising Paul and Linda wanted to get away to 'somewhere sunny' and Africa seemed as far away from rock business aggravation as was possible. But even in Lagos, the McCartneys ran into a spot of bother.

One night Paul and Linda were walking back from a friend's house in the town when a car pulled up and four men jumped out and surrounded them. Said Paul later: 'One of them had a knife and said he would kill us if we didn't hand over everything we had. He was waving a knife about so I decided it wasn't the time to try and reason with him.' The gang took money, cameras and a tape recorder.

As if being mugged wasn't enough, some local musicians tried to claim that Paul had come to Africa to 'rip off' their ideas. After proffering friendship, they sat Paul down in a club one night and said, 'You are stealing our music.' Said Paul: 'I'm not. Come and listen to the tracks. I haven't used any of your musicians.' Apart from the odd cowbell on *Bluebird*, the LP was about as African influenced as a Highland Fling.

The somewhat nerve-wracking atmosphere that prevailed certainly put an edge on Wings' musical output, as was evident on the final product. But the albums Paul has released over the years are only the visible tip of an iceberg of material. Says Robert Ellis: 'Paul has an absolute mania for recording. Sometimes it caused even Paul and Linda to be at loggerheads. She would say, "Why do you have to go to the recording studio every day from ten in the morning

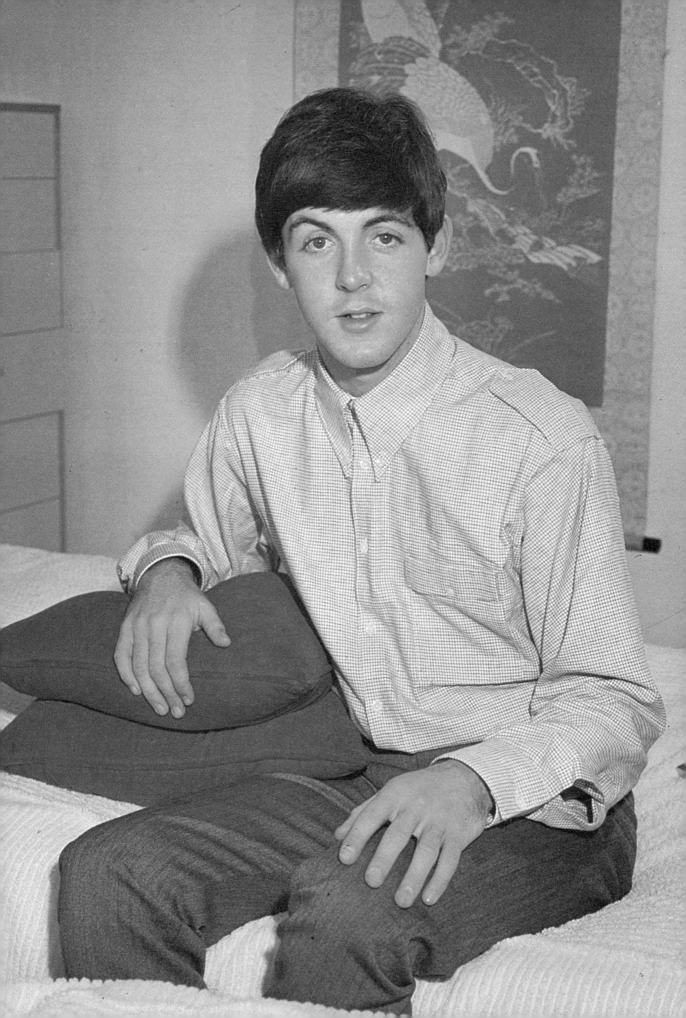

until eight at night? I have to drag along after you when I'd much rather be out riding than sitting around in a recording studio." That sort of thing. She'd be very disillusioned by the whole arduous process of making music. It's Paul's all-consuming passion and there were periods when she felt alone. After 1976, there was sometimes a feeling of "What are we doing all this recording for?"

'But Paul likes to go into the studio and record hundreds and hundreds of tunes that will never see the light of day. Sometimes he'll spend a week just working on one part of a backing track, and then scrap the whole thing! The prodigious effort that goes into his recording is quite frightening because it isn't necessary for a man of his ability to spend so much effort and time. But he does. He actually LOVES doing it and he has such a creative output of ideas, he has to keep laying these ideas down on tape.

'After 1976, his main interest was to be recording rather than playing the music live. He preferred to spend vast sums of money on making video films of the music to promote it, rather than get up there and play himself. He always spent a lot on videos but it got more intense as the years went by. The one thing that was very difficult for all those involved in working with McCartney was to realise the fact that money was NO object. When you were doing something for him, money really was not a problem. It didn't matter what it cost, you did it! He would spend frightening sums of money to achieve what he wanted. The only criteria was success. As long as you gave him what he wanted it really didn't matter what it cost.'

An example of the unlimited cash flow was the story behind the flying lady symbol on the *Wings Greatest* album cover released in December 1978. It was an object that Linda spotted in an auction house catalogue. She sent someone to buy it and it cost a small fortune. It was decided to feature it on the album cover and they hired a photographic studio. Next they wanted to put the flying lady in the snow. 'They set it up and photographed it and it didn't look right' says Bob Ellis, 'so they decided to fly the whole team, photographer and designer, out to the Alps. They hired a helicopter and spent a week in the Alps with all expenses paid for a whole group of twelve people, as well as the family. They hired diggers to excavate a snowdrift to create the scene you see on the cover and then flew the helicopter to take the shots. It didn't matter what it cost, and when you look at the album sleeve it might as well have been done in someone's back garden.'

Later during the tour of America, it was suggested that the Wings emblem be painted on the tour trucks. There were, by then, five in use and Paul hired an art studio team to come along and paint in multicolours along the sides of the trucks the emblem and the words 'Wings Over America' spread out, a word a truck. Then they hired another helicopter to fly over and photograph the top of the trucks from the air while they were travelling through the Arizona desert.

'Paul wanted everything photographed. You only had to move a muscle and he'd say, "I want a photographer here." It didn't matter where they were, or what they were doing. The photographer might have to be flown half way round the world to be there. He wanted everything documented. He started his own magazine, Club Sandwich, so he could use up some of the pictures that weren't being used. It became a newsletter for his own Fan Club!

'Club Sandwich was produced in broadsheet form in full colour at enormous expense – to give away to the fans. The money spent on that was astronomical. Thousands of pounds. But he felt that giving the fans an intimate picture of what he was doing and being documented in his own terms was better than giving interviews to the press. He could give them something he could control and he has a mania for control! Over everything. He'd say, "I don't care what you do with it, but I must have control". The whole purpose of Wings was that he could do things under his control. He could document and deal with the whole thing all along the line in his own way.'

Paul and Linda arrive for the royal premiere of *Live and Let Die* in London, 1973.

One of Paul's better photographic ideas came when he conceived the *Band On The Run* cover. He invited a whole gaggle of celebrities to lunch and had them pictured in prison garb up against a wall. They were Clement Freud, Michael Parkinson, James Coburn, Christopher Lee, John Conteh and Kenny Lynch, all favourite McCartney personalities.

On their return to London from Africa, the three remaining Wings began sessions for a projected Linda solo album to be called *Suzie And The Red Stripes*. Apart from a single *Seaside Woman*, which came out in 1977, taken from these sessions, the album was not completed.

In December, 1973, Linda and Paul decided to go visiting and called on the author to discuss their activities, bringing baby Stella in tow and dispensing charm and good cheer. For a couple who had been up to their necks in turmoil and upsets, they seemed supremely happy.

Paul was calm, caring and his dry laconic humour spiced anecdotes and reminiscences in a way that was both subtle and relaxing. We had never met before, yet he seemed like an old friend. And for anyone of the Beatle generation – of course, in a sense, he was.

Paul recalled how he had gone calling on music business people when The Beatles first arrived in London from Liverpool. 'We went to see Robert Stigwood at his office and he wouldn't see us. Never been struck on him since.'

The couple told how they had enjoyed themselves in Lagos, 'eventually.' First they had to adjust to the different climate and food. 'It was like going to Spain for the first time,' said Paul. 'It was the end of the rainy season. We thought it was going to be tropical and warm. It turned out to be torrential monsoons! Then we got robbed. Some guys with a knife took our tape recorder and cameras. We were out walking late at night and you are not supposed to do that. Then Fela Ransome Kuti accused us of stealing black African music. So I had to say, "Do us a favour Fela, we do okay. We alright as it is. We sell a couple of records here and there. African music is very nice – but you are welcome to it!" He did have a great live band though.'

While we were talking, a tea lady came in to offer cups of char and to say hello to Linda and Paul. 'It's lovely to see you. You give everyone a lot of pleasure,' she told Paul giving him a kiss, and wishing him a merry Christmas. Paul sent his regards to her family and she seemed very touched.

'They're all our mates,' said Paul after the tea lady had rushed off to her trolley. 'I get people in the street just coming and saying "Ullo Paul. How's it going. Haven't seen you on the box lately."' He did a perfect Cockney accent with a musician's keen ears for cadences.

I asked Paul why they had gone to Lagos to record *Band On The Run*. 'It was for the sunshine! We got a list off EMI of all the studios in the world that they own. It turned out Lagos was free for the three weeks when we wanted to record. It was great -- lying on the beach all day doing nothing and recording at night. Actually it didn't turn out quite like that. But that's why we went. For the adventure. We did seven tracks there and came back and mixed it. We took our engineer Geoff Emerick out there, who did *Abbey Road* and *Sgt. Pepper*. He can't stand insects so a couple of the lads put a spider in his bed. It was all a bit like scout camp. The music was influenced in the sense it was a challenge to be there and very uphill.'

'Linda thought I had died one night. I had a little number in the studio. I thought a lung had collapsed. I went outside to get some air – and there wasn't any. It was a humid, hot tropical night. I collapsed.' Linda laid Paul on the ground and she thought he was on the verge of expiring. He recovered but a doctor warned him he was smoking too much.

Perhaps the biggest shock of the trip came just on the verge of their departure. 'You know two of them left, Henry and Denny Seiwell, who left the hour before we left for Gatwick? He rang up and said he couldn't make the trip. So that was a panic time. Henry left over what we call "musical differences." Actually, it *was* a musical difference. We were rehearsing, asked him to play a certain bit, he was loath to play it, and kinda made an excuse about it "Couldn't be played." Being a bit of a guitarist myself I knew it COULD be played. Rather than let it pass, I decided to confront him with it. He decided to confront ME with it and we had a confrontation. We both left rehearsals a bit choked. He rang up to say, "I'm leaving you."'

And Denny didn't want to come to Africa. That was his thing. Apparently someone had been to his house and made him very nervous about Africa, and he just rang me and said, "I can't make this trip man." Funnily enough, when we got back we found a letter which had been sent to us before we left, warning us there was a cholera outbreak in the area we were due to record. If we had seen the letter, I don't think we would have taken the three kids there.'

Paul explained how he coped with the missing Wingsmen. 'We did the whole album with just the three of us, except for the orchestral overdubs. We got Tony Visconti to help with the arrangements. Ironically enough there is one African from Lagos on the album. Remi Kebaka turned up in Air London studio one night for a loon and we got him on one of the tracks doing a bit of percussion. He's the only other person on the entire album. I played all the drums and bass. Denny sometimes doubled on bass. I laid down the drums first.'

Paul revealed that he had been into the drums for years. 'I always suggested to Ringo things that he might play. I hear drums well. I first got into them listening to *Sweet Little Sixteen*. I'd ask Ringo to play a variation on those sort of drum breaks. At sessions I'd just climb on the drum kit and start having a go. I got the feeling I could do it as long as nothing difficult was required.

'In Hamburg, I used to drum when Tony Sheridan's drummer went sick. I did it for a week for the extra cash. I drummed on a couple of Beatle tracks – I forget which – but mainly we used Ringo because he's a real drummer. But I think the drumming on *Band On The Run* is quite good. There's nothing flash. But I can hold a good beat. I like drumming anyway, so Denny not turning up gave me a chance to fulfil an ambition.'

'Most of the songs were written in Scotland in the summer. There are a couple of riffs you might think are African influenced, but they were all written up north. The idea of the album starts off with a prison escape. The guy is stuck inside four walls and thinks "If I ever get out of here, if I ever get out of

here. . . ." There's a break out and then it's band on the run.

'There is a thread but it's not a concept album. It sorts relates to me escaping. Most bands on tour are bands on the run.'

I asked Paul and Linda how satisfied they were with the progress of Wings. 'Well it got us on the road, for one thing,' said Linda, who had spent most of the time trying to prevent Stella writing on the walls. 'That's what it's about really.'

Said Paul: 'I wanted some way I could feel easy about appearing live again. It was pretty difficult after The Beatles you know. They weren't interested in playing live except on really big gigs and I was more interested in playing small places and getting near audiences again. A bit like pub rock. I wasn't interested in putting things back into the music business. It was selfish reasons entirely. I just wanted to play live. So we got a good British tour out of it and the second half of our European tour was good. We loved the university tour we did because that was real down home. We just turned up and charged fifty pence at the door.'

'We accomplished what we set out to do and the next stage is putting Wings MKII together. We're a bit vague about singles. We don't sit around and consider a policy. We just say: "That would make a good single" and put it out. It's haphazard.'

Paul disputed the idea that Wings was a middle-of-the-road outfit. 'I don't like the idea we play gentle rock. That's not what we are trying to do. We come on rocking "live"! Maybe our singles have been a bit lightweight. I can't categorise our musical approach. We are just into stuff we like and it changes. One minute with me I'm all dead keen on ballads. I went to a club the other night and my favourite track they played all night was Fred Astaire singing *Cheek To Cheek*. Brilliant. I loved it. My musical tastes are vast. I like classical music, Fred Astaire, and Pink Floyd, in the same breath.'

What Paul most wanted out of Wings at this time was to humanise the Paul McCartney image. 'At first it was a bit precious. People were coming to see a legend, and all that stuff. Now they come just to see a band, and that's much nicer. By the time we did our British tour we all felt like we were a working band, and Linda felt like a trouper.'

I asked Paul why he didn't invite star name players to join him in Wings – like Eric Clapton, for instance. 'That might be a bit difficult. For one reason, I don't know him very well. I like him a lot and he's a great guitarist but I never chummed up with him. We're just quietly looking around for a really nice guitarist and drummer. I just like to play with people and see what they are like. I don't know in my mind yet who I want. We went with Henry just because I knew he was a good guitar player. That didn't quite work out. It doesn't worry me too much if we have to keep chopping and changing. But it would be nice to get a steady band. The public like to see you settled with a band. We just took Jimmy McCulloch, who is a really nice guy and nice guitarist to Paris to do a couple of tracks. It was a great loon. We went in the van and took the ferry and drove into Paris. The same night we went into the studio until 8 a.m.'

The tracks were Suzie and The Red Stripes, Linda being Suzie and The Stripes consisting of Jimmy, Paul and Denny Laine. Red Stripe was their favourite Jamaican beer. The idea was to do a Derek & The Dominos. Anonymity without trying to hide anything. Linda had written a few songs and she said: 'I'm not Gershwin or anything but I thought I'd have a bit of fun and put it out.'

Interestingly at this time, Paul was able to foresee large changes in the future of rock, away from the superstar image towards a smaller scale affair, emanating from the pubs and colleges. The change did come, just two years later with the emergence of Punk Rock in 1976. 'Rock is becoming too intellectualised. But the good thing is with every movement in that direction there is a counter movement. Someone, somewhere starts up. Like the pub rock bands. It's a small scene but it's healthy. It starts to counteract the big deal of it all. Our university tour was very well received. We weren't the greatest band in the world but just the fact we were there went down well.

'I just think of myself as a hack writer. People just ring up. Rod Stewart rang me up and asked me to write a song for him so I did *Mine For Me* for his album. Then they asked me to write the theme for the James Bond movie. The idea just has to appeal to me and

I'll do it. I don't like to feel that I'm "a major influence on the music scene". I don't believe that. I'd begin to feel very unsafe if I began to believe that. But I love the music scene. We spent a night in Scotland together planning a club. We still have the plans. It would have been a fantastic place.

'What I really want for myself is the freedom to play to 56,000 people and be able to manage that and the next night go and play a pub somewhere. My favourite way of working is to be close to people. We played a few European gigs where Henry would invite people out of the audience. In Rotterdam, a chick got up on stage from the front row and danced. The bouncers panicked but it was such a nice evening. It was like a party. One lousy thing with being big is there is a feeling you have to be big, no matter what. And of course, no one is all big, no matter who they are, Mick Jagger, Rod Stewart or me.'

Many stars in Paul's position became recluses and lived in their own tiny world. Yet he went out of his way to be accessible and meet people. Did he ever feel the need to hide away?

'Immediately after the break up of The Beatles I felt "What am I gonna do?" I then went into a period when everybody started to call me a hermit in isolation. All sorts of little snide articles started to appear. "He's sitting up in Scotland looking into his mirror admiring his own image". Not at all true. I was planting trees up there, doing something for a change. I was trying to get normal again, and giving myself time to think, what do I want to do?'

Paul agreed that he felt abnormal and on the verge of a breakdown after The Beatles. 'Oh definitely. I'm sure when Eric Clapton was being called God, that it got to him. But really I felt normal inside. When I was in The Beatles I could never understand when they said: "What are you going to do when the bubble bursts?" It was a joke question. We always used to say "We'll burst with it – ha, ha."'

'It was the only thing we could think of, just to answer the thing. But I never took it in. I never understand what they meant. What does it mean "when the bubble bursts." When it bursts, I'll be dead. Never understood the question really. I never took it in until The Beatles broke up. And they were always going on about "the pressures." I could see there were pressures. I couldn't feel them! I was just a rocker. People kept saying "Oh, what about all these pressures?" I didn't begin to feel any until the big, dramatic break up of the Beatles. The simple answer is, it is all play and I don't give a shit. Because it doesn't matter anyway. Then you can start to come out with some music and enjoy things, that's the way I feel now.'

'I'm not sweating about getting Wings into an almighty supergroup. It could happen. Easily. And on our British tour we began to have a really good band. One chapter

of Wings has finished and we'll just take it easy. Do music. Play live with people.'

I suggested Paul was now in control of his working environment, where before he wasn't in The Beatles. 'No, I think that's journalese. It's nice to think that's what happened. But we were always pretty much in control. People used to say that a lot, how we were so manipulated. We were NEVER manipulated, I don't think. Maybe subtly.

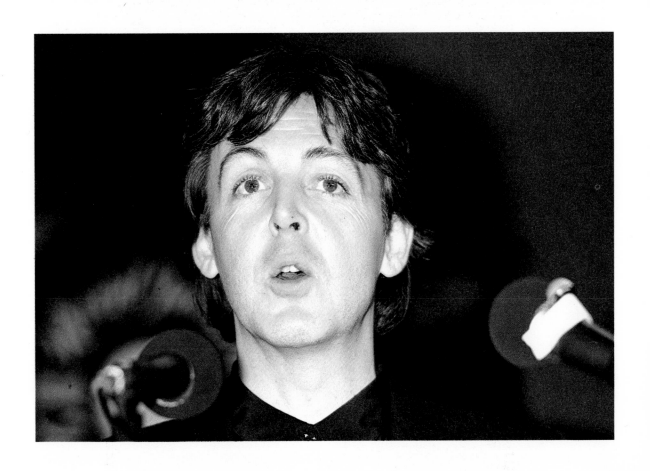

We were certainly manipulated businesswise because we just didn't know anything about business. Brian Epstein came up to us once and said: "I'm going to sell you to Bernard Delfont." We said: "Right man, if you do that, we'll never play another note. We'll just play the national anthem. Every record will be "God Save The Queen." See how you like that, if you pull one on us." That was an attempt at manipulation, half way through The Beatles. We were big. It was getting a bit too much for Brian and he thought, "I'll sell out". He wanted to put us with a good agency, so he had discharged his responsibilities. We always used to talk about how sharp the Grades were as agents. But we just didn't like the idea of being sold. Eventually, of course, we got Apple and *gave* it all away, as Roger Daltrey says in his song.

'The Apple story was very long and involved and if anyone ever gets it down, it'll be very interesting. But from my point of view, it just showed that from the minute Klein came in he was crooked. And very obviously so. I first found out about him when I had been talking to him and he seemed very straight and almost reasonable. He could have had us. He really could have had us if he had just been a bit smarter. The first time I realised he was pulling a number was when he and John called Rolling Stone magazine. In fact, he got John to ring them and there was a lot of manipulation there.... when I wasn't around. There were all sorts of little contracts signed which I still haven't seen. Lots of little companies formed here and there with rights being signed over.'

'They phoned Rolling Stone and said: "McCartney says I can take forty percent if I want, he doesn't care, he says he's got such faith in me, he doesn't care what deal he does with me. Sure they're all behind me. I'm their man now!" Of course, at the time I was having an argument a day with him saying, "Hey man, no WAY forty percent. Maybe ten?" Christ, we were BIG. We were a bloody big group. Why the hell should we give Klein twenty or forty percent? That's what Brian Epstein used to get when we were nothing.'

'Klein said: "Times change." I said: "Sure they have. We are in the bargaining seat now." Then I noticed this thing by him saying: "McCartney says I can have anything." I realised, "Oh shit, he's playing two games at once." That's when I really went against him and started the battle. Earlier, we had got Jagger round to Apple and said: "Mick, what's the story on Klein?" And he said: "He's okay if you watch him!" That meant nothing. Then Mick rang up and said: "Well, er, we're not that struck on him" and stuff. By that time the other three Beatles had signed, and I hadn't. Thank you Lord that I didn't sign. Now the others realise he was a total rip off. He's so despicable, I can't stand the sight of him. I'm just glad that he's out.

'I advise anybody who has written a song to own it themselves. But no publisher will let you own the copyright. I always harp on about *Yesterday* because it is a big song of mine, the only big one that I did on my own. I don't own the copyright of that. It belongs to Lew Grade. No fault of his. He's a good businessman and it was up for sale. So I say to anyone new coming into the business, check it out with your accountant or lawyer and set it up so you can own your own song.'

'During the two years that Allan Klein was manager of The Beatles, none of us took anything out of the company except living expenses. Klein, though, took four million dollars in management fees and claimed another five million. He thinks he's worth ten million and The Beatles were worth nothing. It's wrong. Any schoolkid will tell you it's wrong.' Paul explained that even when the Sixties rock stars set up their own publishing companies, complete with office and secretary, only five percent of the royalties was coming their way. 'It's a trick that publishers have. They say they'll give you your own company. They set up a subsidiary in which they give you small rights and let you name the company after yourself. "Macca Productions" they say, there's your own company. And you say, "Yeah of course! My own little office." But of course when you check into it, the money isn't coming your way.'

After the Christmas holidays, Paul and Linda set about forming Wings MKII, as they had promised. They held some unique auditions for a drummer which yielded Geoff Britton, the new recruit alongside guitarist Jimmy McCulloch, who was finally declared an official Wingsman. It seemed like all Paul's troubles were far away, and they could all get down to some happy music making. But even with Paul's pati-ence, skill and enthusiasm, the course of Wings over the ensuing twelve months would not run smooth. If Paul thought he had seen the last of personality clashes, he was to be in for a few shocks during 1974.

Chapter Seven
THE BATTLE OF WINGS

After *Band On The Run*, Paul's prestige and wealth began a steady upward spiral. But he was always inclined to play down the 'millionaire genius' tag. He would sooner describe himself as a 'rocker' or even 'a hack.' He left it to others to make judgements while he got on with his life and music.

Says Bill Harry: 'Paul is a songwriter in the classic vein, probably the greatest of the twentieth century. When The Beatles chapter closed there was Paul with a great voice, musical and songwriting ability, able to start a new chapter on his own and create something from the ground floor. In Paul's character, is a built-in politeness and love for the family and respect for aunties and uncles and all the rest. He had all the values we expect from an English family. That's why he wanted to bring Linda into it. If he was going to express something, she was going to be a part of it. Now he was able to express himself fully and choose the musicians he wanted. He couldn't do that in The Beatles. Now he was head of the Wings family. He was the godfather who dictated what happened and had full creative rein.'

As 1974 went by, Paul might well have muttered: 'Would that this were true.' He wasn't a dictator, more an Ombudsman trying to deal with warring factions that marred what should have been a dream band. It seemed extraordinary. Paul was offering the greatest opportunity a Seventies rock musician could ask for. He had avoided choosing superstar musicians he could so easily have booked to avoid superstar tantrums. But tantrums he got, as soon as Wings were let loose in America.

At the start of the year, he set up some

unique auditions at a London theatre to find a new drummer. Paul had enjoyed the drumming sessions for *Band On The Run* but knew he needed to find a regular drummer for future tours. He had already found his guitarist, twenty-one year-old Jimmy McCulloch, who had played so well on the Paris sessions for Suzie and The Red Stripes.

Jimmy was a brilliant musician who could be very charming and likeable but was cursed with a fiery temperament. Just over five foot tall, he tried to make up for his lack of height with a show of bravado. Raised in Glasgow, he had early on learned how to defend himself with a lashing tongue. A combination of Scottish temperament, musical frustration and too much whisky would make him an explosive, hell-raising human timebomb ticking away in the ranks.

And yet for most people in the London based music business, Jimmy had been a cheery, good looking kid with tremendous potential. This had been spotted when he left home at the age of thirteen to become a musician and came to town with his Scots group, One In A Million. He was spotted by The Who's Pete Townshend and made an early appearance on Ready, Steady, Go!. The Who hailed him as a genius and later he was chosen to play with Thunderclap Newman, a bizarre band built around pianist Andy Newman, and featured on Track Records' hit *Something In The Air* in 1969. Later Jimmy joined Stone The Crows, where he replaced guitarist Les Harvey, and was working with Blue when Paul asked him to go to Paris.

Jimmy was very proud of his new job with Wings. It seemed like the crowning achievement of his career to play with an ex-Beatle. He proclaimed: 'I've been in the business a long time but it never occurred to me I'd ever play with McCartney. I met a guy who worked in a studio and he told me Paul was looking for a guitarist to work on some sessions. I went along to chat about it but it was like some kind of dream.'

'Paul was there chatting happily and I just kept staring at him and thinking to myself "Christ, he used to be a Beatle. And here he is talking to me like i matter."'

Wings' new drummer also thought he was living in a dream and found himself gawping at the man who had plucked him from the grind of the workaday circuit into the kind of starry world rock musicians dream about. Geoff Britton got the job that dozens of top drummers had fought for and lost. He was a good drummer. Above all he was a rocker, a man who revered the names of Buddy Holly, Bill Haley and Elvis Presley. Perhaps subconsciously Paul thought of him as a younger, brasher Ringo. But there was one important difference. Geoff was a Londoner, born and bred. He was no laid-back Scouse but an upfront Cockney, with his own brand of cheek and humour.

Wings now consisted of a Liverpudlian superstar, his American wife, a Brummie muso, a Glaswegian tearaway and South London karate champion. As Geoff conceded later: 'The chemistry was doomed.'

Even to outsiders, with only the faintest inkling of what was going on, it seemed a strange line-up. It could still have worked but for the ways of human nature. When the band played they rocked as perhaps no Wings unit had rocked before or since. Geoff Britton, a keep fit and karate fanatic, played with a driving power that had earlier sparked such well respected outfits as East Of Eden and The Wild Angels, early rock revivalists. He used massive drum sticks that Ginger Baker had once pronounced as unplayable and as Geoff said proudly: 'There was nothing I couldn't handle' when it came to playing along with Wings. But he only survived a few months and was subsequently dropped, leaving an eloquent and articulate man with feelings of disappointment that would haunt him for many years afterwards.

Geoff was teaching a karate class in Maidstone in early 1974. One of his pupils was Clifford Davies, the ex-manager of Fleetwood Mac. During a break in classes he mentioned that Wings were holding auditions for a drummer. Geoff called Alan Crowther who was setting up the auditions and, with his usual assurance, promised he would be 'just right for the band. No problems!' He was invited to the Albery Theatre in St. Martin's Lane on April 26 and turned up on a Honda motorcycle, wearing a leather jacket and Wild Angels tee shirt. He even brought another drummer friend along and insisted that he be given a chance to audition as well. Rob Townshend, the drummer with Family was playing on stage with a

group of hired session musicians.

Each drummer had to play the same five tunes with the band while Paul and Linda sat in the audience and watched. The tunes chosen included Duke Ellington's *Caravan* which gave the drummer a chance to play some breaks and cope with tempo changes. This number floored Geoff's friend. But Britton found it easy after early experience as a cabaret drummer in St. Moritz, Switzerland.

'I did the business. Right up my street. I had done three years of summer seasons and knew the stuff backwards.' He also coped with a Kansas City style blues shuffle and rock songs.

Geoff then joined his prospective employers in the audience to watch the next contestant, who turned out to be Jimi Hendrix' old drummer. Geoff and his mate both yelled out, 'Oh no, not Mitch Mitchell!' They expected to be wiped out. But recalls Geoff: 'Mitch must have been having a bad day because he was awful. He couldn't keep time, hopeless. When it came to the fill-ins he was beautiful. But the tempos didn't happen and he didn't get the gig. All the drummers had to shout out their names which was a bit embarrassing. Fortunately, I had my Angels T shirt so they knew who I was and didn't have to shout!'

A few days later Geoff got a 'phone call. The McCartney people were happy with him and invited him along to a proper audition with Wings. There were six drummers on the short list, among them Aynsley Dunbar, who 'phoned from America and didn't want to make the auditions in person. A ballroom in Camden Town was hired and three days were spent testing the brace of drummers. Geoff taped these historic sessions, lent the tape to a friend and never got it back.

'It was great. We played *Lucille* and really rocked away. Then Brian Brolley their manager gave me the third degree. He was sussing me out. By now I had got really nervous. I began to think.. "I might be a contender!"'

On May 16, Geoff was out on a running track doing some training when his wife called out that Paul McCartney was on the 'phone saying "You've got the gig." The excitement was almost physical. After years as a struggling musician without much money to support his wife, it at last seemed as if fortune had smiled on them. But instead of feeling unmitigated joy, Geoff was smitten with anxieties.

'I was feeling concerned. The Wild Angels had been up to some mischief in Glasgow and we had a court case waiting. We had been involved in some naughty activities when we toured up there and we had to appear in court. Basically, we had been jibbing hotels. I had a ticket to go to Nashville and there was a court case against me. I dare not tell anyone. I didn't breath a word of it. I took the train to Scotland and we went to court.'

Geoff discovered that Scottish law had three possible verdicts in such a case, guilty, not guilty and not proven. To their immense relief they were found 'not proven.' It was months after the Angels' tour and memories had faded on vital aspects of the case.

'The old beak really hated us Southern rock and rollers. He said if we had been found guilty we would have been put away which would have blown my gig completely. I was quaking in the dock when he started to sum up.' Geoff had already done 'porridge' for stealing cars, as a wild and less then angelic teenager. He felt great relief when he walked free from the court.

Wings were all set to go to Nashville to rehearse and record and make a film called *One Hand Clapping* showing Wings at work. It was the home of the country, hillbilly and rock 'n' roll music Geoff had been raised on in the days when he hung around the jukebox in his local cafe. This was his jukebox dream come to life.

'It was my first time in America and I didn't want to go home. I met a chick out there of course and I just was blown away by the whole place.' They stayed at a ranch with hundreds of acres and a lake. They used a garage to rehearse in and spent their days either playing, or riding motorbikes and going to barbecues. 'It was just marvellous. All the country stars called by like Roy Orbison, Chet Atkins and Floyd Cramer. We were in a place called Lebanon in a dry state. There was no liquor allowed and there was moonshining in the hills around us. Guys came into town in old pick-up trucks and did their whittling with bits of wood. It was

Wings with Ringo Starr.

straight out of a movie. Brilliant.'

It wasn't all play. Wings recorded *Junior's Farm* and *Sally G*, later issued on a single which got to Number Sixteen in the chart, and stayed high for ten weeks.

Geoff was in awe of Paul and held him in great respect. But as a young rocker he could not entirely submerge his own well-defined personality. 'Paul and I got on fine. We were the same sort of age. We came out of the same musical heritage. I felt when we were alone and rapped, the relationship was really fine.' But it soon became apparent the relationship could not run smoothly.

'Unfortunately for Paul it's hard to be one of the world's biggest superstars and not be affected by it. It was such an imbalance between everybody else in the band and him.'

'I'd catch myself, when we were rehearsing, looking at him and it seemed like a dream. But I was used to controlling my own destiny in a band by virtue of being an

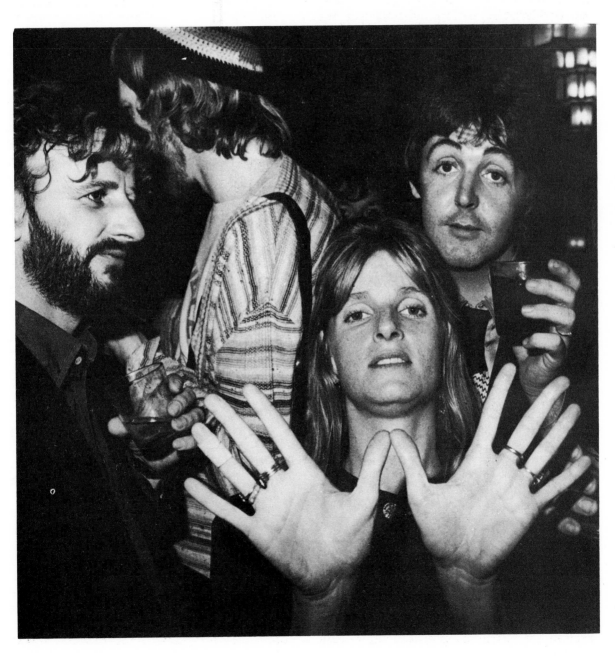

upstart and a bit pushy. And of course, that doesn't go down too well when you've got Paul in the band. You have to realise your position in the hierarchy and that was quite hard for me to do. Paul liked that at first. He looked on me as a novelty. He got off on my little world and I could see he was fascinated by it. Also I didn't go to pieces in his presence, like some of the other drummers had done.'

'We'd lark around and it was all taken for granted. And yet there were times when having grown up on his music and been awestruck by it, it used to affect me privately. When we were together playing *Hey Jude* it was beautiful. But he was subject to so many pressures. His whole world was pressing in on him. And in those conditions – well you are not a normal person.'

While the band were adjusting to life down on the farm, gradually word got around that Wings were in town. At first, they could come and go without being hassled but then sightseers hung around the gate. Off-duty policemen put a twenty-four hour guard on the premises. But even in the farmhouse they were not unmolested.

'The 'phones would go and there would be endless requests to appear on shows. There would be all sorts of celebrities asking favours. David Cassidy would come on the 'phone pouring out his troubles. The stars all came to Paul for help and advice. He was a very respected guy.'

Geoff could see that for all Paul's brave words about The Beatles break up, even by 1974, it was still a source of pain. The constant rumours of a Beatles reunion did nothing to help Paul, trying hard to re-estabish Wings and his solo career.

'The Beatles bust up was a tragedy. He felt strongly about it. There were times of depression and there would be a little conflict between Linda and him and she would say he missed the other three.'

'The Beatles were all equals. They had all come from nothing together and been elevated to this incredible status, unprecedented in the music industry. Of course, they had outgrown their old haunts and friends. But they needed each other. He didn't seem to have any old friends anymore. I felt that Paul didn't have anybody around who could tell him when he was out

of order, or to fuck off. You need that. It doesn't matter who you are. This was possibly my strength, and failing, within the band.'

'I'd get a bit up front about things. Sometimes I'd bite my tongue but basically no, I wouldn't. Because I think it's good for the guy and any relationship to be up front and honest. If you think someone is a bastard you tell them, whether they are a multi-millionaire or not. He needed a lot of that at times. He'd go off the rails and think everything he said was pure wisdom. He didn't think of himself like that but it happened subtly.'

'It's alright if a band has come up together and they are all millionaires. They can talk to each other as equals. But with Wings there were these incredible imbalances which manifest themselves in many ways. For example, we were offered a gig there to play a festival with Stevie Wonder for half an hour. The money being offered was a fortune. I instinctively said "Let's do it!" My cut of that would have bought me a house! I said "Fucking great!" Paul didn't want to do it. So I didn't do any live gigs with the band. A lot of the time was spent making a film. After that, we went to New Orleans to start the *Venus And Mars* album and that's when I got marched out, and that was the end of it.'

In fact, it was the second time the outspoken rocker had been sacked from Wings. The first trauma was in Nashville soon after they arrived.

'There was a controversy over the day's rehearsal. Everyone got a bit stoned and then it got heavy. Jimmy insulted Linda and there were tears. Then I said what I thought of Jimmy.'

After this outburst the management announced that they wanted to 'reassess' Geoff. The drummer, perhaps wishing he had bitten his tongue instead of stoking Scottish fires went to the bandroom and told the crew: 'I think it's all over for me. Can I have some money? I'll take off and see the States before I go back home.' He was bitterly disappointed but put on a brave show of taking it all in his stride. The crew tried to reason with him and offered words of encouragement. 'I'm not going back in there. I'm either the drummer in the band or I'm not.'

Next morning, Paul and Linda, greatly concerned, came to see Geoff for a morale-boosting chat. Paul explained how he wanted them all to pull together and make a success of the band. A wave of relief swept over Geoff and he gladly went back to the studio to carry on rehearsals with Jimmy and Denny.

'It was wonderful for the next few days. And then someone would do something and it was all blown again. It was very fragile. Words would be said and Linda would get upset. Jimmy would say something about the chords being wrong, and the worst thing you can do to a musician who is struggling is to put them under pressure.'

'This is why black musicians succeed, because they are so loose. Fears don't even enter their heads. They're not hung up about playing. Linda would be ultra-sensitive and Jimmy being tactless would put the downers on her. He would be short with Denny too about the tuning. If he came in wrecked and hung over everything about him would be negative. If he was on an up, then we'd rock away for hours and it would be absolute magic and I would be loving it.'

Geoff admitted his own faults but put much of the blame for his final departure squarely on Jimmy McCulloch and Denny Laine. 'At the bottom line they were the cause. They put the spoke in for me. It was a shame. Because at the time when the spoke could have been put in for their gig, I protected and covered for them. Unfortunately, I just got blasted out. I've got my keepsakes and momentos from my days with Wings but it's a shame it ended so quickly. I got on fine with Linda and Paul, but the whole band was very unhappy.'

'Linda was very insecure then. As a keyboard player she was still finding her feet and she was sensitive to the fact she wasn't a great musician. But she improved immensely. She wanted to be in there and was intrigued by being in a band. Paul wanted her there because they were inseparable. She was everything to him. He'd lost his friends and she was a tower of strength when his morale was low. When The Beatles fell apart it was crushing and she was there to help. They were in love. He was the world's richest superstar and a good looking guy. For her, the whole package was

mindblowing. She dug being on stage, but she had to work for it, in terms of getting her chops together.'

Geoff's relationship with Denny and Jimmy deteriorated rapidly. 'They definitely thought I was a fly boy, a bit of an 'erbert. They were musos of the old era who got pissed together. Pretty ignorant guys really, just good players and that was it. They were into heavy drinking and over-the-top drugs. And of course, me with all my sport activities, I didn't participate in anything.'

'People are very funny. You learn all the time. If you are out of step with your immediate society, even if you are morally right, then you are the odd dog in the pack and the others turn on you.'

'You would think they would respect you and let you get on with your own lifestyle. It doesn't work that way. We would go to parties and the tables would be laid out with coke and anything you wanted was there. So everybody got absolutely legless, on the knowledge that I would drive them all home, and I would be straight. I would keep an eye on everybody to see there was no trouble and that was great. But it wasn't.'

'Because I wasn't getting stoned and legless with them we had this barrier between us. I didn't erect a barrier. They did. Now it is much more acceptable not to be party to the drugs and drink syndrome. Now a jogging suit is a national fashion and it is "in" to be doing karate. I would have thought it was a blessing to have someone like me around but it didn't work out like that.'

'Unfortunately I let it slip a few times, with the Londoners attitude, about the "thick Northerners." Ha, ha! And they had this Southern herbert thing as well about me. And I definitely thought they were thick Northerners – that's for sure. Well they WERE thick Northerners. There's no hiding facts.'

'Jimmy was a lovely guitar player and a very talented boy and his passing is subject to much mystery.' (Jimmy McCulloch died in September 1979). 'It's quite weird. When he was straight he was a nice little lad. But a typical Glaswegian. You shove something inside him and he wants to kill the world. Being five foot nothing it was even worse in his case. He was a really hard, aggressive "Hey Jimmy" type. But he didn't need to be

like that. His playing made up for his lack of height.'

Jimmy left Wings in 1977. Says Geoff: 'He had fallen foul of the band and done one tantrum too many and wrecked one of the rooms he was living in on Paul's farm. He'd gone berserk and Paul said that was enough. He used to get so bloody violent when he went over the top. It was the booze and the uppers and downers. You get so burnt out and tired, and you deprive your body of the B vitamins with booze and amphetamine. You shorten the nerves and if you are temperamental as well, you are feeding the fire.'

Paul showed amazing tolerance in putting up with so much from his errant bandsmen, as Geoff is the first to agree. 'Absolutely. He used to come to me and bellyache about the other two and say he wanted to get other people in the band. But I would say that every band had these problems and we could work a way round it. I'd say, "If we all have confidence and respect in each other this can be our strength!" I sincerely believed that. No band is perfect. There is always a problem with someone. That band could still be together now. People don't know how to handle success or other people. It's really down to ignorance, age and opportunities lost. Denny hasn't done anything since. Jimmy might have done. It's hard to say.'

'They weren't doing their homework on that gig. You can be honest with someone without being deferential. You've gotta have a good relationship or you have blown it right down the line. It was in the make-up of the guys.'

'They were bent on blowing it no matter what. Realistically, it's not a gig, it's a multi-million pound industry. It will forgive a rock musician a few things. You can have a booze or drug problem. You can steal and do anything short of rape and be allowed to get away with it. If you start blowing your gig, then the ranks will close on you.'

'Once you go down the avenue of getting pissed and stoned every five minutes, it becomes counter-productive and you start destroying yourself. They should have waited until the band had ironed out all its problems and done it with a clear head. Then they could have got stoned. But they were bent on letting it all hang out, before there was anything to hang out.'

'Paul was one of the boys too, but he was a very dignified person. He likes sitting at home in the evening and watching the telly. Or he'll go and buy a Chinese takeaway and eat it in the car. Very low profile stuff.'

Not all the time was spent feuding. There was one wonderful and productive night spent in Printer's Alley, a Soho style district of Nashville with lots of bars and poolrooms. There they met Waylon Jennings playing a pin table who was invited over to chat to Paul and Geoff and talk about the old days with Buddy Holly. The next day, Geoff found Paul sitting on the stoop by the farmhouse with a guitar in his hand. He called out: "What do you think of this?" He began playing a song which turned out to be *Sally G*.

Says Geoff: 'It was about the friendly state of Tennessee and Printer's Alley and it was literally about the events of the night before. Here was a song, being created. He had it! No messing about. The storyline, the lyrics and melody were all done. It was almost involuntary, like something from within.'

'Fortunately, he has the musical awareness and creativity to handle this gift. In anybody else it might have driven them mad. He has the musicianship to match his creative talent. It almost happened in spite of him. There was this person and there was this talent, joined together. He works and suffers, but it just *flows.*'

'Think of what a song is. Once we've heard a piece of music we can identify it. But before it is there – nothing. Space. Someone has to invent – to create – to fill the space. Well the wealth of stuff Paul has invented and created is just awesome. It now spans two decades and it doesn't look like its going to dry up.'

'Artists like Chuck Berry are very creative but peak in four years and after that are never quite the same again. Paul has gone on which makes his talent and genius all the more exceptional. With Paul, it's like a volcano that bubbles to the surface. He would do something, go somewhere and that would be the song. Somebody else might relate things in a painting, poem or story. For Paul, it's a song.'

'He has incredible pitch and can just pick up a guitar or play the piano and come up with a lovely phrase. He has inspired a whole generation with his music and he is the embodiment of so many unique characteristics. But he is a rock and roller at heart. And Paul has worked consistently over the years. The other Beatles went into different orbits. Lennon and George did a few things, then bosh, they just closed down, and got on with their private lives. Paul never closed down. He just kept going. With Wings he wanted to prove he could go out and do it himself. He didn't want to be anonymous, but he wanted to be part of a band. He wanted Wings to stand up in its own right. He was trying to rebuild what he had with The Beatles. But there was no way this would be allowed. Come interview time, it was only Paul they wanted to talk to. Why should they want to talk to me? I said that if ever there was a chance of The Beatles reforming, I'd willingly step down. Historical-ly, my contribution was insignificant compared to Ringo's.'

'The Wings thing was all very well but really he was one of The Beatles as far as I was concerned. Did he want The Beatles back? I think, desperately. I really feel that. You see they grew up together. They went through the rough times and there is no replacing that. They were friends. If they could have got the Kleins of this world out of the way, and the Lindas and Yokos, got them all out the way, and got the four boys together and thrash it out, it could have been done. And in later years they did gradually get to see each other.'

'Paul was obviously cut in half by The Beatles thing. He was reading nasty things about himself and John was writing songs. And I think Paul needed that. He *was* a bully to work for. He did give the other members of the band a hard time. As The Beatles grew richer and more important, then they could tell him to fuck off. But when there are people hanging around it all gets taken out of context. Dignity is hurt and faces are put out. It could have been cured and remedied. One Beatle might have been more talented than the others but each made a vital contribution. There was obviously a lot of love at one time and it can't have gone completely.' Wings returned to Britain.

The crunch for Geoff came when it was time for the group to fly to New Orleans to start recording tracks for *Venus And Mars*. In fact, they had already done some in *Abbey Road* and Geoff was included on *Love In Song*, *Letting Go* and *Medicine Jar*. While they were back in London, Paul and Linda made an unexpected guest appearance with Rod Stewart and the Faces at Lewisham Odeon. It was the night of November 27, 1974 and said Rod to a wondering crowd: 'My brother and sister are here and I'd like you to meet them.' Out came a girl in green and a man in a loud check jacket. They put their arms around Rod and up went a cheer of disbelief and pleasure as the crowd recognised Paul and Linda. They sang *Mine For Me*, the song Paul had written for Rod's *Smiler* album. Watching from the wings was Geoff Britton.

Said Geoff: 'I was so depressed. I dreaded going to New Orleans with them. It should have been the happiest time of my life. But I was miserable and hated it. There was no

Left to right: David Essex, Paul McCartney and Steve Harley, in Copenhagen.

sincerity in the band and every day it was a fight for survival, a fight to re-establish yourself.'

'I had just come from The Wild Angels, a band where there was a real camaraderie. We were all in it together and it was fun. Paul wanted a band. He genuinely did. Unfortunately, he picked the wrong people. In my opinion, the chemistry wasn't right. I was sensitive to it. I couldn't believe all the hassles. We were at each other's throats.'

'With hindsight, looking back, it was doomed. But I didn't know that until I lived with these people. I was unhappy and you can't fool yourself. I told my wife, which only added to her insecurities. So she 'phoned me in New Orleans and said she wanted a divorce, which really blew me away at the time. We had been through lots of hard times in our life together with me being a musician, and this was a time when it looked like we had finally cracked it, and here was me, the breadwinner, saying he was unhappy and didn't like the gig.'

'So I came back to England. I had lost my gig, my marriage, and then somebody stole my car. It was incredible. I took time out for a reappraisal of my life.' Geoff stopped drumming and went back to school for nine months to study.

He explained the sequence of events which led to his departure. 'We flew to New Orleans individually. We stayed at a lovely hotel in the French quarter; then started work in the studio. When I listen to the tracks we did, I don't think there was anything wrong with my playing. But I could tell by then that I just didn't have any rapport with Jimmy and Denny. They were unapproachable. There was nothing musically I couldn't handle.... they just didn't like me. And to me, it was very apparent. I came out of the studio one night and saw this look on Denny's face. Denny could be very cruel. Him and Jimmy were supposed to be close muckers who would go out boozing together and yet, when the chips were down, he tried to get Jimmy shafted out with a knife in the back. He's a bastard. I should have chinned him. I regret it.'

'I saw him going up to Paul and say: ''I want just you and me to run the band''. I saw the conversation go down and the next day Paul and Linda came into my room and said

I had been terminated. There were no heart-rending scenes. It was his group and he had to make these decisions. I didn't say: ''It's all a mistake!'' or crawl on my knees. I wasn't happy in the band but I knew it was a great loss.'

Geoff greatly regretted his departure from Wings. 'I should never have allowed it to happen. Knowing what I know now, if I could put the clock back, I would have played the whole gig completely differently. I think of it as a lost opportunity, but a priceless experience. It might sound like I am bellyaching but to me it was a privilege to have grown up as a Beatle fan, and then to have found myself rocking out *Hey Jude*, with Paul McCartney singing it. I was struck by that occasion. Now I think what an idiot I was. I should have played it differently, but I can't get over the fact I was unhappy with my position in the band.'

'When I first joined, I was promised royalties and we talked in telephone numbers. Then it became session fees and bonuses. But it was a waste to have let such a golden opportunity become such a bad experience. Maybe I should have given Jimmy McCulloch and Denny Laine the pasting they both deserved. Maybe Jimmy wouldn't be dead now and we'd all still be in Wings.'

In New Orleans, Wings found a new drummer, American Joe English. He fitted in easily and finished off the *Venus And Mars* sessions. The next project was to be a massive tour of the world, one of the biggest in rock history, which would run for thirteen months. It was due to start in England on September 9, 1975 and last until October 21, 1976. Apart from three nights at Wembley Arena, it would include ten other countries reaching two million people. It was all a far cry from the fifty pence gigs on the college tour, and even further removed from another of Paul's early plans.

He had wanted to use the extensive basement of his new McCartney Productions office in London's Soho Square as a lunchtime studio. It would have been equipped with a small stage and trestle tables to sell hamburgers and Pepsis. London office workers would stroll in to see Wings at play. It would have been the Casbah Club or the Jackaranda all over again. But manager Brian Brolley was forced to point out the impracticalities of such a scheme. 'Paul secretly wanted to go back,' says Geoff Britton. 'He wanted the joys of playing, free of the paranoia, of going on a big stage and putting his reputation on the line. If he failed it would be a big story. Big gigs. Big problems. I was all for the lunchtime gigs. It would have been priceless.'

Whether he liked it or not, Paul was heading once again for the spotlights and the screaming crowd, not to mention the fierce attention of the world's media. Once again his work would be put under scrutiny and his every move observed.

It was just ironic that after all the problems with the break up of The Beatles, Paul should have suffered again so many personality problems with Wings.

Says Geoff: 'He could have picked the great musicians of the day but there was no way he could control them. It was a problem. He wanted good players and auditioned the ones he thought could handle his music. But he picked the wrong guys.'

Chapter Eight
WORLD DOMINATION

During the summer of 1975, Paul and Linda took a holiday in America to see Linda's father. Then Wings began gathering for the tour, which was hailed in advance as the first time Paul would sing Beatle songs since their split. It was also the first Wings' concerts at home since 1973. By the time the tour was over, Wings, despite a barrage of media interest in old Beatle connections, had established its own powerful identity. Said Paul: 'This tour established Wings, not re-established me!'

The *Venus & Mars* album was released in May and Paul and Linda celebrated the completion of recording sessions by throwing an enormous party in Los Angeles. They hired the old British liner, the Queen Mary, resting at Long Beach Harbour. Among the guests were Davey Jones, Joni Mitchell, Cher, Michael Jackson, Dean Martin, Bob Dylan and Tatum O'Neil. The stars formed a wild conga line around the decks, and when George Harrison arrived; he was greeted with fervent hugs from Paul.

After the celebration, Wings got down to planning the tour, a massive operation in which efficiency and organisation would be the watchwords. This would be no re-run of the Magical Mystery Tour, when The Beatles forgot to book hotels and studios and just turned up, expecting everything to happen – by magic. This time Paul's management organisation swung into action behind the band. There was an American sound crew and musical director. There were lighting men, photographers, publicists, wardrobe ladies, roadies and drivers.

Wings was augmented for the tour with a brass section featuring old Liverpool mate Howie Casey on tenor sax, Steve 'Tex' Howard on trumpet, Thaddeus Richard, soprano and alto sax, and Tony Dorsey on trombone. Tony wrote their arrangements and had worked with Paul on the making of *Venus & Mars* in New Orleans.

The British dates started at the Southampton Gaumont on September 9, 1975 and went on to Bristol Hippodrome (10), Cardiff Capitol (11), Manchester Free Trade Hall (12), Birmingham Hippodrome (13), Liverpool Empire (15), Newcastle City Hall (16), and London's Hammersmith Odeon (17 & 18).

They also played dates in Scotland, Edinburgh (20), Glasgow (22) and Dundee (23). To accompany the tour, a new single was released: *Letting Go* from the album, which Paul habitually referred to as 'Letingo'. After the British dates, they were due to go to Australia, Japan and America, playing a two hour show night after night featuring songs from Wings' back catalogue.

Many saw the tour as a stiff test of Linda's musical ability. Said one music paper on its front page: 'When she appeared on the band's last tour she was strongly criticised. Since then her keyboard playing has contributed to the success of *Band On The Run* and *Venus & Mars*. According to friends, her musical talent has considerably matured.'

The national press was obsessed by the possibility of a Beatles reformation and could not accept that one Beatle at least was already out there and working.

American promoter, Bob Arum talked about offering twenty million pounds for the group to reform, including a million for each Beatle just for one show. It was claimed that relations within the group were back to normal and it was time for a reunion. 'This is one offer The Beatles just cannot refuse,' claimed the promoter. He was wrong, but persisted in saying: 'The time is ripe for a deal. All four have intimated there is no basic obstacle to getting together again.'

Commented Paul: 'We're friends, old pals. It was only logical that we'd eventually get together again. But it's too early to say whether we'll work together. We would never be permanently together, but there might well be ventures we could re-assemble for again. I wouldn't rule it out. None of us are enemies by a long shot.'

But Paul was just being polite. Paul told me in March 1976: 'Maybe in America one night we'll all loon down to a studio. I'm just playing it by ear. The main thing about this huge offer.... THE HUGE OFFER.... well the man's an embarrassment. If I were a fellow back in Liverpool aged eighteen doing me first job, well I'd think "Nobody can refuse that can they? It's just too much money." Even if we were terrible it would be worth it – right?'

'Well for me, the trouble is I've always been so proud of The Beatles and the embarrassment of the thing is that so much money is being offered, most people in the world would say: "You have to accept". But I wouldn't want it that way. It's what people said when we split up. All the wiseacres, all the Jack the lads said: "They'll be back soon enough, as soon as they feel the pinch." I hate that. It's a drag. In fact, I haven't even talked to the other three about it. I talked to John the other night. Just happened to be talking to him on the phone. We chatted for about an hour and a half. He was in New York, I was in London. We just chatted and rambled, about politics, whatever we were interested in. A natter. And we never once mentioned the reunion or the offer.

'I thought about it after we got off the phone. We just didn't even mention it. I understand how most people in the world think we'd have to accept such an offer. For me, the only way The Beatles could come back together again would be if we wanted to do something musically, not lukewarm just for the money.

'We could do it to make a lot of money, but it would be the wrong motive and this is

what bugs me. It would be a total cop out. It would ruin the whole Beatles thing for me. If the four of us were really keen on the idea, or something in the next year makes us keen on it, or I just talk to the others and find out they are really keen secretly, then I must feel I ought to do something about it.

'But John and I talked on the phone and he didn't even mention it. And I'd read in the papers which said John Lennon was the hottest on this. I spoke to the bugger and he didn't even mention it. Where do you go from there?'

The answer was – out on the road with Wings.

Sometimes Paul's exasperation with end-

less Beatle stories boiled over, and he wrote a letter to Ray Coleman, editor of Melody Maker, which was published and also framed and put up on the office wall. It read: 'In order to put out of its misery the limping dog of a news story which has been dragging itself across your pages for the past year, my answer to the question "Will The Beatles get together again" is no.' Under Paul's signature was a drawing of a Cheshire cat smile.

Normally Paul shows great calm in his dealings with the press. Smoking endless cigarettes helps soothe his nerves. He had a lot to worry about on the road. Wings was a bedlam of screaming children, yelling musi-cians and crew. Everyone was either impatient or had a problem that needed solving. The whole entourage took an age to round up each day and be packed into limousines and coaches for the trip down the motorways of Britain in September 1975.

I joined the party in Bristol and went on the road with Wings observing them at work and play. Travelling on the coach with Paul and Linda, I felt and recognised their need for normal friendship and trust. After each concert, Paul read the reviews and was hurt and baffled by some of the comments which he read aloud. Just chatting, Paul relaxed into an informality that was touching. He seemed strangely vulnerable, a mortal

soul in need of protection. Some of the remarks that greeted his concerts ranged from the patronising to the cutting. He was called 'a grand old man at thirty three.' Others stated: 'McCartney is a throw back' or advised 'Paul should go solo.'

'What do they mean?' he demanded, his face contorted with pain, bewilderment and resignation. 'Don't they think I'm the centre of the show already? But I think I can see what this guy means when he says I'm a throwback. Yes – I suppose I am from another age....' Whenever Paul referred to the press he made a symbolic screwing motion.

The band played its opening concert in Southampton and I caught up with them at the Post House Hotel, outside Bristol. The hotel, with a swimming pool, fountains and low beams was made their base camp. Among those staying was Rose, the McCartney children's nanny, a tutor for Heather and a body guard.

With the staff of promoter Mel Bush and the American road crew taking up all the rooms, it meant I had to find a room in another hotel which locked me out the first night. I had stayed up until 2 a.m. watching Woody Allen's *Play It Again Sam* at the Wings' nightly film show in their portable cinema. Feeling like a vagrant, I tried to sleep in the lounge of the Post House until 8 a.m. when a surly porter rousted me out, and later threatened to call the police. I trudged back to the other hotel and waited outside until dawn, when a woman appeared, to unlock the doors and prepared breakfast. I managed to catch up on enough sleep during the day to make the concert that evening at Bristol Hippodrome.

Fans jammed the old theatre and the show started promptly at 8pm and ran for two solid hours without a break or support act. The audience was a mixture of young fans, married couples and teenagers and there was a strong family atmosphere as they all sang along to the words of songs like *Venus & Mars* and *Band On The Run*.

The band was set up on stage with the brass section at the back and Linda's array of keyboards parked sideways to the right. Jimmy McCulloch and Denny Laine were spread out in front of Joe English's small drum kit. Paul sat at a grand piano and

occasionally moved up front to join Jimmy and Denny. It was a clever layout. Nobody appeared to dominate anybody else.

They used the *Venus & Mars* theme to open and went into *Rock Show*, *Jet* and *Let Me Roll It*. In my review later I wrote: 'As the concert picked up momentum it became apparent that all past hints of amateurism and stories of incompetence have been expunged.''

It was obvious that a lot of rehearsal had gone into getting the music right, and Wings at times managed to sound more like an orchestra than a basic rock group. Linda's role was to add Moog synthesiser effects, tonal colours, introductions and themes.

Linda and Paul barely communicated with each other while the work of performing went ahead, only exchanging smiles when there was a particularly thunderous burst of applause. Linda enjoyed her own burst of cheers and wolf whistles when she stepped up front with a tambourine wearing a snazzy dress covered in Venus And Mars symbols.

Spirits Of Ancient Egypt was a number that gave Jimmy a chance to blaze away on a rocking solo, while *C Moon* introduced a touch of reggae. 'See if you remember this one,' said Paul and *Lady Madonna* had the entire audience clapping to the beat. Later the band switched from electric to acoustic guitars, which Denny Laine referred to as their 'skiffle' set. They played *Picasso's Last Words* and *Richard Corey* by Paul Simon. The beautiful *Blue Bird* from *Band On The Run* was delivered with the aid of a rhythm box. Next came *Yesterday*, listened to in rapt silence, even though the first notes were buried in a roar of recognition. In the emotionally charged atmosphere, the sound of voice and acoustic guitar was enough to bring a tear to the eye. Paul nodded appreciatively when the audience was released from tension in an explosion of cheers.

Wings returned to the power of electricity for *You Gave Me The Answer* and *Magneto And Titanium Man* with Linda singing back up vocals. The show rolled on with *Letting Go*, *Live And Let Die*, *Call Me Back Again*, *My Love*, *Listen To What The Man Said*, and *Band On The Run*. They quit the stage and the audience stamped and cheered like football fans. 'All right – a bit of rock and roll' yelled

Denny Laine on the band's return, and they launched into *Hi Hi Hi*, doubling the tempo for a shattering finale.

After the show, the band returned to the Post House for another film show (*Blazing Saddles*) and rest. The next morning they rose quite early but, nevertheless, looked bleary-eyed when it came to facing the cameras of BBC and Harlech TV for lunch-time interviews at the hotel. While the band was being assembled, one of the TV crew said nervously: 'It's like waiting for an audience with the Pope – or General Amin.'

Eventually, their PR Tony Brainsby arrived beaming through glasses and singing 'We won't be long!' to an old Beatles tune. 'Right – yer on. No screaming.' Paul and Linda came into the lounge, Linda muttering 'Am I ready for this?' The rest of the band followed including Denny Laine's baby, known to everyone as 'Lainey', who struck up a line of conversation with Paul which consisted entirely of them blowing raspberries at each other.

'Okay, quiet please,' demanded the head of the TV crew after a particularly violent outbreak of raspberry blowing. It was agreed beforehand that the interviewers would stick to asking about the Wings tour and include the other members of the band. In the event, the cameras stayed firmly on Paul, who parried questions with practised ease. He was asked, as one of the most famous men in the world and a rich ex-Beatle, why he carried on touring. Just what kept him going?

'Drugs,' said Paul earnestly. 'I must have them. No.... I just like music.' Was he looking forward to playing in Cardiff!' 'Of course,' began Paul, but there was a rumble from Denny Laine who said to nobody in particular: 'When are they going to start speaking English there?' End of first interview. Another tried his hand. What could Paul achieve now?

'I don't know – that's a bit heavy that

question. What do YOU want to do? I want to make really great records. Maybe your ambition is to do a really great interview and when you do, well you won't want to give up will you? You don't ever give up. Everyone goes on.'

The TV men packed up, suitably chastened, and Paul and Linda dived into a black Rolls Royce to drive to Cardiff and the afternoon sound check. As we drove along the motorway, the TV crew zoomed alongside, filming through the window.

The McCartneys weren't angry but seemed perplexed at the constant interest in the past when they had something new and exciting to offer. None of the TV or national newspaper reviewers seemed to have taken in the success of Wings at their concerts and the reaction they were provoking among audiences. 'Why are you doing it?' The press kept asking. The answer was plain to see at each night's concert. But as Linda observed: 'They'll be asking if The Beatles will reform when we're old and grey.' Said Paul: 'That guy asked me what was there left to achieve, as if I'd done it all.' Paul kept muttering to himself: 'What is there left to achieve?'

Wings impressed with their technical professionalism as well as the sheer quality and variety of Paul's songs. 'In the old days of The Beatles we might rehearse for three days. But we've spent months rehearsing Wings. And it's all been better than I thought it would be.'

'We hadn't played to anybody for years and we were a bit nervous. We saw Dave Mason play a concert and he tuned up between every number and I used to think that was death. We rehearsed the band down in Rye in Sussex, in an old cinema all summer learning all the numbers. We could have rehearsed the chat between numbers too but that would have been too formal. We weren't going to have ad-lib chatting, but the audiences didn't seem to mind. They all seem to be Wings fans. After the Beatles, I didn't think anybody could be Wings fans. The TV man kept asking me why I kept going and I wish I had told him about Wings fans. That's what's left for me to do.'

Said Linda: 'Paul could go on talking about The Beatles forever and all four of them get so bored with it.'

'Why can't they let us get on with something new?', demanded Paul.

Said Linda: 'They're still talking about "George is the religious one and John is the nasty one and Ringo is making movies." They don't seem interested in the fact this is a working band. But the people are up to date. It's the press who don't know what's going on.'

'Do you still see John?' said Paul, rhetorically peering out of the window of the car. 'I always feel a bit weedy when I answer those kind of questions. Maybe I should send him a telegram. You know I can't think of anything that the word "Press" means that is nice.'

We drew up at the stage door and as Paul leapt out of the Rolls, he was surrounded by fans clamouring for autographs. 'What makes me want to go on tour again – is a decent audience.'

Paul emphasised to me the need he felt to relate to all kinds of audiences, not just the hip critics and ultra cool rock fans. He recalled the 'James Paul McCartney' TV special when it seemed like he was going to become a middle-of-the-road family entertainer.

'The funny thing was only the hip people didn't like it. It wasn't a hip show at all. So it wasn't a good show. What do you want from a real, live person? God? But we got millions of letters from mid-America saying they loved the show, I've got to remind myself that the main thing is to enjoy yourself. Sometimes I feel as if I have a ten ton weight on my shoulders. And you can't entertain so well unless the weight is off your shoulders. There's many a person has committed suicide over the fact that his Special wasn't so good. But I wouldn't give a crap.'

Paul explained that his motivating force was to get things done, better. 'It's one of the biggest factors in life. I've come home from some rehearsals with Wings and just got the terrible feeling "It's not right, God we could do so much more. We've got to get a producer." But I just have to say to myself: "Get a grip on yourself son. Don't think THAT. You're doing okay." Then you meet someone the next day who says "Oh gee, never heard you sing so good." And you are saved, you are bloody well saved from the jaws of death. I find I'm so susceptible to that. But on this tour I'm keeping cool. I'm

surprised at myself. When I go out on stage, if I see anyone walk out or light a cigarette I think "Oh God, I've lost 'em." You see I misread situations so badly, all the time.

'Obviously, I can't be doing too badly. 'Cos I'm all right. Not as bad as that fellow who had to commit suicide last week because he read the situation so badly. But silly things affect me and that's why I keep insisting that I'm ordinary because I am so bloody ordinary it's annoying. Oh no, there's none of yer: "I am now Paul McCartney, rich and famous and this is it." When interviewers say: "What else can you do?" What else – is to try and get myself together – at some point.

'If I do see someone leaving the theatre while I'm singing I've got to remind myself they might be going to the bog. It really could be that. Instinctively, I just think: "Oh no, they hate me. They hate me. I'm no good." I'm just a born worrier. Which is not a good thing.'

Paul told how his father was similarly assailed by doubts. 'He'll get down about something when really everything is on a huge up. If only he could train himself to see how up it is. It's like the old Indian saying: "I walk down the street and I'm crying because I have no shoes, and then I see a man with no feet. I must try and remind myself that I've got feet.'

'Obviously, in our profession what pisses you off is when you get someone saying: "He's a throw back". And it could be that the critic who said it was pissed, or his wife stamped on him and he's in a right state. 'He comes to my show and thinks: "Who is this bastard? Who does he think he is?" And if we go down well there's still a chance he's going to say: "Ahh – nothing." Anyone can do that you know. I used to know a guy on the way to school who used to say every morning, whatever the weather was: "Bah!" He was always moaning and no one used to sit near him! Just because he was such a downer – all the time. You could never a laugh with him. And you're a bit susceptible in our position. George is in a very dodgy position. John Lennon goes to a club, gets pissed, like EVERYONE does when they go to a club. He'll be a bit rowdy and then everyone will notice, it's HIM and wow, dangerous.

'A soldier gets pissed in a club in Hamburg, gets thumped up, a gas gun at his head, and it's not news. So, to be the newsworthy person is quite a drag at times.'

Paul has always shown great care and diplomacy in his dealings with the press over the years which has earned him the 'PR' tag. From Paul's point of view, this has always been a 'no win' situation. 'That always seemed to be the easy way out,' he explained. 'I always take the path of least resistance. John always believed the best way was to say piss off. I agree with it in a way because then at least they know where they stand and everything is clear. You've offended someone but so what? John is supposed to be a loony according to some people, and I know he isn't. It's just that life gets crazy and you've gotta handle it your own way. IF YOU ASK ME, THE BEATLES ARE VERY SANE. But they're cheeky with it. They're not about to buckle under because someone says: "That's naughty".'

Paul, with a musician's ear for accents, traits and mannerisms is very good at imagining other people's conversations -- about himself. 'He's proved he can still sing, pull an audience and sell out. So he's proved that. Now – goodnight! I'm only kidding. I'm always saying these things to people. With The Beatles our great "in joke" was always that whenever we split up, we would do a Wembley concert and John was going to do this big thing like shout "Fuck the Queen!" It was going to be the final own up, everything all the vee signs, all the ruderies, and it was going to be on "live" television. We were really going to blow it! It was a beautiful dream.' (Just a year later, The Sex Pistols launched an act which virtually built itself on this hypothesis).

Why didn't The Beatles do it? 'You're joking aren't you?' said Paul, as our coach rumbled steadily north towards Manchester. 'Up on the roof at Apple was probably the last time we played together. I can't remember. I'm not a great Beatle-ologist. The Sixties for me are a blur. Nineteen sixty-three is the same as nineteen sixty-seven. It was all one big time. I read the Hunter Davies book and bits of Alan Williams' book too which John gave me a copy of last time I saw him. That's a laugh that one. I mean, blimey that's slightly exaggerated to put it mildly. *The Man Who Gave The Beatles Away* Eh? My brother was thinking of writing one called: *The Man Who Couldn't Give The Beatles Away!*

'Oh, it's terrible. It's a travesty. There are all the legends but it's all exaggerated. Every word is a swear word. Okay we swore, but somehow he hasn't caught the atmosphere. And there are all these stories about peeing on nuns. And that actually comes from two separate stories. One was peeing out of the window, which is a fine old Shakespearian ceremony. It wasn't me folks – I don't do that kind of thing – but it was a drunken friend of mine, peeing out of the window one time.

'And there was another wholly unrelated affair where there happened to be some nuns passing which joins together in the great legend of peeing on the nuns. And Alan's sort of saying: "I don't want to spoil anything for the lads, but they did pee on the nuns." I suggested it sounded like a good follow up to *Band On The Run*.

'Yeah – *Pee On The Nun*.'

At last, the power and impact of the new Wings began to filter through to the press and the reviews turned from the sour to the ecstatic. 'Paul is still the greatest!' 'Paul Soars With Wings!', 'Superlatives Are Superfluous' and 'It's Super-Mac!' By the time the group got to London's Hammersmith Odeon, Wings were playing with the roaring precision of a highly tuned sports car. The cheering and cries for encores were overwhelming and the chants for 'We Want Paul' were vindication for all McCartney's struggles and determination. 'The last word is professionalism!' announced reviewers firmly, noting that after three encores at the Odeon, the crowd were still calling for 'More!' There was still some dissent within the ranks however. The new drummer Joe English was variously described as either 'inept' or 'terrifyingly sharp'.

In October, the band set off for Perth, Australia for sell out concerts and an ecstatic reception. But not all the world was convinced of Mr. McCartney's stature and importance. An angry reader wrote to the London Evening News (now defunct). 'I read with disgust that a Jumbo Jet with a hundred passengers was delayed for an hour, not for royalty but for Paul McCartney. Who is he? Heathrow's priorities have gone berserk.'

Paul had overslept at his St. Johns Wood home and the Quantas flight to Australia was courteously delayed until Paul, Linda, Stella, Heather and Mary could board the plane. Paul is notoriously bad at getting out of bed.

A Franklin cartoon appeared in The Sun with the caption 'We regret having to turn back. Mr. McCartney has forgotten his toothbrush.'

But there were more serious problems when the band tried to visit Japan for more concerts. Paul discovered he was banned from entering Japan because of a previous conviction for a drug offence, two years earlier. The concerts due there on November 19 and 21 were cancelled. Paul would renew his attempts to play in Japan a few years later with disastrous results.

All he had to cope with in Australia were scowling pressmen who asked: 'Aren't you too old for all this' or wanted, inevitably to know about the possibility of a Beatles reunion. They were fuelled by an offer from Hollywood promoter, Bill Sargent to pay the old group thirty million dollars to come out of retirement for one night only and to play 'any place they chose.' Bellowed the Daily Mirror back home, 'Will 1976 be the year The Beatles get back together?'

Paul's answer was swift. 'Money can't buy The Beatles. If we played, it would then be for the wrong motives.' He was busy planning the assault on America with Wings. The US tour was due to start on April 8, 1976. It would include thirty one performances in twenty cities and would mark Paul's first American stage appearances in ten years. It would be the country's first chance to see a Beatle in action for six years.

There were two concerts lined up at the Los Angeles Forum. Before they were officially announced, thirty six thousand tickets sold out within three and a half hours – in one day. There were also two nights booked for the Cow Palace, San Francisco and two at Madison Square Garden, New York. The band had sophisticated new sound and lighting systems to cope with these huge venues, a far cry from the Capitol, Cardiff.

In spite of these elaborate plans and Wings fever breaking out in America, the British press affected not to notice. For them the 'real story' was still a Beatles' reunion. Paul was driven to distraction by this nonsense but made non-commital grunts when the Daily Mirror's columnist confidently claimed: 'The Beatles are significantly nearer to their first reunion. It seems likely the great togetherness will take place in the Olympic Stadium, Montreal for fifteen million pounds.'

Paul had more troubles to concern him however. Jimmy McCulloch had one of his infrequent accidents. He had fallen over in the bathroom and broken his finger. Without the guitarist there could be no show. It happened after the band had played to ten thousand fans in Paris on the last date of the European tour. The American tour had to be postponed and re-scheduled for May. While Jimmy had treatment, the rest of the band went on holiday. Before Paul took off, I met him in London for a bottle of beer and a sandwich. It was a chance to catch up on the McCartney view of The Beatles' reunion and the row over his cancelled trip to Japan.

It's not surprising Paul savours a quiet life in Scotland when he gets a chance. He is normally surrounded by dozens of people all trying to nail him down. When I found Paul, Linda and Denny in a West End hotel, they were busy fending off invitations to dinner, Paul unleashing various warning signals and the cutting edge of his tongue at persistent pests. But he was relaxed and happy enough to talk about Wings At The Speed Of Sound and their trip around the world.

'We had fab fun in Australia. It was the first real tour we'd done for a while. The audiences were great and we just dug playing. It was more like a holiday. The trip to Japan was cancelled and that was the Minister of Justice's fault. I suppose he'd say it was my fault for having smoked some of the deadly weed. But we had our visas signed by the London Japanese Embassy. Everything had been cleared. David Bailey was coming over to do a film and we were in

Australia, just about a week from going to Japan when a note arrived saying "No". They're still old fashioned out there. There's a generation gap and the wrong end of the gap is in the Ministry of Justice, as it is here.

'The older folks see a great danger in allowing in an alien who has admitted smoking marijuana and supposedly they're trying to stamp it out, using all the wrong methods as usual.'

I asked Paul if he was angered by the ban.

'Oh yeah, a bit over the top. It was just one of those things, but we felt a bit sick about it. It's so short-sighted.'

After their Australian tour, Wings sent a video of their show to Japan. It was turned into a current affairs programme with people discussing the merits of marijuana. 'In a way we had become martyrs for the cause, which is a drag,' said Paul, showing signs of irritation.

At least the cancelled Japanese trip gave Paul more time to think about music. Hence the new album. 'We managed to fit it in. We had a great holiday in Hawaii and I got the album together there in my head. We started recording it in January – or February, I'm a bit hazy. The album didn't take long. But we didn't rush it – just let the ideas blossom.

'There were a few things I especially wanted to do. I put a backing track down and then got the idea of getting Joe English to do it because he's got a very good voice. Linda's got this track called *Cook Of The House*, so I thought it would be good to give one to Joe. When he'd done it we were all surprised. He sings well. The band came together for rehearsals at Elstree and a nice thing was the way the brass players worked out a bit for a song called *Silly Love Songs*. They can really get behind it because it's theirs. We also used two euphoniums on *Warm And Beautiful*.

I asked Paul whether he was deliberately trying to push the other members of the band and he said: 'That's always the object with anything I do, and to try and get out of a rut and do something different. When I was in Jamaica, I heard a reggae record which featured a trombone all on its own. It sounded daft and fruity and I filed it away in the back of my mind that I'd love to use a trombone.

'And, of course, now we have Tony

Dorsey who plays trombone for us, so we could use it as a solo instrument on the album.'

A doorbell was used on the opening track, Let 'Em In and I wondered if they were the McCartney household chimes.

'Well, as it happens, it is our actual door-bell which our drummer bought for us, so it has a group significance. And it seemed a good introduction to the album. I don't think of particular themes for an album. There wasn't one on Venus & Mars. I thought of a bunch of tunes. They have a sort of family, love-ish, warm-ish feel. Well.... I can never analyse me own stuff. I hope the reviewers like it, but if they don't, I hope the people like it.'

Paul selected only three songs from the new album for that year's tour, Beware My Love, Silly Love Songs and Let 'Em In, all up tempo. One of the most popular items on the album was Linda's Cook Of The House, and it was inspired by a stay at a house rented in Adelaide. After the concert each night, Linda and Paul would end up in the kitchen having a bite to eat.

'We had all these pots of sage and onion lined up, all the condiments of the season. That's a joke that. Well, all this stuff was lined up and I took everything I saw and tried to work it into the song. Every line in the song was about something in the kitchen.'

Sizzling noises were heard in the intro-duction. The couple went round the house with a mobile recording unit to capture the sounds of Linda cooking. 'The results sounded like applause,' said Paul. 'We used an E flat bacon pan and Selmer chips. The song is high school orientated because that was Linda's scene as a kid in America. In England, we didn' have all that dating and taking chicks out in cars at the age of seven-teen. The most we had was a hop on the back of a tandem and we'd have records in the classroom at the end of term.' Paul began to reminisce about his teenage years at school:

'I remember one day when the guy in the Remo Four brought a guitar. I brought a guitar and George brought in his guitar and we went into the history room, Cliff Edge's room. The teacher's name was Mr. Edge see, and we called him Cliff. I remember doing Long Tall Sally and all the old stuff and that

was the nearest we ever got to a high school hop.'

I asked Paul why he didn't do an album of old pop hits?

'Listen – don't get me on projects. There are so many of those to do. I've got a head full of that. A Buddy Holly album, an album of old pop tunes – there are millions of ideas like that.'

Paul's hands were more than full with Wings' activity and solo albums would have to wait. He was still thrilled at the success of his band. 'Wings is growing and it surprises me in a way because I half expected it not to happen. It was a question of follow that, after The Beatles. But it's established and the main thing is we are enjoying playing and can get off on it which is a great advantage over a lot of older groups.'

Did Paul get tired of being asked about a Beatles reunion?

'I don't mind. We are going to America with Wings and I'm looking forward to that. But I don't count out anything else.'

Reviews for Wings At The Speed Of Sound were mixed. In my review I wrote: 'Paul has a brilliant knack of taking an ordinary, daily statement and imbuing it with intrigue. "Somebody's knocking at the door, some-body's ringing at the bell. Open the door and let them in." It's the kind of thing you or I must say once a day, assuming one has (a) a door, and (b) a bell. My door frequently vibrates to the thud and clamour of callers, but as the din often warns of approaching insurance salesmen, the household usually responds with whispered cries of "Turn out the lights. Pretend we are out." Paul and Linda and Wings are much more accomo-dating. They welcome us into their front sitting room to hear a new phase in their musical career. This album will undoubted-ly increase the worldwide appeal of Wings.'

But said Barbara Charone in Sounds: 'A major disappointment. And it was sup-posed to be a triumph.' As for Albert Wat-son of the South Wales Echo, his feeling was 'Beatlemania is back, yeah, yeah, yeah!' But he was more concerned with the fact that thanks to an EMI campaign, some twenty two old Beatles singles including Yesterday and Hey Jude were back in the Top Hundred. Who was buying all these old Beatle re-cords? 'Humans I should think,' said Paul.

Once again, Paul had to explain to the world why he was now a member of Wings and no longer a Beatle. Said Paul to Hunter Davies: 'When The Beatles split up, I felt on the rocks. I've been accused of walking out on them but I never did. It's something I'd never do. One day John left and that was the last straw. It was the signal for the others to leave. The Beatles were a blanket of security. When the job folded beneath me, suddenly I didn't have a career anymore. I wasn't earning anything. All my money was in Apple. I couldn't get it because I'd signed it all away. I stayed up all night drinking and smoking and watching TV. I lost all my security. I had no idea what to do, there seemed no point in me joining another group.'

Paul explained that he thought what really angered the other Beatles was his attempt to bring in his inlaws, the Eastman family. 'I couldn't believe it. After what we'd been through in ten years. I thought they'd know I wouldn't do anything for those reasons. I was told to get free. I couldn't sue Klein. I had to sue John, George and Ringo instead. What a trauma. Unemployed and up to my ears in a High Court case.

'We were all pretty weird at the time. I'd ring John and he'd say, "Don't bother me." I rang George and he came out with some effing and blinding, not at all Hare Krishna. We weren't normal to each other at the time. I feel very secure with Wings now. I even sing Beatle songs.'

At last, the band was ready to tour America and Jimmy McCulloch returned to the fold, remarking: 'What can I say? I'm sorry.' It was later hinted that the accident with his broken finger had not taken place 'in a bathroom', but in a hotel lobby during a friendly tussle with Wings' fan, David Cassidy.

The band were encouraged by news that a track taken from the new album *Wings At The Speed Of Sound* called: *Silly Love Songs* released on April 30, had got to Number Two in the British chart.

There was nothing silly about Wings' success in America during those arduous, frantic weeks of touring. On the surface it seemed an extravaganza of accolades, celebrations and record breaking statistics. Behind the scenes there were tensions and pressures building up. Paul could take the life style. After The Beatles, this was just a family outing. After all, Wings had all the benefits The Beatles had lacked, superb sound systems, efficient management and modern facilities. There were occasional problems with acoustics in the massive venues, but critics agreed most of the shows were a triumph of rock entertainment. America cheered itself hoarse. On stage, Paul wore a black suit and a white scarf. A typical show, at the L.A. Forum began with clouds of smoke, bubbles and fireworks, heralding the opening strains of the dramatic *Live And Let Die* theme. Next came *Rock Show, Silly Love Songs, Let 'Em In, My Love* and *Long And Winding Road*. When they played *Band On The Run*, a film featuring the stars on the original album cover was projected. The whole smooth running production was stripped down each night and transported across the continent in its convoy of monster trucks, usually without a hitch.

Rumours of a Beatle reunion during the tour hit an all time high when Ringo Starr flew out to see Paul. He was most impressed by the Los Angeles show and presented Paul with a bouquet of flowers.

Among the stars cheering in the audience were Diana Ross, Harry Nilsson, Dennis Wilson, Elton John, Cher, Leo Sayer, Adam Faith and John Bonham. The illuminati of rock were paying homage to a man who as far as artists and musicians were concerned commanded respect for his efforts to be free.

At last, one British newspaper got the message. Said the Daily Express: 'Forget the rumours that The Beatles are getting together again. Wings have taken off.' Paul told a reporter in Detroit: 'Look mate, it's 1976. I don't think most of the people here care about what happened ten years ago. All they are interested in is what I am doing now. The past is gone and it won't come back.'

There was a moment of panic when Paul escaped serious injury by inches when a piece of scaffolding fell from above the stage during a concert in Houston, Texas. Roadie Trevor Jones was hit on the head and needed thirteen stitches. When they arrived in New York, there were hysterical Beatlemania style scenes. Some twenty thousand fans let off rockets and fire crackers in Madison Square Garden and among them were one hundred and fifty British fans who had flown over specially for the concert. Girls sobbed as once more Paul signed autographs.

'Everything I have done since The Beatles split has been leading up to this show,' Paul said backstage. When he played at Washington's Capital Centre, the audience screamed its way through the first three numbers, without stopping. Out in the audience, trying hard to listen above the uproar were The Eagles, Linda Ronstadt and Peter Asher.

One of the most extraordinary concerts on the tour was held at the King Dome, Seattle. The band played to sixty seven thousand claimed to be the largest audience for a single act at an indoor auditorium. It was held on June 10, 1976 and the first twenty one thousand tickets sold out in twenty four hours. The whole show was filmed for a movie which was not released for a couple of years afterwards. Subsequent changes in the line-up of Wings made Paul wonder whether to issue the film and he spent a long time editing it between recording sessions.

The King Dome is enormous, so big it has its own climate and internal weather which has to be combatted by air conditioning. For the Wings concert, a huge video screen was constructed over the stage to give everyone a good view. It was the same size as the stage, and yet from the back of the hall it looked like a matchbox. Everything about the tour seemed to take on a dream-like air for those working with the band. It all came to an end with a glorious Hollywood party on June 23rd. It cost over two hundred thousand dollars to set up in the house and gardens built by silent movie star Harold Lloyd, which had never previously been open to inspection.

It was organised by the tour promoters, Caribou Concerts West and, at Paul's behest, all the guests wore white. Even the photographers had to wear white. There were armed guards to prevent gate crashers and protect the millionaire guests who included Jack Nicklaus, Henry Fonda, Elton John, Diana Ross, David Cassidy, Roman Polanski, Cher, Mick and Bianca Jagger, The Eagles, Steve McQueen, Bob Dylan, Joni Mitchell, Dustin Hoffman, Olivia Newton-John, The Jacksons, Ringo, George, Rod Stewart and Warren Beatty.

The guests were ferried up from the gates by minibus, to be greeted by an astonishing and bizarre array of entertainments. But it was all done in the best possible taste. A song, et lumiere, string quartets, and even the Los Angeles Ballet brought a touch of culture. Dinner was served in a marquee and a Busby Berkely style water ballet was performed in the pool. There was palm reading sessions, and an artist flown in from Mexico hand painted the guests' white tee shirts.

The visitors responded to all this in markedly different ways. Bob Dylan sat in a tree throughout and pondered the meaning of life. One guest poured drink over himself. Paul and Linda watched proceedings with quiet detachment. Nobody went near a small stage set up with drums guitars and amplifiers for a jam session that never happened.

At the end of the evening, the guests strolled back to their cars to find on every dashboard a single white rose and a note 'Thank you for coming, Paul and Linda.'

By the time the world tour was over, Wings had played in seven European countries, and in Australia, Canada and America. Including the final dates at Wembley in England, they had given sixty six concerts which had reached an astonishing two million people. Said the Liverpool Echo, dutifully charting the progress of the city's favourite son: 'Gone are the days when everything Paul wrote was accompanied by the tag 'Ex-Beatle'. He is now fully established in his own right as a leading songwriter and musician.'

The Jewish Chronicle noted that Wings' success and the revival of interest in old Beatle records had helped lift EMI's full year profits from thirty four million to fifty nine million pounds.

Sid Bernstein, The Beatles' American concert promoter, came up with an even bigger 'Great Beatles Reunion Offer'. He planned a simultaneous cinema screen presentation throughout the Western world with fifteen million dollars in it for the lads.

Paul: 'A great idea, if we were getting together, again. But we're not.'

Throughout the American tour, Wings' lead guitar player had been giving cause for alarm. 'Jimmy had a lot of personal problems which made it difficult for him to form a lasting relationship!', said one of Wings' staff. 'He couldn't find a girlfriend, or even a boyfriend. Paul likes to be able to understand the people he works with and their problems, but he found Jimmy difficult to understand. He had been given maximum opportunities in the kind of musical setting most young guitarists dreamt about. But he couldn't handle the heavy touring. He was a classic example of a rock musician unable to cope with fame, money and pressures. His family tried to help him and everybody gave him a lot of attention. A big effort was made to look after him and keep away undesirables. Nobody threw him to the lions. But all the help didn't protect him. He wouldn't accept help. Sometimes he was together, but a lot of the time he was playing the concerts semi-conscious from too much whiskey. He could be surly, unpleasant and a real bastard. But many members of the entourage behaved like that.'

Paul would talk to Jimmy in the backs of planes as they flew around America, but in the end the pep talks were to no avail. For Jimmy, the writing was on the wall.

To be sure, the show was polished and presented with all the machine perfection of a 'rock show', but such shows were presented almost weekly during the seventies by The Who, Elton John and every heavy rock outfit that could buy a smoke generator. Wings' appeal had rested in their warm family feeling and close contact with audiences. Rockbiz overkill negated this. I missed the easy spontaneity of Wings' shows a year before, and the genuine excitement this has had engendered.

I wrote a review, as if couched by the social secretary of a Northern club, one Arnold Clutterbuck, who 'couldn't see what all the bluddy fuss was about.' It had to be read with a Mancunian accent. I added under my own byline that I thought a touch of boredom had set in which was hard to explain:

'I liked the songs and who can fail to be moved on hearing *Yesterday* at least once a year? The band played beautifully, and I was thoroughly entranced. But eventually the show began to sag. The atmosphere was slow to ignite. *Lady Madonna* got the first

cheer. But the concert went on so long, that for all their polish, it began to seem we had been sitting on hard, uncomfortable seats, listening to Wings forever. The Empire Pool induced the feeling we were watching some distant event, an ice spectacular, glamorous but cold. This fellow is never satisfied, I can hear the distant rumble of discontent.'

I went on to rave about how well drilled the band had become, how they did a brilliant job in recreating their album tracks. Returning once more to 'humour', I predicted that despite the grumbles of social secretary, Arnold Clutterbuck, there was 'a bright future for this top pop group on the club circuit.'

It was harmless enough. But it was a mistake. Linda did not like it. She was under the impression I was saying that Paul would go on singing *Yesterday* for ever. Even Paul misread the tone of the article. It wasn't the criticism that mattered. It had seemed like an act of treachery.

Chapter Nine
COOK OF THE HOUSE

'Life with Paul is great in so many ways. I love being married to him just for the way he is. And that's beautiful.' Linda Eastman had a tough job on her hands when she became Linda McCartney. Life with Paul may have been beautiful after their marriage in 1969, but she was in for a rough ride. Fortunately, she had the strength to cope with the demands and stresses affecting Paul, maintain her own identity and put up with a lot of personal abuse. They made a great team. A shared love for family life, a sense of humour and determination to carry on working.... together they could cope with most things.

Linda is easy going, affectionate and supportive. Her anger is roused only when she sees Paul attacked, or when her own self-confidence is threatened by assaults on her role and capabilities. As a photographer, musician and mother she has walked the tightrope of dependence and independence with admirable skill. An American, living in a strange land with a slice of national property, she showed tact and restraint. She is what the British in an earlier, gentler age, might have called 'a good sport.' But she can react strongly towards people who fail in some way in their dealings with Paul. They have made strenuous efforts over the years to be pleasant, outgoing and generous. Understandably, they sometimes lose patience or faith in others.

Linda has a tenderness, intelligence and sense of fun that makes her irresistible. Such a combination appeals to musicians who tend to find themselves confronted with vacuous groupies or steely-eyed gold diggers. Linda was neither of these but when she beamed unspoken signals of understanding, they found their mark in Paul when they met at a New York press reception.

It was 1968 and The Beatles were launching Apple. Journalist Lillian Roxon, famed for her Rock Encyclopedia had rung Linda and said: 'Why don't you come along', doubtless enjoying her role as matchmaker. At the reception, Linda couldn't get near to Paul as dozens of guests milled around. But she wrote her phone number on a piece of paper and slipped it to him. As Paul was about to leave she rushed up and kissed him on the cheek. He smiled and left. The same night he called her up and invited her to the flat where he was staying with John Lennon. Next day The Beatles returned to London, leaving Linda behind.

A month later, Paul flew to California and called Linda on his arrival and she flew to the west coast to meet him. It was the start of an inseparable relationship. The first time they had met was in London in the Bag O'Nails Club, a regular haunt of rock musicians. Jimi Hendrix played there – one of Linda's faves. Publicist Bill Harry saw Linda and Paul and was struck by their togetherness – literally.

'I was sitting at a table in the Bag O'Nails with Paul and Chas Chandler. We were all watching Georgie Fame & The Blue Flames on stage. Linda came over and squeezed in between us. She grabbed Paul's arm. Every picture I've ever seen of them since, Linda has Paul by the arm. Nothing sinister about it – they were just very close.'

Linda was a working girl when Paul met her. Born September, 24, 1942, she had started taking pictures at Tucson Art Centre, Arizona. She had got a job as a receptionist on a New York magazine and was in the office when an invitation came in to meet The Rolling Stones on a yacht on the Hudson River. She took her camera and was the only photographer and among her subjects were Jimi Hendrix, Brian Jones, and The Beach Boys. She was married to geologist Melvyn See and they had a daughter Heather, born on December 31, 1963. Heather would become part of the happy McCartney family which grew to considerable size. 'I'm good with babies. I like the idea of having one in the house,' she joked. Said Paul: 'The idea of a big family is to have a band.'

Mary was born on August 28, 1969 and named after Paul's mother. Stella was born on September 13, 1971 and named after Linda's mother who was killed in a plane crash. Her father Lee Eastman, apart from being a top New York lawyer who helped Paul with advice dring the difficult Beatles bust up, was also a noted art collector. James McCartney was born on September 12, 1977 by caesarian operation.

From the start of their marriage, Paul and Linda were determined to be free of the trappings of stardom and to enjoy themselves. They once spent a week unrecognised in a Blackpool boarding house, soaking up the atmosphere of childhood English holidays. Their home in London was a four storey Victorian house with a backyard full of animals and described by some as 'a mud bath.' Life on their farm in Scotland was even more primitive and muddy. They once paid a cab driver one hundred pounds to transport some chickens from St. Johns Wood to Scotland, leaving behind the ducks, geese and four dogs.

It was on the walls of St. Johns Wood that Linda first experienced graffiti from fans, angered and disappointed that Paul had not married Jane Asher. But Linda's charm soon won over the old Beatle fans and she became a hero when Wings hit the road with Linda bravely playing the keyboards.

Linda set about being Mrs. McCartney with a will. High Park Farm near Cambeltown, was set in some six hundred acres of moor. It was poor soil, windswept and no good for agriculture. But Linda loved the colours in the landscapes and set to work on improving the two bedroomed farmhouse. She supervised the decorating while an estate manager took care of the heavy work. On the farm the children could ride around on horseback, while Linda went shopping in Cambeltown, with Paul driving her to town in their Landrover 'Helen Wheels.' It was the only vehicle capable of making it up a rough road, kept deliberately untended to discourage sightseers.

When Paul and Linda first went off to Scotland in 1969, the press began to call them 'recluses' but said Linda: 'I couldn't think of anything I'd rather do than live there growing my own vegetables and looking after the sheep and getting covered in mud. I'm a country girl at heart.' They put up a greenhouse to help with the produce and said Paul: 'She's the lead gardener. I'm the rhythm gardener!'

They settled down to a pleasant routine with Paul lighting the fire and doing the washing up and Linda preparing the meals. After a trip out riding across the moors, they'd go into the barn to work on some songs, have supper, watch TV and go to bed.

'We were not cut off from the world. We were never hermits', insisted Linda. 'We were only ten minutes from Cambeltown, but we like the quiet, simple life.' But it wasn't that quiet. In March 1973, Paul was fined a hundred pounds at Cambeltown for cultivating cannabis in his greenhouse. They had been spotted by a visiting crime prevention officer. All five plants had withered, which didn't say much for their gardening skills.

There was more disruption to the McCartney married bliss when Martha, their old English sheep dog, was the subject of complaints from neighbours. They objected to her barking in the garden at St. John's Wood. Said Paul: 'They're a load of old colonels!' Martha had given birth to eight puppies which explained the day and night barking. There was an exchange of words with the neighbours and Linda responded: 'We're gonna start a zoo next!'

Although Linda has never lost her American accent, she can speak in the broadest Cockney when the mood takes her, and is very knowledgable about English working class pursuits like football, which she watches avidly on the telly. As a kid growing up she watched baseball and the Brooklyn Dodgers. 'I never had much time for sports except horse riding,' she told me during time off from a Wings tour. 'All my teen years were spent with an ear to the radio listening to pop. I loved Buddy Holly, the Everly Brothers and Chuck Berry. In high school with a few other girls we used to cut classes every now and then and go up to the music block to fool around. But I never saw myself becoming a musician.'

Linda revealed that she thought people felt they had to say bad things about her when she became a full member of Wings. 'But it doesn't prey on me. It's funny, before I married Paul I got on really great with people. Then I married Paul and all of a sudden I was this ogre. I became a perfect foil. I was just a perfect person to knock in every way.'

Some had suggested she was responsible for the frequent line up changes in Wings and she said: 'Yeah, well there was always somebody in Wings who couldn't keep it together and I always felt very strongly about it myself, because I'm very aware of what's going on around me. When I started photography it made me very aware of everything. Paul didn't feel confidence in the band at first.'

By the 1975-76 tour, Linda was playing Mellotron, Moog organ and piano. 'At first I was really worried about them. On *Maybe I'm Amazed*, I played organ and then Mellotron and organ again. Now it doesn't worry me because I know what I'm doing. It's like a camera. I don't really know how a synthesiser works, but I know how to use it.'

Linda explained that Paul hadn't given her any lessons on the keyboards. 'He has no patience. I had to learn it myself. The few things he'd show me, if I didn't get it right, he'd get really angry. So I said, like forget it!' Linda had a tutor who called in the mornings to go over the arrangements.

She shared the surprise that many felt on discovering Paul's range of musical talents. 'Paul is a really great drummer. And you should hear him play electric guitar. It turns out apparently on a lot of the early Beatles albums he played the guitar solos, like on *Taxman*, which George wrote. Paul played the lead bit on that one. That lead bit on *Blue Bird*? That's him.

'On *Maybe I'm Amazed* on the McCartney album, you can get a little idea but until you meet Paul you don't realise he is such a good musician.

'You think he's a great face maybe, and there's not much behind it. He's a great keyboard player, as good as any of the New Orleans players. He plays great stuff! That's why he's lucky. I think he'll always make music. Like Picasso when he was ninety and still painting. I think Paul will be playing when he's ninety.'

Linda helps Paul in his writing as much as possible and says: 'He doesn't lock himself away. We can be sitting watching television and he might just get up and play and all of a sudden there's another song there. He writes a lot of stuff on acoustic guitar, mainly when we're on holiday, if there's no piano. I'm amazed at how it comes to him. I've written a few songs of my own but I'm very shy about it. I did the first white reggae track, *Seaside Woman* years ago. I was always afraid to release it!

'After the Beatles break up, he was very unsure what to do, and I helped and still do help. They were really difficult times and I didn't always appreciate how difficult, because I didn't appreciate what a career was. We were being sued for a million pounds because the music publishers said I was incapable of writing a song. I'd had no training. But Paul had no training either. So he said, right, get out there to our studio at home, and write a song!

'I was mad keen on reggae because we'd just been to Jamaica and this was before it became big here. I was just mad on it and wrote this song called *Seaside Woman*, which was based on how they speak in Jamaica.'

Linda enjoyed being 'one of the boys' in the band on the road. 'I like them all. They are really nice people. If I didn't think I fitted in then I wouldn't do it. When I was a photographer, I used to go on the road. I went on the road with Blue Cheer, all the way through the mid-West.'

She and Paul shared interests in many hobbies and activities apart from music. 'He's very good at a lot of things. He does a lot of drawing and painting. And he likes farming.

'He clips the sheep and goes out on the tractor. He likes carpentry. Sometimes there

are pressures on us but most of the time things get better. The earliest pressure was not having a good band. The biggest pressure for me is that I find I get very aggravated about what the papers say about us. How can they criticise Paul when he's written some of the greatest songs that have made so many people happy? That frustrates me and makes me want to say: "Look, let's make this a better world." It's not just Paul, it's all the knocking some great artists get. I feel we should build them up. Great painters like Magritte have been knocked – forever. I'd like to change all that.

'I can't stand the way critics never enjoy themselves. But the people buy our records and they must like them!'

Linda has managed to balance being a musician and a mother without actually organising her life in a strictly regimented way. 'I don't have a schedule. I have the most fun living life at random. I could live with very little. I don't need a lot. Too much hinders you and in a way we have too much but what can you do? I wouldn't mind just living a very normal life. I don't enjoy the trappings of stardom, not at all. I'm just not like that.

'I did when I was a teenager and very materialistic, I must own up. Now I realise that isn't what makes you happy. I think love is the only thing, giving it and taking it. It's really the only important thing for me. And the whole spiritual thing. And that means being settled in life. I do believe in God and I'm in tune with life. So I can feel confident. Life keeps going on and it's been going on a long time.'

Linda found great happiness in her marriage to Paul but says she was happy before she got married. 'I was happy when I found photography and found something I wanted to do, and I've been happy ever since then. Before that, I was not confused, exactly but rock 'n' roll was the only thing I liked before that. Now I can do all the things I love.'

Linda was undoubtedly the most creative of all the Beatle wives, most seriously interested in maintaining her career. She worked in unpretentious but effective ways, at both photography and music. When James McCartney was born, this prevented Wings from touring, but she increased her photographic output. Apart from an annual book of 'Linda's Pics', she also produced a hardback volume of her best studies, published at £7.50 by MPL Communications Ltd in 1976. It had shots of Paul at home in Scotland, engaged in domestic pursuits, like painting a roof, and earlier shots from her rock photography days, showing Brian Jones, Hendrix and The Beach Boys.

One of her most intriguing and candid pictures showed a business meeting between Allan Klein, John Lennon, Yoko Ono and Paul, the latter pulling a warning smile which seemed to say 'The shark has pearly teeth dear.' Yoko manages to look both quizzical and imperious.

Linda had a second book of photographs published to coincide with her fortieth birthday in September 1982, and some were displayed at a London gallery, with shots of John Lennon to the fore.

Linda has also made two cartoon films, with the aid of expert animators, *Oriental Nightfish*, which was entered at the Cannes Film Festival and *Seaside Woman*, which won a prize there in 1980.

In recent years, she had helped Paul with his film and video work, notably shouting 'Fire!' during the *Say, Say, Say* promotion video with Michael Jackson. After fourteen years of McCartney marriage – she is still a good sport.

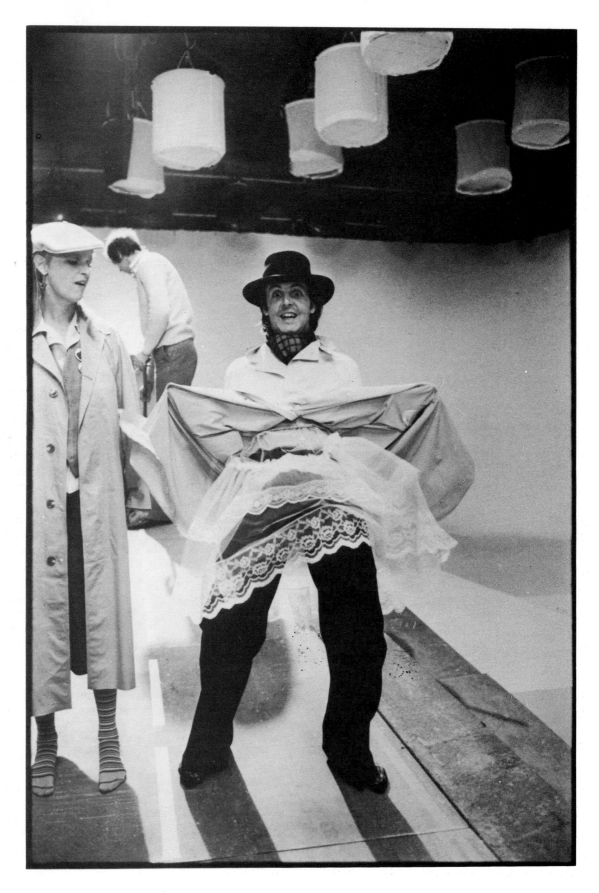

Chapter Ten

WAR AND PEACE

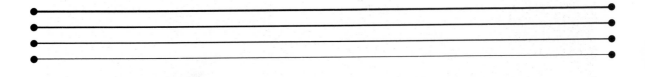

A birthday party was held at the end of the last Empire Pool show in honour of McCartney Productions' managing director Brian Brolly. The guests bombarded each other with cream cakes. It was the very sort of behaviour to be swiped at as 'decadent' by a new breed of moralising purists who suddenly emerged with the birth of Punk Rock in the summer of 1976.

The attitudes and outspoken comments of The Sex Pistols swept through rock, chilling the hearts of the Establishment and bringing into question long accepted values. Much was the soul searching and agonising, particularly among those groups who had always fondly imagined themselves to be the authentic voice of teenage rebellion. All that was about to change. But of all the artists who had for so long dominated the media and record industry with an apparently unalienable 'right to rule', Paul McCartney was the least affected by the uproar.

His answer to The Sex Pistols was to release a lilting Scottish ballad of his own creation which would become one of the biggest selling singles of all time. *Mull Of Kintyre* was the smash hit of Christmas 1977 and a thousand leagues away from *Never Mind The Bollocks*. Yet strangely enough, there was a fleeting moment in Paul's previous recorded output which seemed to anticipate the revolutionary punk style, as epitomised by Johnny Rotten's singing with The Sex Pistols.

In the middle of *Rock Show* on the *Venus & Mars* album of 1975, there appears a curious break in proceedings. Wings adopt a jerky, angular beat, and Paul distorts his voice into a Cockney accent. Linda chants 'Oi' in the background, while Paul sings 'In my green metal suit I'm preparing to shoot up the city, and the ring at the end of my nose makes me look rather pretty.' He goes on to introduce a character called 'Kitty', for the sake of an easy rhyme. The heavy emphasis on 'pretty' and 'kitty' are the broken syllables Londoners use to add deliberation and menace to their speech; the same phrasing made memorable by Johnny Rotten on *Pretty Vacant*.

Rock Show reverts to its regular beat and theme of 'long hair and Madison Square', which so upset critic Charles Shaar Murray on his New Musical Express review, when he tore the song and the entire album to bits. He hated its patronising tone. Yet it seemed Paul and Linda were actually inventing Punk and Oi, at least two years ahead of schedule, complete with Wings.

On December 10, 1976, Paul released *Wings Over America*, a triple album package which represented a complete concert from nine hundred tapes of thirty US shows. Bob Ellis, photographer on the tour feels it was the climax of Paul's performing career. 'It was the pinnacle of what he wanted to achieve out of Wings. After every concert he would say "See you next year!", with a fist in the air, waving to all the kids. Yet everybody knew he wasn't coming back the next year.

'The tour was a tremendously successful culmination of all those years of hard work to promote the Wings image. After that, he really felt that he had done it and didn't want to do it again. When he set out in 1971, he wanted to go through that whole procedure up to the level of being an internationally successful band. He achieved that, without question. It wasn't so much the big show, as having the acceptance by the mass record buying public, which was even more important than the critical acclaim heaped on the band in later years.'

'The Wings concept was basically Paul McCartney in a different guise. In 1976 people were already saying to him that he should go solo. What did he need Wings for? But he was terribly insecure about his own individuality. He really didn't want to have the whole show on his shoulders. And he didn't go back to America on tour again after 1976.'

'There was a lot of discussion about what format Wings would take and indeed he did another tour of Britain in 1979 with the last formation of Wings a relatively low key affair, with a clubby atmosphere. At the time, they were discussing doing a film of *Band On The Run*. They wanted to use the touring situation to film sequences for a movie but it never happened. The tour went ahead without the film. Later Paul just shelved Wings and was increasingly disinclined to tour, but Denny Laine got itchy feet because he wanted to get out there and work. Linda felt she didn't want to go on the road anymore and thought Paul should put his attention to different enterprises. They both felt that.'

The same month that *Wings Over America* was released, John Lennon, Yoko Ono and George Harrison sued Allen Klein, alleging 'bad management'. It was claimed his management had led to The Beatles' split. He sued them back for twenty million dollars, for fees, commissions and expenses incurred when he managed The Beatles. Paul could afford an inward chuckle of 'I told you so.' As if to rub salt in the wounds of the old group and its cherished memory, a Beatles Christmas Convention for fans held at Alexandra Palace, London was described as 'the most embarrassing fiasco ever linked to The Beatles name.'

In January 1977, Yoko helped settle the legal battles with Klein and all actions were dropped after three years of feuding. Commented Paul when it was all over: 'He's been stopped, if you call getting four million quid being stopped. And part of that money

was mine!' Klein praised Yoko for her 'Kissinger-like negotiating brilliance.' At least Paul had the consolation of knowing that in the first two years of Wings' existence he had earned more money than he ever did with The Beatles, a fact which astonished those who assumed Beatlemania had brought them all riches beyond imagining. But Paul's earnings up until the release of *Band On The Run* went to Apple. The first song he owned was *My Love*, published in April 1973. His most famous ballad, *Yesterday*, which has at the last count one thousand two hundred cover versions, was owned by Lord Grade. Paul claims he was never asked if he wanted to sell the song. It was in the light of such financial jiggery-pokery that Paul set up McCartney Productions, first housed in a one room office up four flights of stairs in Soho Square and then swiftly expanded into an entire building.

The McCartney family was also undergoing expansion. In June 1977, as Paul departed for a trip to New York, he announced Linda was expecting a baby, and thought it would probably be a girl. 'We're used to girls,' he said.

Linda had her fourth child, James Louis, at the London Hospital on September 12, 1977. Said Linda: 'He's a contented baby who sleeps through the night. He's got Paul's big eyes and my colour hair. He's beautiful.' Said Paul: 'We have named all our children after people we've loved very much. Our new baby boy is named James after my father and Louis after Linda's grandfather. I don't know if James will go into the music business – he's certainly got a powerful pair of lungs!'

During the summer, Wings embarked on one of its most adventurous recording sessions – on board boats moored at sea off the Virgin Islands. Even more curious, it resulted in an album called *London Town*, which came out the following year complete with a picture of Tower Bridge on the cover and not a hint of its semi-tropical origins.

The band enjoyed themselves on the 'floating studio' built by McCartney Productions on board the charter yacht *Fair Coral*. Musical instruments were shipped out and a converted minesweeper, the *Samala* was used to accommodate the band, Denny, Jimmy and Joe with ten other assistants. *El*

Toro, another yacht, served as home for Paul, pregnant Linda and the three daughters.

Paul explained the idea: 'We wanted to create a situation that would take the sweat out of work. I hate the grind of trying to seek inspiration.' Life afloat was fun. Between recording sessions there was sunbathing and swimming. The only set back was when they were fined fifteen dollars for playing amplified music after ten at night.

The original idea came from Denny Laine who had visited a floating studio in Los Angeles when Rod Stewart had been cutting a track. Denny, a boating enthusiast, put the idea to Paul. He wasn't sure if it would work but liked sunshine and scenery. In the event, the sun was so hot on board ship that eggs cooked themselves on the plates. Whenever recording got too warm for comfort, Wings slipped over the side into the ocean. There were no Caribbean pirates to disturb them and the only visitors were bats and flying fish. Denny Laine, the sailing fan, suffered sunburn and had to be taken back to the island for medical attention, by water ambulance. Paul cut his knee and bruised his leg in a fall, and another of the party broke a heel falling down a stairwell and had to be shipped to hospital. To cheer themselves up after these mishaps, a video of the Cup Final between Liverpool and Manchester United was sent out from London. When he wasn't actually recording or swimming, Paul also sat down to play the captain's mini piano while the McCartney children danced around the cabin.

'It's alright for some, eh?', said Paul when I saw him in London in November that year, and he recalled the boating expedition. It was the first time I'd seen him since the Empire Pool gig and it gave him a chance for a go back about my review.

'Prat!.... Pranny!' were among the heartfelt adjectives he used about the alleged slagging off of *Yesterday*. I hadn't said anything about the song except that Paul would have to sing it every time Wings performed, implying its perennial appeal. But the tone of the piece, and in particular its headline 'Jet Lagged', rankled.

'I thought your review was shit,' he said pleasantly enough, as we met at the number two studio in Abbey Road. The studio was decorated like a Parisian cafe with tables, umbrellas and plants. 'Just to give a little atmosphere' explained Paul.

Paul was actually more amused than angry at the review but he said firmly enough: 'All that stuff about *Yesterday*. It's engraved on me forehead. I'll never play it again!'

Paul talked cheerfully about the effects of punk rock, the departure of Jimmy and Joe and the floating recording sessions. First he told me how Heather had gone to see the Stranglers. 'She came back a changed person, over the moon, just loved it. And the next week a review appeared and it was like a terrible review. "The bass player was inefficient" .... the same old technical crap .... reviews are always wrong.'

Many thought 1977 had been a quiet year for Wings but said Paul: 'No, not inactive. Very active. But in the studio and on boats. We didn't have any trouble with salt water in the machines or sharks attacking us. At night there was much merriment, leaping from top decks into uncharted waters and stuff. I had a couple too many one night and nearly broke something jumping from one boat to another. But then you always break yourself up on holiday.'

'The studio worked out incredibly well and the very first day we got a track down. There was a nice free feeling. We'd swim in the day and record at night. We had written most of the songs beforehand. Denny and I wrote a lot of stuff last summer. We stayed a month on the boat and by the time we recorded it, the songs just seemed to work.'

'We got moved on for being naughty rock'n'roll people infesting the waters. We moored at the US Virgin Island called St. Johns and it's a national park. One of the rules is you must not play amplified music. I think they mean trannies. But we had a whole thing going. You could hear it for miles. We got fined fifteen dollars.'

Paul was somewhat reticent in talking about the tracks, which later became *London Town*, and he gave the impression of not quite knowing what to do with them. 'I never really like talking about albums in advance. People who have heard it like it. It's just a new studio album with a lot of songs, and no big concept. But you never can tell you know. *Sgt. Pepper* wasn't supposed to be a concept. That was just a collection of songs. There's no title for the album. I didn't get where I am today by giving titles ahead of time.'

Joe English and Jimmy McCulloch had quit after the sessions and Wings was once again reduced to a three piece. Said Paul: 'Jimmy and Joe did all their stuff before they split. They were on the boat and then Denny and I finished off the album. A couple of years ago I used to worry if anyone left – "Oh God, I can't keep a group together." But now I don't worry. There is no need to keep it together all the time. I'm more interested in the music and if we can do that, I don't mind how it has to be done.'

Paul explained he didn't want to tour again until they had new material ready. 'We wanna go out with some new stuff. I mean YOU didn't like us playing all the old stuff. Yes, I could quote your bloody review to you Welch. We'll get some new stuff together and think about going out again. We're not too worried at the moment. Joe needed to go back to America because he is extremely American and isn't struck on Britain. It's not everyone you can persuade Britain is an okay place to live y'know. He's used to things like late night telly and hamburgers. Linda is not really American in inverted commas. She doesn't miss any of that at all, so she tells me anyway.

'Jimmy wanted to make a move. A bit like football really. He's a good lad Jimmy, a good guitar player, but sometimes he's a bit hard to live with. That's pretty well known in the Biz and we just decided it would be better if we didn't bother anymore. It got a bit fraught up in Scotland. He's with the Small Faces now but he's done a lot of nice guitar on the new album and on the boat he was incredibly together. He's really into playing heavy rock.'

Jimmy had been with the band for four years and his violent temper tantrums were his undoing. Paul was in no hurry to replace him and certainly didn't want a repetition of the mass auditions of a couple of years before which he felt had been a mistake.

'I'm getting letters from guitar players. But me and Denny both play guitar and if it's not live we can work out the guitar things. And if we need to overdub I can play drums too. I did the drumming on *Band On*

The Run and that did all right. I can't drum technically very well but I can hold the beat and to me that's what you should be able to do if you're a drummer. I like a drummer who holds the beat dead solid. So here we are.... back to the trio! No sweat. We'll just continue like this. It's easier now there are less people to deal with. We can make decisions quicker among ourselves.'

Paul explained that with Linda expecting a baby he didn't fancy touring anyway. 'I didn't want her on stage at the Peterborough Empire and having to rush off to hospital. It's a big number having a baby. So we decided to get on with recording. We'll go out live next year and pick up a drummer and guitarist. We could always go out with me and Denny on acoustics. We'd have a laff anyway. Denny and I wrote together on previous albums but never more than one tune. Then in summer 1976, we sat down and wrote a bunch together. It's good to have someone to bounce off. We haven't really got into songwriting together yet, but we did write a few where we'd patch each other's songs up. We haven't tried sitting down and writing from square one.'

When Denny Laine walked into the studio and joined us for the interview, Paul looked up and said: 'This is that bastard who gave us that bad review. Fuckin' 'it 'im.'

'No hard feelings,' said Denny, who sat down and began strumming his guitar, at exactly the spot where, as Paul pointed out, *Love Me Do* had been recorded by The Beatles fifteen years earlier. There would be

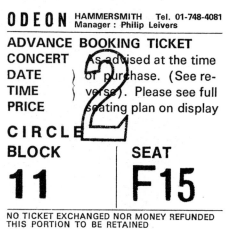

ODEON HAMMERSMITH Tel. 01-748-4081
Manager : Philip Leivers

ADVANCE BOOKING TICKET
CONCERT As advised at the time
DATE) of purchase. (See reverse).
TIME) Please see full
PRICE seating plan on display

CIRCLE
BLOCK
11   SEAT
                      F15

NO TICKET EXCHANGED NOR MONEY REFUNDED
THIS PORTION TO BE RETAINED

many more dramatic events before the twentieth anniversary was celebrated.

On that chilly November afternoon, Paul revealed that his new single was *Mull Of Kintyre* and said Paul simply: 'It's Scottish. It sounds so different from the songs we did on the boat, we thought it should be a single and it sounds very Christmassy and New Yeary. It's a kind of glass of ale in your hand, leaning up against the bar tune. We had the local pipe band join in and we took a mobile studio up to Scotland and put the equipment in the old barn. We had the Cambeltown Band and they were great – just pipes and drums. It was interesting writing for them. You can't just write any old tune. They can't play every note in a normal scale. They've got the drone going all the time so you have to be careful what chord you change over the drone. So it's a very simple song. I had to conduct them very heavily. It's a waltz and an attempt at writing a new Scottish tune. All the other Scottish tunes are old traditional stuff, and I like bagpipes anyway.'

Mull Of Kintyre was a double A side, with *Girls School* as a good hearty rocker. Paul was in some quandry about which side was the most suitable for the public as his photographer, Bob Ellis, recalls.

'Wings were recording at De Lane Lea studios in Wembley. I was there photographing another band. McCartney was next door doing some overdubs for the film *Wings Over America*. I went in to say hello and sit around. Suddenly one of the tour managers walked in with the acetate of what was to be *Mull Of Kintyre*. Paul was delighted. We found a record player and stuck it on. He played both sides and wanted to know what everybody thought. He didn't know if it would be a hit. He hadn't had much success at that point and he didn't know which side to release as an A side and didn't know which could be a hit.'

'He thought probably *Mull Of Kintyre*, but he was being very open about it and tried not to influence people's minds about what should be done with the single. He was pleased with it of course. He was proud of all his work. Yet he wasn't that confident in it. Sure it was different, but then he had done all sorts of varied stuff, and all sorts of weird things, most of which had never seen the light of day.'

Paul was still committed to the idea of touring, even if his sidemen had a habit of quitting, but his ideas were changing.

'There was one point where we felt we had to be on stage every night. If we were going to be any good. But when it comes around to the right time, we'll do it – go out and play. We actually fancy playing in some small, steamy clubs and get back to the people right there and play to them for a laugh. We keep wanting to do a residency. We'd like to get a little club somewhere and build an audience. We'd like to get a great little scene going for a couple of weeks.'

'We did it on our university tour, the first thing we did, and cheap tickets. I love all that – if we could charge fifty pence or something. We'd like to get away from the situation of "You are now coming to see an extremely expensive group. I'd much rather have people come in at lunch time or after work, have a little dance and a cheese roll. It's not so precious as when it gets big. You get trapped in tinsel and glitter which is what the punks are against. The first thing you want to do when you see someone on a pedestal is knock 'em down, isn't it? We've actually done quite well despite all the slagging off and bad reviews. The main thing is the music. It's not the bread and it's not the fame. It's not the acclaim, it's not even the reviews, it's down to whether you like the music or not. And the stuff we do now WE LIKE.'

Girls School was a hit, particularly with Americans. It's lyrics were all about a pornographic St. Trinians. Paul drew his inspiration from the back pages of American entertainment guides which featured films like *School Mistress* and *The Woman Trainer*. But it was *Mull Of Kintyre* which seemed to sweep the world within a matter of days of its release.

Even before the block busting *Mull* was released, Paul had sold the most records of any artist during 1976. And over a few years in America, Wings had been awarded with seven gold singles, eight gold albums, six platinum and three double platinum albums. *Wings Over America* was the first triple album by a band to make Number One in America. The Woodstock album of the famed festival was the previous winner in the triple album stakes. In one year – 1976 – Wings were awarded two gold singles, two gold LPs and two platinum LPs.

Mull Of Kintyre was released on November 11, 1977 and went to Number One within days. It stayed in the charts for seventeen weeks. At its peak it was selling around twenty thousand copies a day. At a special awards ceremony at a London club, Paul was presented with gold and silver discs for the singles *Silly Love Songs*, *Let 'Em In* and *Venus And Mars* and for the albums *Wings Over America* and *Wings At The Speed Of Sound*.

But it was *Mull* which grabbed the headlines. The plaintive quality of the pipes, lilting melody and Paul's heartfelt vocals made it irresistible, as far as the public was concerned, during the sentimental Christmas season. The song was done in one night with seven pipers and ten drummers. The knock on effects were enormous. The pipe band became world famous over night and the whole area of the Mull Of Kintyre became a tourist attraction. The pipers were besieged by reporters. Said one: 'We don't see much of Paul around the area, but he's a proper gentleman. Very professional.'

Wings held a Scottish style reception for the record's launch complete with haggis, Scotch salmon, cheese and beer. Paul was delighted at the success of *Mull* and said: 'It's been a long time coming. We have been close before, but this will just about make our Christmas.' *Mull* sales topping four hundred and fifty thousand had given Wings their first Number One in the British charts, although the band had topped American charts four times during 1977.

Some Americans were baffled by the unfamiliar name and dashed to their atlases to discover that 'The Mull Of Kintyre is a sparsely populated peninsula at the mouth of the Firth Of Clyde.' The residents of Cambeltown were delighted at being thus honoured and queued at the local record shop to order copies and send them to relatives overseas.

Sales of *Mull* eventually topped two million in the UK, replacing The Beatles' *She Loves You* as the largest selling single in British history. It was Number One in Germany, Holland, Belguim and a big seller in Australia. Paul's earnings during 1977 were already topping sixteen million pounds with Wings' American tour chipping a handy two million pounds. Earnings from *Mull* were estimated at two hundred thousand pounds. Not bad for a song which Paul himself described as a 'cross between *Sailing* and *Amazing Grace*.' It was noted that only sixteen singles had ever sold more than a million copies since the record charts began and *Mull* was now the seventeenth.

Despite all this impressive success, Paul could not shake off the endless Beatles' reunion rumours. This time they were supposed to get together for a benefit concert to help 'Save The Whales.'

Said Paul: 'People keep on saying "When are you getting back together again?" They don't realise I can't. There was a play on in the West End called *John, Paul, George, Ringo & Bert*. . . . which made out that all the others wanted to keep it going. In the play John is saying in a thick Liverpool accent: "For the sake of the group Paullie, let's stick together." For one thing, he never called me Paullie and for another it was totally opposite to the way it really happened. It set me down in history as the one who broke the group up. The opposite is true. Ringo left first because he didn't think he was drumming well enough, and we persuaded him he was the best. Then George left during *Let It Be*. They had all left. . . .' No matter how many times he said it, Paul couldn't seem to get his message across. George Harrison tried to help his old partner, saying: 'If you want to see The Beatles, go and see Wings.'

From merely badgering Paul, increasingly hostile and inexplicably vicious attacks were mounted on his talent and personality from those seeking chinks in the armour.

In one onslaught, writer Charles Shaar Murray explained that he felt Paul was 'essentially uncommitted to rock 'n' roll.' It marked a sudden change of heart from Charles who had previously claimed that Wings could do no wrong. Nevertheless he boldly described *Venus And Mars* as a 'terrible record' and thought that Paul angled his music at mums and dads and came off poorly in comparison with the gritty honesty of John Lennon. Putting the boot in with obvious relish, Murray went on to call Paul a 'swot, teacher's pet, soppy sneak, and grouchy spoil sport.' Paul was guilty of allowing his talent to fall into decay and was prone to vapid, shallow prettiness. Charles castigated him for selling himself short by refusing to extend his talent and for taking the easy way out. It was a devastating attack, which Paul found deeply wounding.

More joined in the sport. Sunday Times writer Philip Norman penned an ode. 'O deified Scouse, with unmusical spouse, for the cliches and clay you unload, to an anodyne tune may they bury you soon, in the middlemost 'midst of the road.'

In March, Paul released London Town and with his determination to enjoy himself with the music business undented by endless chastisement, he organised a boat trip up the Thames complete with a fish and chip supper. And he celebrated the first anniversary of Club Sandwich, their bi-monthly paper for the members of the Wings Fan Club. Linda baked a cake for the small celebration party. Charles Shaar Murray and Philip Norman were not invited.

Paul thought about the criticism levelled at such songs as Rock Show and agreed that perhaps it hadn't quite come off. 'I really wanted it to be sweaty,' he told critic Colin Irwin. 'We had a lot of trouble with the drummer. But it doesn't help when someone else comes along and says "Wimpish – middle of the road." It's like in school. You write an essay and you try to do something for the buggers and they turn round and say "You were late for school again." Hell man, give me some encouragement. Don't do that to me.'

'I've worked me bloody way into the record business and now I've got teachers again, slapping me wrists every time I don't quite pull it off.'

In July, contrary to rumours that Wings were splitting up for good, Paul announced two new members, twenty four-year-old Steve Holley, a drummer from Staines, and twenty five-year-old Laurence Juber, a session guitarist, who had worked with Cleo Laine. He had impressed Denny Laine when he backed him singing Go Now, his old Moody Blues hit, on a TV show. Holley had previously been with G. T. Moore and the Reggae Guitars. The new boys were given their baptism of fire recording in the family barn studio in Scotland. Fortunately, it was summer and not winter. Said Laur-

ence: 'Paul was one of my earliest influences. I have tremendous respect for him. When I went for the audition I was quite surprised – I wasn't nervous!' Between rehearsals with the new band, Paul was spending his time at Twickenham studios working on the film of the last Wings tour.

All seemed to be brightening up for the McCartney camp. Beatle reformation rumours had died down and the heaviest McCartney critics had moved on to other targets. Paul busied himself with his concept of Buddy Holly Week. He had recently acquired the Holly song catalogue and wanted to keep alive the singer's memory as a tribute to one of his early favourites. The highlight of that year's Holly Week was the release of the film The Buddy Holly Story. But tragedy cast a shadow over the celebrations. Keith Moon, The Who's drummer and one of Paul's oldest rock biz mates was found dead at his Mayfair flat, just hours after attending the premie 're.

On Thursday, September 7, 1978 Keith went to a party hosted by Paul at the Peppermint Park in London's West End. The guests included both old and New Wave stars. Keith went with his girlfriend Annette Walter Lax and seemed in sober mood. He chatted cheerfully enough to Paul and fellow guest TV star David Frost. He even announced his engagement to Annette. The party transferred to a cinema to see the film, but after forty-five minutes, Keith told Annette: 'I don't think I can take much more of this.'

The couple left to go to the flat which Moon rented from Harry Nilsson. He insisted that Annette cook him a meal while he watched a video horror movie. He went to sleep and woke up the next morning, still hungry. After steak, champagne and pills he went back to sleep, while Annette dozed on a couch in their living room. In the afternoon she found Keith still apparently asleep. But by the eerie stillness of the room, she knew that he was dead. He was taken to Middlesex Hospital and was pronounced dead on arrival. It was discovered at the subsequent autopsy that he had taken an overdose of sedative tablets designed to combat alcoholism. Keith was just thirty three years old, a victim of the rock lifestyle he had come to epitomise.

'He was a desperate man. He didn't even stay to the end of the Buddy Holly film.'

In October 1978, Paul sprang one of his frequent surprises by organising the kind of dream rock session that would have caused hysterics at any time up until the Punk Rock boom. He hired No. 2 studio in EMI Abbey Road and assembled a dazzling array of talent. This included Pete Townshend, Dave Gilmour (guitarist with Pink Floyd), Eric Clapton and Hank B. Marvin, together with John Bonham, Kenny Jones, John Paul Jones (of Led Zeppelin), Ronnie Lane and a horde of brass and percussion players. They were dubbed the Rockestra and contributed two tracks to *Back To the Egg*, an album released in 1979, which made surprisingly little impact. But Paul was pleased with the Rockestra: 'It's amazing how tight they played.'

In January 1979 Denny Laine, the old stalwart from the earliest days of Wings, announced that he was 'fed up' and wanted to go on the road. 'I'm desperate to be on tour' he said. 'I get twitchy sitting around in a studio. I am quite sure we will be touring soon, otherwise I honestly feel that I wouldn't be able to stay in Wings.'

In April, BBC TV showed the seventy-five minute *Wings Over The World* film of the band's 1975-6 tour. It was three years overdue. Said Paul: 'I know its confusing because we have a different line-up now. But I had to make a decision about that film. I either presented it late or did nothing at all.' He revealed that he was planning a British tour combining large venues and small gigs, with his new line up featuring Laurence Juber and Steve Holley.

Then came another tragedy. A year after the death of Keith Moon, Jimmy McCulloch, the fiery ex-Wings guitarist was found dead at his flat in Maida Vale on September 27. The body was discovered by his brother Jack who had to break into the flat, after Jimmy had failed to turn up for rehearsals with a new band – The Dukes.

Recalls Geoff Britton: 'Jimmy had a band he put together. They'd just done a deal with Warner Brothers and they were coming up to their first ever gig. Jimmy had gone missing for a couple of days and hadn't made the rehearsals. They got no response from his phone so they went round to his flat and kicked the door down and there was Jimmy dead. He was sitting up. Someone had been there in the flat and left him. There were a lot of unanswered questions. Someone had been with him, panicked and run off. I don't think he was bumped off but he was left alone. What a waste of talent.'

Said Paul: 'He was a great guitar player. I am very, very sad.'

Jimmy was just twenty six years old. Medical experts claimed they were baffled by his death, as there were no signs of injury, but then it was said he died from morphine poisoning. Jimmy was not an addict. An open verdict on his death was returned by the Coroner and the police said as there was no suspicion of foul play their inquiries were concluded. The funeral was held on October 4.

Jimmy's death was a great tragedy and seemed to reflect the increasing air of gloom in the music industry and the whole country. The decade which had begun with such high hopes had turned sour. The recession, which had reared its head as far back as 1977, had grown beyond a pundit's prediction in sudden harsh reality. Britain seemed in danger of being cast back into the Thirties, with mass unemployment, factory closures and increasing violence in the air. Within a couple of years of EMI making huge sums from hit albums like *Wings Over America* and the single *Mull Of Kintyre*, their profits slumped and the largest recording organisation in the world was hit by a financial crisis. It was taken over by the Thorn Electrical group and at the same time another British record giant, Decca, was merged with Polygram. Throughout the world record sales dived and *Back To The Egg* felt the pinch.

In the midst of all this, perhaps it was not surprising that Paul harked back to his roots and memories of happier days. There was no chance of a Beatle reunion but Wings would come out to play once more, and go back to Liverpool for the start of a tour. It was to be an emotional, nostalgic homecoming, even more so than their last visit when they played Liverpool Empire in 1975. This time Paul was planning a free concert at the Royal Court Theatre for the pupils of his old school.

Wings' 1979 British tour was described by some as a 'low key affair.' Paul had wanted to carry out his much cherished scheme to play in small clubs, just like the old days in Hamburg and Liverpool. But practicalities dictated otherwise. Promoter Harvey Goldsmith suggested to Paul it would make more sense to play at Britain's chain of cinemas and city halls, which in any case were more intimate than the vast sports arenas of America. Certainly there was less ballyhoo about the tour once it got underway. After each show, Paul drove all the way home, except when they were in Scotland and they stayed in a hotel, where an 'end of tour' party was held. The organisation ran smoothly and there were no temper tantrums.

Outside in the streets there were scenes of enthusiasm bordering on hysteria which showed how strong and consistent Paul's grassroots appeal was, despite wild fluctuations in the chart department, changes within Wings, and the worst the press could throw at him.

The tour started with a free concert on November 23 at the Royal Court Theatre, Liverpool, followed by three concerts on November 24, 25 and 26. The rest of the tour dates were Manchester Apollo (28, 29), Southampton Gaumont (December 1), Brighton Centre (2), Lewisham Odeon (3), The Rainbow, Finsbury Park (5), Wembley Arena (7,8,9,10), Birmingham Odeon (12), Newcastle City Hall (14), Edinburgh Odeon (15) and Glasgow Apollo (16, 17). It was Wings' first UK tour in three years and marked the debut of Laurence Juber and Steve Holley. The horn section of Howie Casey, Tony Dorsey, Steve Howard and Thaddeus Richard was retained. But the hundred strong crew of previous tours was cut down to forty.

Paul had promised in January to play at the Royal Court Theatre, which had been running into financial trouble. He had donated five thousand pounds to their survival fund. 'It's a great boost for the theatre,' said their spokesman, Sir Henry Livermore. Labour councillors had been less grateful and, with petty spite, blocked a motion to convey the thanks of Liverpool Council.

Said one of them: 'I don't see why Paul McCartney should be singled out for special praise. The Beatles could have given a million and not missed it. They made their millions and we have not seen them since.'

In point of fact, The Beatles had given more millions in taxation to the country than they received. Paul was no longer a Beatle, the group didn't exist, he gave considerably more to charity than was publicly acknowledged, and he *was* coming back to Liverpool, to give a free concert at the theatre for the pupils of his old school, Liverpool Institute. Later the city changed its attitude to The Beatles in the wake of the death of John Lennon, the Toxteth riots and the decay of the city's industries and prestige. They started naming streets after them.

Paul was constantly advised by lawyers to live abroad to reduce his 98 per cent tax burden. His answer to that was swift and always the same. 'I just hate the idea that you have to live where it's convenient for your money. We like it in England. We love the country. It's a great place to bring up children.'

However patriotic, Paul was not immune from attack from the curmudgeons of society. When folk thought perhaps there should be a statue erected in honour of The Beatles, an irate reader of the Liverpool Echo wrote to the paper: 'To erect a statue of The Beatles would be an insult to the great city of Liverpool and to the many thousands of good people who have brought great credit to the city. The Beatles represented all that was bad in society in the sixties. They conned the public with their music, such as it was. It was a phenomenon that is best forgotten.'

It was not a view shared by the average Liverpudlian however, nor did it reflect feelings through the country at large. There were thousands literally fighting to get their hands on the all important bits of paper that would allow them to hear the music of McCartney, the Beatle who came back.

As tickets for the tour went on sale, there were amazing scenes. Thousands queued outside the Royal Court and theatres all over the country. After waiting all night in freezing temperatures in Liverpool, a thousand fans were disappointed and angry to find that all four thousand five hundred tickets had been sold. They had gone in four hours. Ticket touts were attacked in scuffles outside the Manchester Apollo when tickets were offered at ten times their face value.

The fans had been camping out for three days in lines three deep and half a mile long. Some four hundred were turned away when all five thousand three hundred seats were sold within four hours. No one who arrived at the scene after 7 a.m. stood any chance of getting one, but the persistent stuck it out, trying to keep warm under sheets of polythene and in sleeping bags.

In Birmingham, fans besieged the cinema when they were told all the tickets had been sold by postal application. In Glasgow, six thousand waited for hours in bitter weather only to find the tickets had all gone. In Bristol, forty thousand applied for tickets, nine times the capacity of the venue. Liverpool's Royal Court denied they were responsible for ticket sales, which only left disappointed fans even more angry and frustrated. One man at least seemed pleased with the turn of events.

Mr. Bertram Parker, headmaster of Liverpool Institute and once Paul's Geography teacher, was delighted with the idea of the free concert. 'It's a marvellous gesture by a famous old boy.'

Said Paul: 'It's my way of saying "thank you" for some very happy years. Everyone seems to knock their school days but for me they have fond memories.'

Special buses were laid on for the pupils who arrived in school uniform. But once the curtain went up there were screams and whistles that would have earned detention and lines in Paul's school days. Mr. Parker – 'Blip' to his pupils – sat in the stalls and tried to recall what the superstar had been like as a spotty kid doing dirty drawings in class. His reverie was interrupted by a voice booming over the PA from the stage: 'Hello Blip – nice to see you.'

There was no doubt that Paul found it a heartwarming occasion, as much a treat for him as for the kids. 'I feel I am not judged with the same harshness by the people here as elsewhere' he told a reporter.

Back in London, however, the cynics hadn't changed. Wings joined other bands, including The Who and Led Zeppelin in a charity concert for the stricken people of Kampuchea. 'A spectacular, shambling mess,' was one reviewer's verdict.

The Wings' single for November 1979 *Wonderful Christmas Time* was called part of 'The great Xmas crap pumping machine.'

Back To The Egg, released in June was slated as 'a horrendous little omelette' and described as 'a muddled bag of half baked concepts.' It would be the last album credited to Wings.

Paul acknowledged that sales of the 'Egg' album were down. Its release coincided with a sudden huge slump in American and worldwide record sales. Many thought that the entire music business was at last coming to a halt. And for Paul it looked like The End had come in the New Year when he unexpectedly found himself incarcerated in a Japanese jail.

The headlines screamed the world over. 'Beatle Paul Held Over Drugs. Marijuana found in airport search!' Paul McCartney was arrested for allegedly possessing drugs at Tokyo airport on Wednesday, January 16, 1980. Customs men had found a large quantity of what American airline hostesses invariably call 'smoking materials' in his suitcase.

Paul, Linda, their four children and the entire Wings entourage had just arrived for the two week tour of Japan that had been talked about for years. All past attempts to enter the country had been foiled because the Japanese authorities were aware of Paul's previous 'drugs bust' convictions. They had relented and granted a visa because they appreciated his popularity with Japanese fans. In view of the well known severity of the local drugs laws, it was amazingly daft of Paul to come in with his own supply, not even properly concealed, when he could have easily 'scored', once safely through the police and customs net.

Just as Paul was cheerfully strolling through customs, he was stopped and searched. His subsequent arrest was shown on 'live' television, laid on to cover his historic visit. Linda and the band were allowed to go to their hotels. Turmoil and near panic reigned in the McCartney camp when it was realised he could face a long jail sentence. This wasn't rock 'n' roll fantasy but harsh reality.

Wings were due to play eleven concerts and all were sold out. The fans were devastated and so was the promoter. The first pictures arrived in newspaper offices of Paul making his Japanese debut – in handcuffs.

There had been nothing quite so sensational since the jailing of Mick Jagger. Paul McCartney M.B.E. was formally charged with drug smuggling. In vain he explained: 'I just brought in some hash for smoking.'

Linda, unhappy and upset, was increasingly concerned. It seemed all McCartney's power and status could not shield him from the wrath of the law. After nine hours in jail, the tour was cancelled. 'It's all a mistake, a serious mistake' said Paul, as the guards carted him off. Weeping girls arriving at the jail began chanting 'Free Paul', but the hours turned to days and there seemed no sign that he would be released. It was an extraordinary situation. Paul sat in his cell, sending out messages for food and fresh clothes. Back home, the Daily Star, attempting to emulate The Times of thirteen years earlier (which had sprung to the defence of Jagger), trumpeted in uncertain English: 'Putting him in chains is ludicrous. Japan, which purports to be a modern industrial nation, should learn to behave in a civilised fashion.' Japan patently *was* a modern industrialised nation and had a civilisation considerably older than Britain's, but it did seem they were being unduly harsh with a man who had come to entertain them and not start a smuggling operation. The fact remains that Paul had laid himself wide open. British promoter Harvey Goldsmith was furious with the authorities. Paul was shattered. The Japanese promoter, Seijiro Udo was in tears. He had lost two hundred thousand pounds following cancellation of a tour which had taken him years to set up. He had made repeated requests for Paul's visa. With uncharacteristic passion he announced that Paul had 'betrayed' him.

Each morning, Paul was roused from his mattress at 6 a.m. and taken to the drugs agency H.Q. for questioning, after a breakfast of beanpaste soup. Then it was back to the 8' x 4' cell to ponder his fate until lights out at 8 p.m. After the fourth night, the Japanese promoter announced he was going to sue McCartney. Linda and family grew even more depressed, back at the hotel. The band felt there was little point in hanging around and flew back to England. Only a handful of his employees loyally stuck out the ordeal, waiting patiently for news.

Denny Laine was not among them. He had gone off to MIDEM, the annual music business junket in the South of France. The news was all bad. Japanese radio and TV officially banned the playing of all Wings songs on their networks. In America, a fan was killed by the police at Miami Airport. Twenty nine year-old Kenneth Lambert had planned to fly to Japan to 'free Paul', possibly with the aid of the toy gun he had been foolishly waving at the cops. He had no money for a ticket and had started a row. The police opened fire when he pointed his toy gun at them. Meanwhile, back in Japan, Paul prepared to spend his sixth night in jail and the fans were singing *Yesterday* outside his window. He had his first visit from Linda and later she said: 'It's a strain.... the authorities tell us nothing.'

By now, the ever adaptable Paul was beginning to learn how to cope with prison life. He was moved and touched by the letters and telegrams that poured in. The hours of interrogation were obviously designed to obtain maximum 'loss of face', considered a great disgrace in the East. Paul was more concerned about the washing facilities. There was no bath and he had to wash in the same water supplied to the lavatory. He called for a visit by the British Consul, a cheerful soul called Mr. Doland Warren-Knott, who chatted and joked with him for fifteen minutes without managing to obtain his release. It seemed McCartney was becoming a permanent fixture at the Metropolitan Jail and said his jailer, Yasuji Ariga: 'He is very polite and has made a good impression on the guards.' It was agreed that Paul should be allowed one bath a week and he chose the traditional method, going into the communal tub with other prisoners. There were no musical instruments so he resorted to singing with the other jailbirds. The British Consul was highly amused. He chuckled at the thought of Paul coming all the way to Japan for a tour and ending up singing in jail for his fellow prisoners.

Then on the 25th of January, ten days after his arrest, Paul was released and it was announced that he would be deported. The Tokyo prosecutor's office dropped their investigation and Paul was taken to Narita airport and put on a flight to Amsterdam with Linda and the children. It was a tearful reunion.

Paul recording the guitar and vocal parts of *Mull of Kintyre* at his farm in the highlands. Note the union jack sock serving as a spitscreen.

Paul was released because he had brought the drugs into the country for his own use and not to sell them to others. 'He has been punished enough,' said a spokesman. 'He has shown signs of repentence and apologised.' If he had been convicted of smuggling he could have spent seven years in jail.

But his ordeal was not quite over, even when he finally got on the jet back to Europe. He was pursued by reporters who surrounded him at the airport in Tokyo and again at Amsterdam. Here the Dutch authorities refused to allow him into the country. He took a private jet to Lydd airport in Kent, to return to the comforts of home.

Paul may have shown sign of repentence in the Japanese jail but once back home he said of hash: 'I can take it or leave it. It's silly to say it's wicked. I think we should decriminalise it.' Of his time in jail he said: 'I wasn't badly treated but it was an experience I never want to repeat. It was incredibly dumb, really stupid of me to try to take the hash into Japan. I just wasn't thinking logically. I didn't really try to hide the stuff. It was just sitting there on top of the suitcase.'

In the aftermath Paul had to pay the promoter £200,000 and it cost around ten thousand pounds a day in living expenses and for lawyers fees. He talked to broadcaster Paul Gambaccini and told him 'In the clink I had a lot of time to think.' He revealed that he decided to finish of his solo LP *McCartney II*, which was eventually released in May 1980, together with a clutch of singles. It really seemed as if the sojourn in prison, the nearest perhaps that a rock star can get to isolation in a monastery, had concentrated his mind wonderfully.

McCartney II was an excellent album with some varied, interesting songs, like the extraordinary *Temporary Secretary*, a big chart hit in the autumn, the beautiful *Waterfalls* and the exciting *Coming Up*, a trinity of Paul's finest blockbusters.

The worst punishment for Paul in jail, apart from the threat of being held for seven years, was the boredom. He couldn't sleep and suffered from headaches.

There were no pencils or musical instruments and he couldn't compose but he did some physical exercise, skipping and mental exercise, thinking about his recording plans. As soon as he got back to England he spent two hours a day for ten days writing down his experiences, in long hand.

On *McCartney II*, Paul played all the instruments instead of using Wings and recorded it at home in Sussex and in Scotland. The funky *Coming Up*, an exuberant shout of freedom was built up like many of Paul's songs, from a basic drum track, with guitars, bass and vocals added on later. His vocals were sped up and put through an echo. It got to Number Two in the U.K. charts. A live version by Wings on the B side was a hit in America and had been recorded in Glasgow on their last tour. The American Columbia label had suggested the 'live' version was best suited to U.S. radio audiences. They also wanted it on the solo album but Paul preferred his own studio version.

Paul did a wonderful video to accompany *Coming Up*, on which he appeared as each member of a 'band' called The Plastic Macs, in various guises, including himself as 'Beatle Paul' complete with violin base.

In April 1980, Paul was presented with an Ivor Novello Award for services to the British music by Yul Brynner. It seemed as if the dark tide of shocks and tragedies that had marred recent years was receding.

In the summer he was officially entered in the prestigous Who's Who as McCartney (James) Paul MBE 1965; musician, composer; born Allerton, Liverpool, 18 June 1942. There followed details of his tours, compositions and recordings. Most of the entry of course was devoted to his output with John Lennon and The Beatles. There was even a reference to his early trio with John and George Harrison, The Moondogs, which performed back in 1959. Although Paul had seen less and less of his old partner over the years, when they lived on different sides of the Atlantic, they stayed in touch by phone, and Paul called John at Christmas, 1979. He told a reporter shortly afterwards: 'People are calling John a recluse because he isn't doing what they expect him to do. In fact he's been getting on with being a family man. He's cooking and having a great time. John had told Paul he wasn't doing anything musical, and that he didn't particularly miss playing or recording at that time. But John was emerging from the five years he had deliberately devoted towards raising his son Sean.

John Ono Lennon celebrated his fortieth birthday on October 9, 1980 and announced he was bringing out a new LP, to be called *Double Fantasy*, his first since *Rock 'n' Roll*. John had kept such a low profile that, after a neighbour had shown him the film *Yellow Submarine*, Sean ran home shouting, 'Daddy, were you really a Beatle?'

During the many 'Beatle reunion' scares of the Seventies, Paul had usually kept an open mind on the subject. John remained intransigent. 'Going back to The Beatles would be like going back to school. I was never one for reunions. It's all over.'

While the famous were going about their business, an unknown pudgy youth, with a history of mental illness, Mark David Chapman, was busy buying himself a .38 calibre revolver in a shop in Honolulu. A slogan in the shop read 'Support the 2nd amendment.... the right to keep and bear arms! Buy a gun and get a bang out of life!'

Chapman's life was built on the fantasy that he was not just another American dropout but one of the best loved and most creative figures in popular culture – John Lennon. As a twenty five year-old Beatle fan, he even married a girl with Japanese ancestry and taught himself to play the guitar. Only one flaw prevented him from actually becoming John Lennon. The genuine prototype was alive and well and coming back into public life. To Chapman, who signed his name 'John Lennon', it seemed an imposter was trying to usurp his position, especially one who had just released a single called *Starting Over*.

John, encouraged by record company boss David Geffen had begun recording again at New York's Hit Factory studios. He explained that the tracks were a greeting to those who had lived through the Sixties and Beatle years. 'We're still here and I'm asking: well, how are you? how have you been? this is us, we survived.'

John and Yoko were returning from the recording studio to their apartment in the Dakota Building in New York City on the night of December 8, 1980 when Chapman drew his gun and shot John down. He was rushed to hospital but it was too late. Lennon was dead.

A shockwave of grief, anger and disbelief went around the world. The news broke in

London in the early hours of the following day. It was established that John had died just before 11 p.m. He and Yoko had just arrived at the Dakota on the Upper West Side of Manhattan after a late recording session. Chapman had accosted them and an argument broke out. Chapman had been seen lurking around the building for three days and earlier John had signed a copy of *Double Fantasy* for him. This time he didn't want an autograph. He wanted to kill. He pulled out the .38 and crouching combat style, fired five times. 'Help me,' said John, as he lay dying in his wife's arms.

Paul was told of John's death by his London office staff and he immediately telephoned Yoko and they spoke for several minutes while Paul offered his condolances. The pointless, cruel killing struck at the hearts of all The Beatles and their families. A friend close to Paul said: 'It has been a great emotional upset for him.' After struggling to find the right words to express his feelings, Paul eventually issued a statement to say that he was deeply shocked and saddened at the news. 'He was a great man and will be missed by the whole world and will be remembered for his art, music and contribution to world peace.'

In the confusion of press reports pouring in from America, Paul naturally wondered if he might be in danger and bodyguards mounted a round the clock watch. A tremor of fear went through the whole community of celebrities in an age when the life of The Pope as well as a pop star could be threatened. But the use of bodyguards had a more mundane purpose as well, to protect Paul and his family from the press during the aftermath of the tragedy. Chapman was arrested, tried and jailed.

Paul talked later about his feelings. 'There's one thing about sudden death. There are so many things left unsaid. I was really worried for a few weeks afterwards. There are crazy people everywhere. But I really couldn't live like that (under guard). My attitude is to try and push it out of my mind. I would just like to have seen John the day before and just straightened everything out with us. We found we could talk to each other as long as it was about kids, and stuff like that.'

Paul tried to rationalise the rift between himself and his old songwriting partner, and it was as if talking in public about the depth or otherwise of John's antagonism could lift the pressure and heal the wounds. He told interviewers: 'People say we were worlds apart but we weren't. We actually did know each other. We actually were very close. We had a ding dong in the press especially after the Apple stuff. Yoko told me. how very complimentary he was about me, but he just didn't want to be the cloying, sychopantic sort of guy saying in public "Oh Paul's terrific – he's really great." There was a very competitive thing between us. Yoko says a lot of the slagging off was John taking the mickey. I talked to Yoko the day after he was killed and the first thing she said was "John was really fond of you." He was very jealous and so was I. The last telephone conversation I had with him we were still the best of mates.'

When Paul first heard the news of John's death he was so stunned he couldn't believe it was true, a feeling shared by millions of others around the world who had grown up with Beatle music and shared a part of their life with John, Paul, George and Ringo.

'It was crazy. It was anger. It was fear. It was madness. It was the world coming to an end.'

As Paul mourned the death of his friend, he also reflected on the knowledge that his own obituary had already been written, prepared by Beatles' biographer Hunter Davies for The Times.

'They are ready should I die.'

Chapter Eleven
PIPES OF PEACE

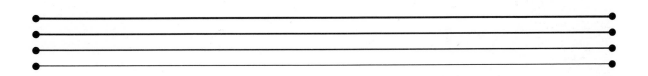

Twin hammer blows of imprisonment and the death of John Lennon gave Paul cause to pause and reflect. But these events served only to hasten changes in his career that many thought inevitable.

Throughout 1981 a self-imposed ban on releasing records served as a silent tribute to his old friend. His subsequent return to musical activities saw greater success than ever. And he seemed happy and determined to go on working, simply because it is his way of life. Said a friend: 'Paul doesn't have an ego like other rock stars. He doesn't need adulation and doesn't work for that reason, which in the rock scene is unusual in itself. He is a perfectionist who likes everything to be right and in that sense he is more like the entertainers of the old school.'

Wings had served him well during the previous decade but now he relinquished this concept and began recording with his musical peers in the way friends and critics had urged him to do for years. He had made his point. Paul had enjoyed the group life denied him by the early shut down of The Beatles. Wings had lasted ten years in one form or another and had provided a sort of musical life support system. Now the concept was redundant. The abortive trip to Japan and the speedy departure of the musicians, leaving Paul to sweat it out in jail had probably hastened its death knell although officially the band had not been broken up. For some time afterwards McCartney press statements would claim: 'Wings IS Paul and Linda.'

Certainly the partnership with Denny Laine came to an abrupt end. His decision to leave Japan and go off to MIDEM while Paul's fate was undetermined could not have helped relations between the two. Says one ex-Wings employee: 'Basically Denny Laine was paid a fortune to help Paul. Although he didn't make a huge musical contribution, he helped keep the band together and raised morale when times were tough. He was the go-between. But he didn't really share the McCartney family circle. Denny was his own man, and unfortunately his girlfriend, Jojo, didn't see eye to eye with Linda.'

Denny was normally a quiet, cheerful and friendly man who had suffered early disappointments in his career when he quit the Moody Blues to form his own band, the Electric String Band. The Moodies went on to enormous financial success and his own group had died the death although it was musically highly innovative. Denny was happy to work with Paul and had found a comfortable niche. But like most musicians he yearned to be his own boss or at least feel he was an important figure in his own right. But in music as in life there are the leaders and the led. McCartney, along with a rare breed that includes the likes of Frank Zappa and Ian Anderson of Jethro Tull, is definitely one of the leaders. Working for Paul was fun, profitable and not too demanding. But like Jimmy McCulloch who took to the bottle, Denny felt the need to exert himself. In August 1980, he made a stab at forming his own band and played at such venues at London's Marquee Club. He made his own record, the aptly titled *Japanese Tears*, with contributions from Jojo – now his wife – and old Wingsmen Denny Seiwell and Henry McCullough.

133

But for Denny life seemed to be getting dangerously complicated. Jojo suffered a drugs overdose at their home in Laleham, Middlesex, in December. She was stricken with grief at the news that her father had died from gunshot wounds in America. She was rushed to hospital but later recovered. Such strain in his personal life left Denny vulnerable to public upsets. Somehow he got involved in a fight in Morton's nightclub in Mayfair. Denny appeared at Marlborough Street magistrates court, accused of assaulting a rock group manager, Jock McDonald. Denny was charged under his real name of Brian Hines. The court case hung over him for weeks before it was finally dropped. Around the same time, he was fined a hundred and seventy five pounds on a drinks driving charge after he crashed his Ferrari into a fence. 'I don't seem to be having much luck lately,' he said ruefully.

In April 1981, he announced his decision to quit Wings and said: 'It was obvious we wouldn't tour again. There has been no row. But touring is the purpose of being in the business as far as I am concerned.' Paul wished him the best of luck but couldn't resist adding: 'He just decided he wanted to go his own way, saying he wanted to go on tour . . . . and he hasn't been on a tour since!' A year later Denny got divorced and went to live in Spain, far from the traumas of the rock business.

Denny Laine had served his time with Wings as a psychological counterpoint to Paul. Although he had his problems, he had been level headed enough to lend the right degree of support. It was always the stated aim that Denny would make major contributions to McCartney's songwriting, but in reality Paul could never allow anybody to take over that vital function.

Wings had been suspended because of the murder of John, and it was the crucial factor in the decision not to tour. But Paul made it plain he'd had enough of trying to wet nurse the band. He said with feeling: 'I hate the pressures of a group. With so many changes in the line up it distracted from the music. I got bored with the whole thing.'

Paul didn't regard this as the end but simply the beginning of a new phase in his career. For a while he toyed with the idea of putting together a super group, with musi- cians like drummer Phil Collins and bassist Stanley Clarke, to do a 'Band On The Run' style tour. But it was easier to get such men into the studio than tempt them on the road with what would essentially be a new version of Wings.

Paul now concentrated all his energy on recording, filming and making promo videos. He seemed to undergo a great burst of creative energy that kept him at the helm of the pop scene in a way he had not enjoyed for years.

In January 1981, Paul and Linda took the Concorde to the Bahamas. Paul was intent on going to the volcanic island of Montserrat, near Antigua, to start work on a new album after his holidays. He had decided to work again with his old chum and confidant, George Martin, who owned the studios there as well as Air Studios in London. In an uncertain world, it seemed most proper that Paul should seek out a man who commanded respect and whose lucky touch seemed to have worked such wonders during The Beatles era. George, the urbane, civilised and dignified Englishman, whose early work on the legendary Goon Show records had once so impressed John Lennon, had produced The Beatles all the way from *Love Me Do* to *Sgt. Pepper*. There was a tremor of excitement throughout the music world at the thought of such a reunion.

Paul explained the decision was 'because I felt there had been something missing from the previous few albums.' Together they would take great care to ensure only music and production of the finest quality would emerge. After all, they both had their reputations on the line. Extra recording equipment by the ton was flown out to the island paradise. But even here there would be no escape from prying eyes. There was to be an all star cast on the new album and on February 15, Ringo Starr and his family flew in followed by Stevie Wonder, clutching the rhythm box he gave to Paul as a present. The world's press were alerted. This was Paul's first recording since the death of John and news editors scented the age old story of a 'Beatle reunion.' This time Paul had had enough. His temper snapped. When he was pursued by photographers along the island roads, he deliberately rammed them with his jeep. 'Monsters!', he shouted at them in fury. He followed this up with a long road-side lecture on the individual's right to privacy. 'There's no story. No reunion!' he stormed. This was the frustrated reaction of a man who was supposedly able to 'manipulate reporters.' It was the human side of Paul which so many claimed was hidden behind a bland veneer. He could rage and lose his temper just like anybody else. But even on this 'mask slipping' occasion, Paul tried to reason with the people who were driving him to distraction. Nobody had given more time to the press than Paul, or put up with so much stick. He is naturally easy going and would rather walk away from potentially disturbing scenes. It is part of the public's perception of Paul that he is open, outgoing, non-reclusive and far removed from the Howard Hughes image of a millionaire. But, says Robert Ellis: 'Oh I think he IS a Howard Hughes character. The public image and the private McCartney are quite different. The real McCartney is much more complex than even the most in-depth interview has ever revealed.'

'I remember when the first Wings albums were slated, he got very defensive and didn't like the fact they were heavily criticised. If people around him were clever, they knew not to criticise him. He was desperate for critical acceptance.'

'On the first tours by Wings, the reviews were read diligently. Good or bad. He was very concerned at that time about the critical slating the band was getting. The point about his public image is he treats it like a profession. He deals with the press in a professional manner and portrays himself as a reticent person, but full of bonhomie. In fact he gives very little away. Nobody ever scratches more than the surface of the man. The more he likes you, the more he tells you.... but only what he wants you to know. There is never any question of letting the barriers down and being frank and honest. He makes quips, comments and serious remarks about his music. But it is practised. He repeats himself endlessly and gives what I would term a glib answer.

'He has been called sly because of this, but he would never go out of his way to hurt or damage people. He's only sly when he had to dodge people, or go around them because he doesn't want to meet them, or

have his picture taken in a particular situation. Instead of saying "No" he avoids a situation by going around it. He will say one thing and do another. He tries to be honest with himself and what he does, but people's impression of him isn't always the right one. So some may think he is being hypocritical. He might say something about a plan or idea when he has no intention of doing it. I think that is a result of the intense pressure of the Beatle years. It must be remembered that everybody thinks that McCartney can do whatever he wants and whatever THEY want. "You've got all this money – surely you don't mind doing this for me!" He's good natured enough not to say, "Fuck off!" He'll say, "Why don't you discuss it with my office and we'll see what can be worked out," when he had already decided he's not gonna do it! "We'll work out the details and see how it can be done."'

'He's a great one for avoiding problems rather than facing them head on. He's no different from everybody else in that respect. He's had so much experience of problems, he doesn't want to deal with them all the time. So he makes excuses to people just to save himself the hassle.'

Once he had shaken off the photographers, Paul could get down to work without interruptions, or the need to worry about PR and images.

Says Robert Ellis: 'Watching Paul McCartney recording is like watching a different person. Aside from his public face, he has a whole different attitude to work. He places

great attention to details. Yet often when he has high hopes for a record it doesn't always live up to his hopes, in terms of sales. Publically, he always displays great enthusiasm for all his work, but he also betrays a lack of confidence, and he is genuinely modest. He hates talking about how his songs are made. He talks about their origins in a make-believe way, and frequently they are untrue. The story of how a song came to be written can change from interview to interview. A lot of his more obtuse songs are simply got up from thin air. And a lot of them are recorded in a very abstract way by putting two or more bits together, then adding on an arrangement later. His method of writing a song is to come up with a fragment of a tune – just a sequence of notes and some garbled words. Usually he writes at the piano first and he is always humming incessantly. Music just pours out of him all the time!''

The March sessions went well and the end result was the critically acclaimed *Tug Of War* album, released in April 1982. It contained the smash hit single *Ebony And Ivory*, with Paul duetting with Stevie Wonder. Ringo Starr drummed on a track and the other guests included friends like sax player Andy Mackay and 10cc star Eric Stewart. The video made to promote *Ebony And Ivory* was one of the most expensive ever made. As Stevie couldn't make the London sessions, the two superstars were filmed separately which seemed ironic to some, in view of the theme of 'perfect harmony.' But the effect and message of the song was simple, unaffected and helped make it a worldwide success story.

After Paul and Stevie cut *Ebony And Ivory*, they jammed together in the studio with Paul on drums and Stevie on synthesiser. The latter is also a fine funky drummer and he was not afraid to tell Paul off for playing 'too busily.' If there is one thing a musician can't stand, it's being told how to play, and for a few seconds Paul felt miffed. Then he realised that the advice was right and proper. He cooled down his drumming ardour and the piece began to live and breath and turned into another song for the album, *What's That You're Doing*, with lyrics and bass added after the jam.

Most moving of the new songs was *Here Today*, which was written with John Lennon

in mind. Paul thought it needed a string quartet to bring out the best in the melody, but felt constrained for fear that it would result in comparisons with *Yesterday*.

Discussions with George Martin followed and then Paul realised they shouldn't hold back from using the strings, simply because they had done something like it once before. In Martin's words: 'The song screamed out for a string quartet.'

Paul felt it was a particularly hard song for him to sing and was later surprised when not many seemed to pick on its significance, nor realise it was about John. 'I wrote it one day when I was just sitting down working on those minor opening chords. I'd never done a song about John before.' He explained that the whole album was about conflict and opposites. 'I don't think I would have used that theme before. I would have been afraid of bringing people down. But I've been growing up and after all, it isn't news there is a tough side to life.'

While *Tug Of War* was making its first impact on the charts, memories of Wings were kept alive by the release of *Rock Show*, a film featuring the band when it appeared at the King Dome, Seattle, during their world tour. It was given a cinema première in April 1981, attended by Lord Snowdon as a guest of Paul and Linda.

Rock Show was Wings as their fans liked to remember them, and it also served as a memorial for the late Jimmy McCulloch. The whole band looked like they were thoroughly enjoying themselves; Linda letting out Indian style whoops from behind her battery of keyboards, Denny and Paul exchanging winks, smiles and asides. The powerful brass section blasting away on *Jet* and *Listen To What The Man Said*, showed how well McCartney songs responded to full-blooded treatment. And Jimmy McCulloch was seen at his best, looking young, handsome and happy, playing superb slide and lead guitar.

Shortly after the première , on April 27, there was another star studded event when Ringo Starr married for the second time. This time his bride was beautiful actress Barbara Bach and the wedding took place at Marylebone Registry office. Paul and Linda were there and so were two hundred yelling fans. It was quite like old times. George Harrison and Olivia were there and so the three ex-Beatles were photographed in public together for the first time since John's death. They went to Rags Club in Mayfair, when a cheerful Ringo surprised the guests by playing not his drum kit, but a guitar. It was revealed that the man who officiated at the service had also married Paul and Linda in the same room in 1969.

When George Harrison recorded his tribute to John *All Those Years Ago*, Paul and Linda added background vocal harmonies and Ringo was the drummer. This was the closest they got to the much yearned-for 'reunion.' But somehow Paul was ever drawn back to his roots, despite the passing of the years. In May 1982, he returned to Penny Lane in Liverpool and the church where he sang as a choirboy. He was best man at the wedding of his brother Mike to Rowena Horne at St. Barnabus. Mike, who had once achieved fame as Mike McGear with the satirical group, Scaffold, had suffered his own share of upsets over the years. He had divorced his first wife and then a fire at his home had destroyed many of his precious souvenirs. Now he had reverted back to using the family surname and had published his own book, Thank U Very Much. One of his biggest hits, *Lily The Pink* was played on the church organ.

After carrying out the marriage ceremony, the Rev. Harrington turned to the Best Man and recalled his days as a choirboy. 'He used to sit up here – making some sort of noise!'

The ex-choirister was secure in the knowledge that *Tug Of War* was selling one hundred and twenty five thousand copies a day. To celebrate, he bought himself a eighteenth century windmill near his home in Sussex. On June 18, he also celebrated his fortieth birthday. He had been a musician for twenty-five years and still the hits and accolades were pouring in. In February 1983, Paul was given the British Record Industry Award for the best UK Male Artist and as the man who had made 'An Outstanding Contribution To Music.' He also received the Sony Award for Technical Excellence, shared with George Martin and Geoff Emerick for their work on *Tug Of War*.

Following the successful collaboration with Stevie Wonder, Paul now teamed with his old friend from the Jackson Five, and now a world superstar, Michael Jackson. In May they cut the single *The Girl Is Mine*, produced by Quincy Jones in Los Angeles. Toto's Jeff Porcaro was on drums and described the excitement of the occasion. 'It was great hearing those two guys singing live. It sounded like a signature tune of both of them. McCartney melody and that old Motown groove from Michael. We worked out the tune in the studio. George Martin was there too.'

In October 1983, Paul and Michael had another huge hit with the insidiously groovy *Say Say Say*, culled from the *Pipes Of Peace* album, again produced by George Martin and with a bunch of star sidemen.

While Paul was busy producing these block-busters, he was also engrossed in making his first major feature film *Give My Regards To Broad Street*, a musical comedy. He wrote the script, score and ten songs and invited friends old and new to join him in the action including Ringo, Linda and Tracey Ullman. Shooting went ahead on locations in London. It was sixteen years since *The Magical Mystery Tour* and McCartney Magic was in no danger of getting lost en route this time.

In December 1983, Paul, George and Ringo met with Yoko Ono at the Dorchester, London to discuss business. The meeting went on for hours and sparked off the age old controversy. Would The Beatles get back together? 'Don't be silly, don't be daft,' was Ringo's admonition to reporters outside. Paul slipped out a side door. There was nothing more he could say on the subject.

Paul McCartney today is still essentially a pop fan, a man who likes to check out the new groups recording at Air Studios, while maintaining enthusiasm for his boyhood idols like Buddy Holly. He has been an inspiration and catalyst. A man, in the words of an old non-McCartney song, whose intentions are good but is so often misunderstood. Fired with enthusiasm and sense of humour, probably his greatest burden is to live up to the world wide image of him as a genius. For him songwriting is the result of long hours of experiment, spurred by those timeless moments of inspiration. It's not a coincidence that one of his favourite painters is Picasso who conducted his work in a similar style. Paul's lifes work has been to channel the bright flashes of light into a constantly flowing current within the accepted structures of pop music. At his best, when constructing a song like *Waterfalls*, the phrase 'genius' is not one that can be readily denied.

Despite the compromises and constraints, despite the necessary failures and occasional diversions, Paul's overriding talent has touched people. No artist can ask for more.

In his case, the success rate easily outstrips work that has slipped by the wayside. The sheer variety and hidden depths in his songs frequently catches people unaware, which helps to explain why so often his record releases are greeted with a mixture of dismay, apathy, misunderstanding or hostility. Songs which appear specious suddenly come back at the listener weeks, months, or even years later – their gem-like beauty fully revealed. Whether they're *Hey Jude*, *Temporary Secretary* or *Coming Up*, McCartney songs need to be played and played.

Much is now made of the riches that Paul has earned from songwriting. At their most vitriolic, new wave rock stars have snarled that McCartney earns too much, an estimated £7 a minute, more than they can earn in a week. 'Why doesn't he do something with it, buy instruments for kids,' was one savage cry.

'He may earn that much in a minute, but he pays almost the same amount back in tax,' said Tony Brainsby, for many years Paul's press adviser. Paul has never flaunted his wealth and has always been at pains to 'stay ordinary', as his father-in-law once advised him.

'Really I try to lead a pretty normal life,' Paul once told me. 'The only abnormality is being Paul McCartney!'

In fact, Paul does give a tremendous amount to charity, often secretly. Often he makes a small public donation while giving larger amounts privately to avoid embarrassing the recipients or endangering their future fund-raising. Its interesting that those who jeer the loudest at Paul for his earnings, probably wouldn't give a brass farthing to charity themselves. Even while punks were castigating McCartney with violent language, Paul was actually busy giving musical instruments, donations to kidney machines, aid to theatres, funds for health clinics and assistance to musicians who have been injured in accidents or hit hard times. Says a friend: 'Paul is often accused of meanness, when he is actually giving thousands behind the scenes. And he is dead against merchandising. He won't sell any products with his name on it, and he won't even wear somebody's tee-shirt.'

Paul is fiercely protective of his family and his achievements. He doesn't enjoy being caught alone in public and dislikes being recognised in the street. But when these occasions arise he deals with it in effortless fashion. He will sign autographs while purposefully walking towards his car and won't actually avoid his fans, as long as his safety isn't threatened. But when you are Paul McCartney, privacy becomes a special joy and walking alone down Oxford Street is not something he would relish. He is happiest at work in the recording studio and one of the most telling pictures of him is on the *McCartney II* album, where baby James is seen tugging at his father's tee-shirt, while he attempts to thread tape on a recording machine.

Says a friend: 'Paul is primarily a family man and even with Wings never went off on a razzle with the boys in the band. His family is his main interest aside from playing. On the road there are always women around making themselves obviously available, but he never makes any advances to anybody else. If he wanted a night out he prefers to organise a big do. He'll have a big knees up and maybe a band. Everybody comes. But it's always under his control. If he has to go to a record company reception or somebody else's do, it is always a major hassle. He arrives late and there are last minute changes about transportation and security.'

A beer, a smoke and a joke are among Paul's simple pleasures, but that hasn't stopped him indulging in a little empire building. Apart from building a large new house on a Sussex hilltop, one of Paul's wisest investments was into music publishing, which began when he acquired the Buddy Holly song catalogue. His MPL company now owns an amazing collection of songs which represent some of the greatest milestones in pop – and jazz history. For example, he owns *The Original Boogie*

Woogie first recorded by pianist Pine Top Smith way back in 1929 and one of the first great dance hits. The big band hits of Woody Herman, including such classics from the 1940s like *Apple Honey*, *Blowing Up A Storm*, *Bijou*, *Goosey Gander* and *North West Passage*, are all Paul's.

There are novelties like *Chopsticks* and *Christopher Columbus*, which formed the basis of the Benny Goodman hit *Sing, Sing, Sing*. There are traditional dixieland jazz standards, *It's Tight Like That*, *Casa Loma Stomp*, *Basin Street Blues*, *Bugle Call Rag*, *Mahogany Hall Stomp*, *Your Feets Too Big*, *Wolverine Blues* and *King Porter Stomp*.

There are songs by Johnny Mercer, Jelly Roll Morton, John Lennon, Truman Capote, John Barry, Ira Gershwin, Harold Arlen, Scott Joplin and Ralph Burns. There is even a song called *Linda* dating from 1944, the theme from the Ed Sullivan TV Show and the hits from a whole clutch of Broadway musicals. These include: *Annie*, *Bye Bye Birdie*, *Mame*, *Peter Pan*, *Hello Dolly!*, *A Chorus Line* and *Grease*.

As a result of the income from these songs, together with royalties from Beatle hits and his own subsequent compositions, it was claimed that, by the early 1980s, Paul's personal fortune was estimated at around two hundred and fifty million pounds and was increasing at a rate of twenty five million. Not bad for a lad who once wanted just one hundred pounds to buy everything he dreamed of owning. With entries in Who's Who and the Guinness Book Of Records, meetings with the Queen and Prince Phillip, and his portrait due to hang in the National Portrait Gallery, it was little wonder that some began calling him Lord Mull Of Kintyre!

But Paul tries not to get bogged down into the debate about whether he earns seven or forty seven pounds a second. 'I try not to talk about it. It's a bit like discovering a gold mine at the bottom of your garden,' he told Ray Connolly. 'It's embarrassing to talk about and there's always the fear if you do, someone will want to take it off you!' He explained that he invested in music publishing because it was a business he understood, unlike hotels or haulage.

'It seemed the perfect choice for me. I was already publishing a lot of Buddy Holly songs. It turned out to be massive. I surprise myself whenever I think about it. We own the rights to all kinds of classics like *Stormy Weather* and *Tenderly*.'

Despite the numbing statistics behind his success, Paul has genuinely managed to remain largely untouched by it all. Says Bill Harry: 'He's always kept in touch with the people. He appeals to them – not the critics. The trouble is a lot of rock stars try to appeal to the critics – and not the people. They always talk about him being a banal, middle-aged rocker. There's always this obsession with age in the press. And the music papers would have you believe that music only belongs to a certain age group. The rest of us are not entitled to music.'

'Once you reach a certain age you are over the hill and a has been and have no right to sensible criticism. The music can't be any good because it's not played by young kids. Now they try to say Paul's music only appeals to middle-aged mums. I know it appeals to kids .... because his records go into the charts! When The Beatles were doing gigs in Liverpool, in the early days before they ever recorded, I remember Paul performing numbers like *Till There Was You* from *The Music Man*. He always loved musicals and artists like Fred Astaire and Jack Buchanan. Of course, it wasn't rock 'n' roll. But he sang *Till There Was You* at the Cavern and all the Liverpool gigs, before Brian Epstein even met them, and he sang it beautifully. When he formed Wings he was given full rein and could sing whatever he liked. In some ways The Beatles restricted him.'

'With Wings, Paul went into popular music and John stayed in Rock with a capital R. All the British music papers went into Rock and anything pop was regarded as wishy washy and worthless. But pop is part of culture too, and one thing Paul didn't want was just to be involved in heavy rock. In his songs you find an expression of his life. *Martha My Dear* for his dog; *Helen Wheels* about the car he drove. Most of his work is autobiographical. It's about his life and evokes nice, comfortable images. There is nothing savage or political about his work. He is a twentieth Century Pop Song writer, probably one of the greatest.'

'Musically I'm a bit of an all-rounder.' When Paul McCartney says that, it seems a wry understatement. Paul is subtle enough not to parade his ability. It is part of his artistry that he can make the music more important than the means of production. He is a populist, not an elitist, but that does not make his work any less important or valuable.

Pop has produced many fine lyricists, poets, balladeers and players. Few manage to combine these roles as artfully as Paul. He listens, absorbs, then brings forth a flow of ideas – words and music sparked off by the people, scenes, feelings and events around him.

When he first started writing with John Lennon, they wanted to be Britain's answer to pop writing teams like Goffin and King. Lennon & McCartney did indeed become one of the most celebrated composing teams of the century and can be fairly included in the pantheon of mainly American names like Gershwin, Kern and Rodgers & Hart. The Liverpool boys were from entirely different backgrounds to the men who had made pop song writing a sophisticated art. The Beatles, weren't writing for Tin Pan Alley or showbusiness. But they wrote about the same subjects, mainly love in its various forms, that appealed to the previous generation of writers.

Paul had begun writing on his own before he met John and his first song was *My Little Girl*, a three chord effort built around his nascent guitar playing. Amazingly, he wrote the classic *When I'm 64*, which made such an impact on *Sgt. Pepper*, years before when he was sixteen and still getting to grips with the piano. He is proud of his

songwriting achievements but modest in the sense he has always shied away from heavy analysis and attempts to elevate him into the rarefied world of 'serious music' criticism. 'I just sit down and try to write a song. Whatever comes out ....', he says, in answer to incessant demands to know where it all comes from.

Paul's contribution to Beatles' music was enormous and legendary. Songs like *Eleanor Rigby*, *Fixing A Hole*, *Hey Jude*, *Yesterday*, *She's Leaving Home* and *Michelle* stood out among the sparkling cascade of Lennon & McCartney songs, marked by their mixture of haunting sentiment, sympathetic observation and flashes of black humour.

Unlike so many pop songs which appear meaningless, when read aloud, out of context of the musical accompaniment, Paul's songs stood up to being stripped of the guitar and drums safety net. It was something that Peter Sellers noticed and used to good effect in his mock Shakespearian reading of The Beatles' hit *A Hard Day's Night* in 1966. *When I'm Sixty-Four* was a particularly well constructed ditty, a young man's amused view of retirement and all the things the old folk who surrounded him held dear, not to mention their stilted style in formal seaside postcards. A fondness for such cozy English institutions has often surfaced in Paul's pronouncements, together with an understanding of loneliness, fate and fortune. And when a song like *Eleanor Rigby* emerged with its despairing images and such haunting phrases as 'wearing the face that she keeps in a jar by the door', it was no wonder eminent musicologists began digging back into the classics to find precedence for such creative outbursts.

If there was songwriting rivalry between John and Paul then certainly they inspired each other to such heights, they helped elevate the whole concept of pop music. In a way pop has been living off the prestige they gave it ever since. Not everything Paul did in The Beatles, even at their peak, was instantly accepted without question. *Maxwell's Silver Hammer*, although just another song as far as Paul was concerned, had a certain indefinable ugliness about it, and was certainly disliked by John when it appeared on the *Abbey Road* album. It was an early sign of the checks and balances of The Beatles being cast aside, and in the aftermath of the breakup, the heady wine of freedom often caused Paul to lose his sense of equilibrium. But from *Blackbird* on the White Album to *Bluebird* on *Band On The Run*, Paul proved that he was able to produce gems of wit and charm with a consistency that is a constant source of surprise and delight. Even when he has stepped out of the singer-songwriter mould to produce a film theme like *Live And Let Die* or a new Scottish folk anthem with *Mull Of Kintyre*, then he is equally adept at grasping the medium and supplying the inspiration. It would be interesting to see the results if Paul in later years took an interest in the church and began writing carols and hymns to replenish the nation's stock.

John and Paul wrote over fifty songs before The Beatles were famous, most of which, with the exception of *Love Me Do*, vanished and were never published. Paul thinks he probably has some of them scribbled down in tatty old exercise books under mountains of junk stored in one of his homes. When they worked together it was a matter of both contributing lyrics, snatches of melody and themes. 'We were trying to find the next beat,' says Paul. 'In the papers it was like *Latin Rock* is the next beat. As soon as we stopped trying to find it, the next beat came along and it was Merseybeat!' But Paul has never categorised his writing or tastes in music since, because he is aware of how much more there is to music than an array of convenient tags and sub-titles.

Paul still writes in a variety of ways. There is no formula, no set way of going about things. He started his composing career

strumming the guitar and inventing songs. Now he'll use the piano as often as the guitar, and his songs can be either studio-built montages, surreal experiments, rocking twelve-bar blues or ballads composed in the conventional way, with a neat set of lyrics carefully set to music. He can be just as effective as a quavering, heartfelt vocalist cracking a few notes along the way while

plucking his acoustic guitar, or as a roaring performer surrounded by blasting trumpets, strings and percussion. And different treatments can drastically alter his original musical intentions.

He cites *All My Loving* as one early Beatles classic which began life as a poem. The melody was tacked on later. *Yesterday*, considered one of his finest songs, turned up as a tune in his head that wouldn't go away when he got out of bed one morning. He went down to breakfast, and 'scrambled egg' seemed to fit the melody line and provided the original working title. More appropriate words were hammered out later. A string quartet added in the studio gave the finishing touch to a song the world

would come to know and love.

George Martin helped put many fresh new Beatle songs into the best settings and Paul and George eventually formed a wonderfully productive partnership which is as relevant today, resulting in albums like *Tug Of War* and *Pipes Of Peace*, as it was in the heyday of *Sgt. Pepper*. Their mutual respect

makes for a perfect working partnership that Paul might find harder to form with another musician. Martin can give guidance and make suggestions without becoming a burden or a rival.

For George there is the obvious delight in sharing Paul's vision of a song and the pleasure of being in the company of an old friend, doing what they both like best – making records.

In the early Beatles days, George often took crucial decisions that resulted in the success of a song. Paul recalls that *Please Please Me* was planned as a slow, dramatic ballad suitable for a singer like Roy Orbison. George thought it sounded better sped up. He was right. There came a point in The Beatles career when so much credit was being given to George for his influence on Beatles' music, that it began to cause tension, and particularly incensed John in his more vitriolic moments. But the passing of the years and much water under the bridge has long since rendered such old arguments about 'who did what' irrelevant. What remains fascinating, however, is Paul's seemingly endless ability to fashion songs. Even those privy to the actual creative process, whether Linda, her family or friends, or Paul's musical compatriots, find the 'plucking from thin air' of a new tune, rather unnerving.

On one famous occasion, the film actor Dustin Hoffman was having dinner with the McCartneys and commented on Paul's ability. Later he set Paul a challenge by quoting him 'Picasso's last words' before his death, as reported in a copy of Time magazine. The phrase was 'Drink to me, drink to my health, you know I can't drink anymore.' Paul grabbed his guitar and within seconds was producing one of the most memorable songs to *Picasso's Last Words*, that would subsequently appear on *Band On The Run*. Dustin Hoffman was so surprised that he began shouting for witnesses. The words on this occasion belonged to Picasso, but the melody was all Paul.

Yet not everyone over the years has accepted that Paul's songs, particularly during the Wings years, were anything to praise to the skies. For every university professor approvingly nodding his head at the McCartney choice of chord, there has been a catcalling mob ready to hurl their mudpies and brickbats.

'It's about time the British record buying public woke up to the fact that McCartney's records are so bloody boring and ordinary,' sneered one reader of a British music paper. 'As an unknown artist his records would have sunk without trace.'

A radio disc jockey described *McCartney II*, which produced such masterworks as *Coming Up, Waterfall* and *Temporary Secretary*, as 'doodling around testing your tape recorder.'

Indeed, many of Paul's records have floated past without causing much beyond a raised eyebrow or two. But if every song he wrote or recorded was as popular and successful as *Yesterday* or *Mull Of Kintyre*, then he would be in danger of being set upon by mobs of frightened peasants, armed with pitchforks, uttering cries of 'witchcraft'. The public has been privy to Paul's private musical scrapbook. He cannot expect to please everyone, especially when most musical tastes are addled with intolerance. Music has many shining facets and Paul is attracted to them all, and as a one man musical workshop it's not surprising some of the experiments are more obvious successes than others. But as he says: 'I've done enough good things to satisfy myself, which is all that most people ask for. I've never felt I'm in any one musical category. I like everything from Fred Astaire to The Sex Pistols!'

Many seeking the answer to Paul's continued success over the years should perhaps look no further than the receptive nature of Paul's attitude to music of all kinds. It is the narrow and stilted who become hidebound and eventually fade away. Many rock artists who became idols and were a huge influence in their day eventually ceased to say anything new and became self-parodies. Many peaked in a spectacular way to high critical acclaim but found themselves names consigned to the pages of the encyclopaedias, dried up without any new inspiration or sense of direction.

Paul has often infuriated critics with his uneven, erratic approach, and he has stood accused of lapses of self-discipline and taste. All this has been his saviour. From *Mary Had A Little Lamb* to *Hey Jude* and from *Eleanor Rigby* to *Say Say Say* it has been one big work out.

Paul's greatest ally is the recording studio, where he spends so much time happily engrossed in the reeling tape gabbling at high speeds across its magnetic heads, carrying the message of his songs and stories. Here he can sit, perhaps on a high stool clutching his guitar, wearing a pair of headphones, converting the songs that come to him at any minute of the day, into productions that might end up anywhere, as a tucked-away album track, a B side, or a world wide smash hit, so successful even the composer is astounded.

Paul is blessed in that, unlike many a would-be composer who scribbles down some lyrics that seem to him quite brilliant, he can turn the dream of a potential hit into a finished product by following through the whole process. His musicianship ensures that ideas are converted into shape, in the most effective way.

Yet many still find it surprising that Paul is such a gifted instrumentalist. Over the years he has developed as a guitarist who can rock out the blues or pick delicate acoustic solos and accompaniment. He is a pianist with a broad command of the keyboard, and a red hot drummer who can take care of business. He is also a very fine bassist, one of the most influential in the development of rock style.

But he points out that he started his musical career as a guitarist. First came the trumpet from his father, which he gave up when he feared his lips might be ruined along with his looks. Then came his first guitar. 'I started out as a guitarist and my first one was a Rosetti Lucky Seven, which was a plank of wood with strings.' When The Beatles first went to Hamburg they went without a drummer and Paul used to say 'the rhythm is in the guitars!' Then one night in Hamburg at the Star Club, Paul went onto piano while Stu Sutcliffe played bass.

'I used to play piano on a lot of Ray Charles numbers like *Don't Let The Sun Catch You Crying*. So really I've been playing the piano for a long time. I should be able to play it by now! I've never really put it around, like the fact I can play piano and pretty good guitar. In fact, I'm putting it around now so I must be insecure or something, but it's true that a lot of Beatles' guitar solos – I played. That intro to *Paperback Writer* and the solo on *Taxman* is me. A lot of stuff I played – and people didn't know. I like to surprise people. I can cover a few instruments and different styles. I'd never say I was a great drummer but in a high moment I can do it.'

'Somehow there is a rather funny image of me, even though on my solo albums I played everything. *McCartney* still wasn't called: 'The album where he plays everything.' It was all done subtly. Rather coy. I always do things a bit coy, because I'd rather do that than be too showy and have it not come off. I know I CAN do it and have confidence in myself.'

The night Paul's first guitar fell apart, during a spot of pre-Pete Townshend violence, he was forced to switch to bass, which was the start of the process of becoming an all rounder. It is a process still going forward.

Throughout the year, Paul has served the cause of popular music with honour. Yet with all the achievements, accolades and statistics of success heaped up behind him, there is still a feeling that Paul has only just begun and that in the years ahead he will just get better. The process can only stop when it ceases to be both a means to fun and fulfilment. The songs yet to come can only enrich an already unique treasury of music. In the meantime, the tunes keep coming. . . . 'I know,' says Paul. 'I can't help it!'

Chapter Thirteen

PAUL ON RECORD – POST BEATLES

McCARTNEY (Apple). Paul's first solo work, released in 1970, the year The Beatles broke up and Apple collapsed. The music represented an oasis of calm reflection in a period of uproar and anger. Paul played all the instruments, yet this seemed to escape the attention of those expecting a kind of superior George Martin/Beatles production. Paul was experimenting, tossing in teasingly attractive melodies and interesting, mysterious sounds. He popped them in between blatantly half finished songs like *Junk*, revelling in his independence and freedom. Not everyone appreciated his approach but in retrospect, it could be seen that Paul was, in effect, reviving the artless joy of a school boy skiffle group, especially on tunes like the two beat *Man We Was Lonely*. All this suggested a man of the Sixties, somewhat shattered, in need of sanity, rest and avoidance of anything that might overtax the brain. Paul pottered about with his guitars, drums and tape machines like Pete Townshend making demos. It was a marshalling of thoughts yet to be developed in the context of a group. The home grown nature of *Oo You* was closer in spirit to US Fifties rock, while *Momma Miss America* had the casual, echoing simplicity of reggae. His one man band was quite impressive. He set up piano and bass riffs, using multi-tracking and pushed himself along with a nice line in heavy rock drumming. Paul ventured an atmospheric drum solo on the native inspired *Kreen-Akrore*, named after a South American tribe. Even the dullest material like *Teddy Boy* had a certain charm and fascination. If John Lennon needed primal scream therapy, this was Paul's own way of clearing out the cobwebs. The results were nothing like as dramatic as John's first solo albums, but this was a slow fuse being lit. One outstanding track was *Maybe I'm Amazed*, a worthy successor to *Hey Jude*, complete with rumbling left hand piano rolls and soulful vocals. It was one song Phil Spector could have refashioned with a big arrangement, without incurring the wrath of the creator.

RAM (Apple). Better recorded and blessed with a louder mix than *McCartney*. This showed Paul was serious about involving Linda as his musical partner. This was Linda's training period and her backing vocals helped Paul out on such rocking items as *3 Legs*, which harked back to the echoing sounds of Gene Vincent and Buddy Holly. This was a nascent Wings in formation with Denny Seiwell on drums, playing not much better than Paul could manage. Released in 1971, the same erratic qualities of the previous album were noted, with tracks fading in and out, which infuriated critics. Although there was a better drum and guitar sound and considerable 'presence' on the curious cut *Ram On*, there was still a throwaway feeling about the whole production, including the packaging, with its 'DIY' style cut-out snaps on the cover. Cottage industry rock, stoned and rural, but like

the 'better mouse trap syndrome' due for expansion. The master musician of the future could be heard emerging on *Dear Boy* – before it came to an abrupt halt. *Uncle Albert**Admiral Halsey was *Yellow Submarine* revisited, the sort of whimsy which Paul finds endearing. A lot of effort went into this, but it was end of the pier stuff. *Smile Away*, a rocker that helped restore some rock earthiness, was marred by lyrics about 'smelly feet'. Experiments and changes of mood gave the album an uncertain feeling, and it seemed Paul wanted to try a variety of styles without settling down to serious music making. On *Heart Of The Country*, Paul sang high pitched vocals and played cotton picking guitar in swing time. *Monkberry Moon Delight* had some rather frantic pre-punk screaming vocals, with enthusiastic backing from Linda and one of those oompah bass lines which insinuate themselves into the subconscious for days. *Eat At Home* once more revived old time rock, and there was certainly nothing here or in *Long Haired Lady* to indicate a great composer at work, despite the noisy arrangement. A smidgeon of *Ram On* was reprised and used as a filler before *The Back Seat Of My Car*, a 'proper' song, albeit not very inspired. Mysterious and expensive strings and brass made a wasted appearance on this disjointed composition which nevertheless, had some nice bits before running wildly out of control. The overall impression was a bad rehearsal. And there was more of the same to come. At least the pump was being primed and Paul was girding up his musical loins.

WINGS WILD LIFE (Parlophone). Completing the hat trick of duff albums that threatened to wipe out Paul's credibility in the early stages of post-Beatles activity, *Wild Life* was the album they said was supposed to have been 'done in a week', just like Bob Dylan had done. Well Dylan was making some pretty awful albums around this time, where established artists were relearning how to play, write and sing to suit the new decade. Rhythm sections in particular were poor in 1971, as most players still had to learn from soul and disco session men how to make the beat tight, syncopated and funky. Engineers had yet to find a way to use all the technology at hand without sounding as if they were working in a mattress factory. This was one of the strangest of Paul's albums. A cover picture of the group amidst pleasant lakeside scenery, without any title or identifying names, suggested the McCartney Skiffle Group was shyly avoiding publicity. But it marked the debut of Wings, with Denny Laine on guitar and vocals and Denny Seiwell retained on drums. The sessions were relaxed all right, like a private musical documentary of a family and friends having fun in the studios. There were a few intriguing songs. The monosyllabic *Bip Bop* was a Gene Vincent style breathless and restrained blue jean bop. Even Paul was amused by the simplic-

147

ity of his lyrics here. And the stretched out, reggae influenced, *Love Is Strange*, was hardly the stuff to inspire a generation of rock fans. Once again Paul was getting riffs, melodies and moods out of his system – singing, playing and having fun with friends and family. *Wild Life*, the title track, had a pendulous beat, but the screaming vocals were frankly a pain. On all these early works, Paul was at his vocal best on the least pretentious, simplest songs like *Some People Never Know* which had an easy tune and unmannered vocals. The same applied to *Tomorrow* and *Dear Friend*. The latter was a rather glum and long drawn out piece with piano accompaniment. Most of the tracks were laid down in three weeks and the album was laid to rest by the public with equal rapidity. Once again, bits of studio out-takes and noise were left on tape, giving the air of unfinished work being casually tossed off. It was time to get down to serious business.

RED ROSE SPEEDWAY (EMI). After some decidedly odd releases, *Red Rose Speedway*, with its enigmatic title and picture of Paul with a rose stuffed in his mouth in front of a shiny motorcycle, seemed in danger of being overlooked. Fortunately, it included one of Paul's best songs in ages, the flawless *My Love*, a standard in the making. Its slow, measured beat, fully orchestrated, provided the perfect showcase for Paul, the ballad singer par excellence. The rise and fall of the melody line and its resolution into a natural climax and strident breast beating finale, more than made up for the years of *Ram On* and *Junk*. This was the second album credited to Wings, released in 1973 and marking the return to a definite musical policy and higher standards all round. Once again, the album packaging was strangely amateur, but included a useful booklet of photographs of Wings on the road, together with details of who played what and the lyrics. The songs certainly deserved closer attention. *One More Kiss* was a jolly country ballad and *Little Lamb Dragonfly* had rich guitar chords from Hugh McCracken. The music was better engineered and mixed with the instruments obtaining a warm balanced sound, except for some rather straggly brass work sneaking in and out. Among the duller songs were *When The Night*, a dirge over a plonking one note piano riff, and *Loup (1st Indian On The Moon)*, an instrumental that was probably fun to make but had no place on a public gramophone record. It was all part of the remaining moments of confusion before the solid achievement of *Band On The Run*. Songs like *Hold Me Tight* and *Lazy Dynamite* were formed into a medley, a device that Paul likes to use, perhaps to speed up the pace of an album. It seems like he was spending more time getting Wings into shape as a band, than polishing and improving his own handicraft. And he sometimes seemed almost suicidally at odds with prevailing musical trends. It took a brave man to release *Hands Of Love*, a sort of music hall ditty in the age of Glam Rock and Techno Flash. And it took a very loyal pioneer member of the Wings Fan Club to put up with it.

BAND ON THE RUN (Apple). Those who heard this on release in late 1973 recall the sense of relief. The strident, confident and impressive chords of the title track served notice that Paul was back on his feet. This was no re-run of happy amateur hour but a powerful collection of great songs, played with a strong sense of purpose. At last, Wings sounded like a band .... yet the strange thing was, most of the band had failed to turn up for the sessions. It was all done by Paul, Linda and Denny with a little help from some brass players and engineer Geoff Emerick. The album had real pace and Wings romped through the songs like seasoned pros out to blast an audience. The sense of 'live' performance reflected their increased experience as touring artists and elevated *Band On The Run* into the pantheon of great Seventies rock albums. Tunes like *Jet* and *Bluebird* would become part of Wings' on the road repertoire. *Bluebird* was beautifully arranged and conceived with delicate use of bells and

percussion. It shows Paul's unerring ability to pluck a melody from his fertile imagination, a new one in a world full of old tunes. Forced by circumstances back into the role of drummer, his playing was beefy and impressive and showed how far he had advanced since *Kreen-Akrore*. He excelled in other instrumental areas. *Mrs. Vanderbilt* was notable for its heavy guitar chord break, contrasting with the overall jollity of the piece. The opening lines, incidentally, paraphrased the catch phrase of a post-war comedian, Cheerful Charlie Chester, and went 'Down in the jungle living in a tent, you don't use money, you don't pay rent.' The original couplet was 'Down in the jungle living in a tent, cheaper than a prefab – no rent!' Presumably it was felt American audiences would fail to understand the phrase 'prefab'. More important was the excellent *Let Me Roll It*, which showed Paul back as one of our best rockers. Here he let rip with the meanest blues since leaving The Beatles. The furiously angry guitar riff echoed the kind of sound John Lennon got in The Plastic Ono Band. This kind of impact was not maintained however and side two began to sag slightly. The oddly titled *Mamunia* had an irresistable hook line and *No Words* had neat vocal harmonies from Paul, Linda and Denny. *Picasso's Last Words (Drink To Me)* was the song Paul composed at the drop of a hint from Dustin Hoffman, and had a strongly alcoholic content and some boozy drums, stumbling towards some new announcements in French and a reprise from *Mrs. Vanderbilt*. Strange, but doubtless all part of some master plan. To round off this hugely successful album was *Nineteen Hundred And Eight-Five* – a rocker with Paul defiantly smashing home bass and piano. VENUS AND MARS (Capitol). Another fine album, well produced with a brace of good songs, it showed that the advent of Wings as a stable unit had given Paul something tangible to write for and about. Like *Band On The Run*, this was all material that could be used on stage and the opening *Venus And Mars* and *Rock Show* were tailor made for the world tour the band embarked on during the year of its release, in 1975. Wings, with Jimmy McCulloch on guitar, sounded hot and ready to do battle with all the other bands that had been dominating the touring circuits in the years since Paul had been off the road. Paul's love of vocal harmonies and doo wop vocals was evident on the rocking *Magneto And Titanium Man*, inspired by American comic book heroes. For those hungry for basic blues there was the haunting and moody *Letting Go*, complimentary to *Let Me Roll It* on the previous album. Paul's best use, thus far, of a brass section was heard on this cut, which had Geoff Britton on drums, providing a socking beat. To reward those who still had fond memories of Paul, the Beatle who loved music hall, there was *You Gave Me The Answer*, which sounded just like it came from a thirties British musical, preferably with Jack Buchanan in the leading role. Full of soft shoe shuffles and nifty rim shots, Paul sang it through what sounds like a megaphone. *Medicine Jar* was a Jimmy McCulloch speciality, that had sadly appropriate lyrics and along with the atmospheric *Spirits Of Ancient Egypt*, became staple fare for the band, as they played to bigger and bigger audiences across America. *Listen To What The Man Said* was an especially happy and successful piece of writing with a soprano sax solo from Tom Scott that perfectly fitted the swinging beat. At last, Paul had found a way to experiment, try different styles and even stick in his little album in-jokes (snatches of conversation, odd bits of song tacked onto the beginning and end of tracks), without sacrificing quality. *Listen To What The Man Said* was deservedly a hit single. On the album it segued into *Treat Her Gently-Lonely Old People*, one of Paul's laments at the piano, richly orchestrated and sincerely performed. Just for fun, Paul tagged onto the end of the album the piece of music he wrote as the theme for the TV series *Crossroads* – actually dropped from the show after protests by televiewers.

WINGS AT THE SPEED OF SOUND (Parlophone). Paul's eagerness to encourage the members of Wings to participate

in full, resulted in several songs on this 1976 release being designed as showcases. Denny Laine was featured on *The Note You Never Wrote*; Jimmy sang *Wino Junko* and Linda the concert party item, *Cook Of The House*, complete with the sound of frying bacon. Even drummer Joe English got into the singing act with Paul's composition for him, *Must Do Something About It*. He sang with surprising range and expertise and threatened to upstage the whole gang of them. He formed his own group in later years, quit Wings and took to religion, perhaps in reaction to hearing Jimmy sing *Wino Junko* every night. The stand out song was Paul's *Let 'Em In* and *Silly Love Songs* was another winner. The former showed his knack of taking an obvious idea and turning it into magic. *Let 'Em In* started with door chimes and went into a rolling march, which led Denny Laine to tote a military snare drum around his waist and wear a military hat during the American tour. There were grumbles from an increasingly truculent and pugnacious rock press about *Silly Love Songs* but it was just as Paul described it, and there was now't wrong with it, especially as he offered in contrast the solid and stomping *Beware My Love*. There was nothing pansy

about the driving bass beat on *Love Songs* and it was probably the sentiments that incurred more hostility than the tune and treatment. It paused for breath, then built up tension, before dancing off into a dream-like reverie. One of the first of Paul's 'modern' productions, it boasted tight disco stomping drums and sophisticated brass and strings. *Speed Of Sound*, with its bold, dramatic cover and smooth production, represented Wings at its most concent and efficient. A contentment best expressed on the hymn-like *Warm And Beautiful*, which would be well worth including in any compendium of hymns, ancient or modern.

WINGS OVER AMERICA (Parlophone). A triple LP block buster, it topped the American charts during 1976-77. Recorded during the band's American tour, Paul's voice is hoarse compared to the relaxed sessions that produced the previous studio album. Nevertheless, he roared his way into a slightly slower than usual *Rock Show* with fervent intensity. The band rocked with a skill grown after gruelling weeks on the road. There were twenty eight songs on the six sides which captured the concert atmosphere without loss of

sound quality. Wings had become a big soul band as the various cuts showed. Trumpets and saxes backed up the guitar and keyboard riffs with shouting accents. Joe English's competent, unflashy drumming more or less followed the guide lines set by Paul, when he drummed on the original versions of the tunes. Jimmy McCulloch made an enormous contribution to the success of Wings in a way that was perhaps not fully appreciated at the time. His fleet fingered guitar steamed through songs like *Medicine Jar* and he roared with pent up fervour on *Let Me Roll It*. The heartfelt cheering that greeted his solos must have soothed his tormented soul. Paul's bass guitar work was equally impressive in a more subtle way. Deep, rich and driving, it kept the band on course. When Paul switched to piano to rumble and roll through *Maybe I'm Amazed*, Denny Laine took over bass duties. Paul's display of musicianship showed what would have gone to waste if he had simply retired from performing after The Beatles, and spent his time in writing alone. This was the integrated group he needed, locked on course. Paul was now confident enough to include a few Beatles classics, as well as the best of his writing since 1970. Thus the band got its teeth into *Lady Madonna* and *The Long And Winding*

Road and Paul sang a poignant *Yesterday*. The film theme, *Live And Let Die*, was pressed into service as a dramatic interlude, while the show peaked on *Letting Go, Band On The Run, Hi Hi Hi* and *Soily*. Linda could be heard offering sympathetic synthesiser and sturdy back up vocals but more interestingly, perhaps, giving the sort of moral encouragement that helped Paul turn Wings from a tentative idea into a colossus of the rock touring circuit. The cheers said it all, but Wings had set themselves high standards even they would now find hard to beat.

LONDON TOWN (Parlophone). A strange piece of work, recorded mostly in the Virgin Islands on board the motor yacht *Fair Carol*, yet given a London theme with Denny, Linda and Paul pictured aboard a boat moored in the Thames with a backdrop of Tower Bridge. Despite the tensions within Wings which resulted in the sudden departures of Jimmy McCulloch and Joe English (their pictures were nowhere to be seen on the elaborate poster insert or cover artwork), the mood was relaxed and romantic. *Girlfriend* was a good example of this loving feeling. Some of the sessions were recorded at EMI London, and perhaps it was the combination of the city rain and tropical sunshine which affected the music, but more likely it was a reaction against the upfront pressures experienced on the road, where all was noise and dissent. Once again Paul unleashed a broth of melodies which crept up and seduced the long term listener, willing to give a heavily panned LP a fair hearing. Some saw it as Paul, once again, experimenting too much and not getting down to the nitty gritty. But *London Town* pioneered many of the sounds and styles in arrangement that would dominate pop music for the next eight years. *With A Little Luck* had the soulful beat that anticipated later collaborations with Michael Jackson and the use of polyphonic synthesisers enriched the Wingsian total texture. Paul also came up with one of his famous comic novelties. *Famous Groupies* had amusing, neatly observed lyrics, that told stories and suggested images in a way that most pop song writing rarely manages to achieve. There were more conventional goodies. *Deliver Your Children* revived the Laine-McCartney skiffle group. It was a home-grown folk tune ideal for performing in cellar clubs for bearded intellectuals. *Name And Address* harked back once more to Buddy Holly and showed that Paul was not entirely wrapped up in writing off the peg hits for Wings to devour on the road. *With A Little Luck* was a chart hit, and there were some other fine songs, including the delicate *I'm Carrying*, and atmospheric *Cafe On The Left Bank*. Denny sang a charming tune too, *Children Children*, which made reference to a 'tiny waterfall', an idea which was later expanded into an even better song.

WINGS GREATEST (Parlophone). While the band underwent drastic personnel changes, it was decided timely to release a compilation of Paul's greatest hits. Issued in December 1978, *Wings Greatest* contained a dozen songs. It served to emphasize that however erratic some of the past albums, there had been a steady stream of high grade composition. It was an opportunity to look back and compare notes. The contrast between *Jet* and *Mull Of Kintyre* and between *My Love* and *Live And Let Die* was astonishing. And the output ranged from the blazing, extrovert excitement of *Band On The Run* and *Junior's Farm* to the relaxed swing of *Hi Hi Hi* and *Let 'Em In*. The selection showed how Paul could write for given situations, create love ballads in the classic mould, or use the manners and influences of rock and folk music to fashion new ideas and melodies. Although Wings had developed into a rock band hungry for material, Paul had still avoided being sucked into becoming a 'rock writer' tied by the ball and chain of convention. Thus, *Mull Of Kintyre* was actually a radical departure for him, and far more successful than *Uncle Albert*Admiral Halsey*, included from *RAM*. Paul was fond of their pair of old buffers, but a better choice would have been *Letting Go* or *Let Me Roll It*. The remaining cuts on the compilation were *Another Day, Silly Love Songs* and *With A Little Luck*. Linda and Paul had some fun preparing the art work. They took one of Linda's favourite pieces, a rather gaudy figure of a girl who looked like she had once adorned the interior walls of the Odeon Leicester Square, draped in some rather hefty looking curtain that sagged from her arms. She was flown out to Switzerland to be photographed on the ski slopes against a snowy background. Meanwhile, Paul began thinking about the next studio album. After the soft rock approach of *Wings At The Speed Of Sound* and *London Town*, he sought a return to the hard rocking style of the previous incarnation of the band. The results, however, would be strangely disappointing.

BACK TO THE EGG (Parlophone). The phrase 'egg' in the context of any venture seems to be somehow jinxed. Certainly this album laid an egg, in terms of sales, much to Paul's surprise. It coincided with the worldwide slump in album sales, EMI's financial troubles, and a recession in the music industry that blew a cold and unexpected draught of reality into the pop dream world. Perhaps the public had a surfeit of Wings albums by any name. Changes in the rock scene rendered much of the music contained on *Back To The Egg* dated and irrelevant by the lights of 1979. The cover was clever and imaginative, showing Wings with new members Laurence Juber and Steve Holley, peering at the planet earth out in space through a hole in the floor of a suburban living room. It suggested an album of space music or perhaps some daring electronics. Instead the songs were rough and crude and intermittent radio broadcasts, slotted between the tracks, didn't help to give any particular theme or style. It seemed like an album that changed its mind every few grooves and ultimately led nowhere. The album's title and even the name of the band were conspicuously absent from the cover and it seemed like Paul was going back to the anonymity of his *Wild Life* period. Instead of properly establishing the new members and giving the band a new identity, matters were confused by the addition of the famed *Rockestra*. This was a great idea – to include such famous rock instrumentalists as Pete Townshend, Kenny Jones, Hank Marvin, and John Bonham together with a big brass section, into a rock orchestra. This leviathan provided *Rockestra Theme*, a glorious rave up, and *So Glad To See You Here*. But that was all. Ideally, the album should have been renamed *Rockestra* and the big band used throughout. But the bulk of the time was given over to nondescript songs like *To You* with a rather messy slide guitar. There was one attractive novelty, *My Baby's Request*, which was a perfect recreation of a lounge style dance band with Barney Kessel style guitar backing. A half way house album, it marked the end of Wings and the start of Paul's artistic renaissance.

McCARTNEY II (Parlophone). The Big One. It tore Paul free of accumulated encumberances of previous years and shot him into the Eighties to greet a new army of fans. Perhaps it was the sojourn in the Japanese jail, or perhaps the ideas had been coming anyway. But he pulled some marvellous new songs and ideas out of his innermost recesses. Released in Spring 1980, it had a striking cover picture of the composer with his name properly displayed on the front for the first time. The sheery simplicity contrasted with all the space and snow scenes of previous cover art, and emphasised that this time Paul had decided to go it alone and get down to business. He played all the instruments, just as he had on the first *McCartney* LP of 1970. He wrote all the lyrics and came up with three block busters – the hits *Coming Up, Waterfalls* and *Temporary Secretary*. The first item stood playing over and over to fully appreciate its irresistible riff, driving beat and all manner of subtleties. Americans objected to Paul's speeded up vocals and preferred a 'live' version recorded in Scotland by Wings on their last tour. But with his unusual vocal treatment, Paul was once again anticipating trends. Such effects would dominate the 'new music' of the new decade. *Temporary Secretary* was even more futuristic, a churning, angular construction that was almost frightening in its intensity, and unrecognisable as a McCartney song. *Waterfalls*, however, was pure vintage McCartney. A shining, beautiful song, undoubtedly one of his most exquisite. Experimental instrumental *Frozen Jap* and the amusing *Bogey Music*, inspired by Fungus the Bogeyman, were fascinating examples of Paul's sense of humour and questing musical spirit. Once again there were complaints of self-indulgence, but then the whole process of creativity could be called an indulgence. Without it, nothing could be achieved. *McCartney II* was a musical self-portrait, not to be consigned to the attic, but to be revealed to as wide an audience as possible.

TUG OF WAR (EMI). Critically acclaimed, rich in hits, 1982's release saw Paul reunited with George Martin. His presence was like switching the lights back on. There was no fiddling about with gimmicks, sidetracking or irrelevancy, just a selection of excellent songs, beautifully performed and given the best possible treatment. Paul had the gentle voice of authority at his elbow, nudging him firmly in the direction of quality and good taste. If *Back To The Egg* had presented Paul at his most confused, then at a stroke *Tug Of War* gave Paul respect and the rightful place in music he deserved with the discipline of the partnership urging him into line. It wasn't that he had failed to come up with great songs in the past. They had gushed forth. But they had often splattered into inconsequential droplets. Wings too had sometimes been a lead weight rather than a source of uplift. On this one, Denny Laine turned up to play some guitar, but the big difference was that at last Paul was playing with musicians who were his equals, men of stature in their own right like Stevie Wonder, Ringo Starr, Andy Mackay, Eric Stewart and Steve Gadd. They infused great strength and quality into proceedings. One of the delights resulting from this collaboration was *What's That You're Doing?*, with Paul on drums backing Stevie on keyboards. There was still plenty of variety, but somehow each song worked and sounded finished, like *Here Today*. Here was a worthy successor to *Yesterday*, sung by Paul with touching sentiment and backed with a string quartet. This must have brought back a lot of emotional memories to the old campaigners of McCartney-Martin. There was even a hint of Beatles about the Mersey beat *Ballroom Dancing*, with Sixties style boogie guitar. *Ebony And Ivory*, a piece of perfectly fashioned pop song writing, had laudible sentiments and was deservedly a hit of great magnitude. *The Pound Is Sinking* was a strange one, but was easily made up for by *Wanderlust*, sung with clever counter melodies and shiny clean brass. The teaming of Carl Perkins with Paul, while not as productive as the link with Stevie Wonder, nevertheless had an air of history in the making about it and resulted in the chirpy, echoing *Get It*. Carl's laughter summed up the happy nature of the union as two of rock's most important influences bounced through the beat like raw young recruits to rock'n'roll, yelling the time honoured battle cry of *Go Cat!*.

PIPES OF PEACE (Parlophone). Paul completed a fourteen year recording cycle with increased brilliance and the benefit of years of experience. Once again, George Martin was beside Paul at the controls, and there was a shining gloss of quality and expertise which made the album an attractive and happy listening experience. More talented friends were prevailed upon to join forces with Paul on his musical explorations and the ideas flowed. The title cut was made the subject of an elaborate and dramatic video film featuring Paul playing a duel role of a British and German officer in the First World War trenches, attempting to fraternise with each other. It was based on the true story of opposing armies playing football amidst the barbed wired to celebrate Christmas. 'What do you say? Will the human race be run in a day? Or will someone save this planet we're playing on? he sang. His flair for creating a provocative couplet was never better displayed than on this potentially gloomy song, that nevertheless has a smile of peace and optimism. In his opening line he wrote: 'I light a candle to our love. In love our problems disappear.' Wishful thinking perhaps, but in battle torn 1983 any call for peace was urgently required. A children's choir echoed Paul's words and strings added a suitably profound coda. The album was rich in well edited, meaningful lyrics. *The Other Me* was a plea for forgiveness, regretting thoughtless hurts and wrongs from that alternative personality that resides in most of us. There was the smash hit *Say Say Say*, with Paul singing with Michael Jackson, and an instrumental jam with bass guitar ace Stanley Clarke. It would have been nice to hear both of them in a bass guitar duet as well. *Average Person* harked back to the sort of song The Beatles used to sing about, lonely, disappointed people, and this time Paul discussed the ambitions of an engine driver, waitress and boxer. Given an almost jokey treatment, the

vaudevillian approach put a brave face on a tragic picture. The brash singalong kazoos had overtones of *Lady Madonna* and the tune stuck in the head in the same relentless way. Thus within the space of a few years, Paul had revitalised his musical output and career, taken personal tragedy, shocks and shake-ups in his stride and emerged strongly productive, sane and very happy. For Paul the quest has not finished, nor perhaps even properly begun. The man who was once a Beatle and had been a Wing, is now at last . . . . himself.

Discography

SINGLES – THE BEATLES

1962

October 5 **LOVE ME DO**/P.S. I Love You *(Parlophone R 4949)*

1963

January 11 **PLEASE PLEASE ME**/Ask Me Why *(Parlophone R 4983)*
April 12 **FROM ME TO YOU**/Thank You Girl *(Parlophone R 5015)*
August 23 **SHE LOVES YOU**/I'll Get You *(Parlophone R 5055)*
November 29 **I WANT TO HOLD YOUR HAND**/This Boy *(Parlophone R 5084)*

1964

March 20 **CAN'T BUY ME LOVE**/You Can't Do That *(Parlophone R 5114)*
July 10 **A HARD DAY'S NIGHT**/Things We Said Today *(Parlophone R 5160)*
November 27 **I FEEL FINE**/She's A Woman *(Parlophone R 5200)*

1965

April 9 **TICKET TO RIDE**/Yes It Is *(Parlophone R 5265)*
July 23 **HELP**/I'm Down *(Parlophone R 5305)*
December 3 **DAY TRIPPER**/We Can Work It Out *(Parlophone R 5389)*

1966

June 10 **PAPERBACK WRITER**/Rain *(Parlophone R 5452)*
August 5 **ELEANOR RIGBY**/YELLOW SUBMARINE *(Parlophone R 5493)*

1967

February 17 **PENNY LANE/STRAWBERRY FIELDS FOREVER** *(Parlophone R 5570)*
July 7 **ALL YOU NEED IS LOVE**/Baby You're A Rich Man *(Parlophone R 5620)*
November 24 **HELLO GOODBYE**/I Am The Walrus *(Parlophone R 5655)*

1968

March 15 **LADY MADONNA**/The Inner Light *(Parlophone R 5675)*
August 26 **HEY JUDE**/Revolution *(Apple R 5722)*

1969

April 11 **GET BACK**/Don't Let Me Down *(Apple R 5777)*
October 30 **SOMETHING**/Come Together *(Apple R 5814)*

1970

March 6 **LET IT BE**/You Know My Name (Look Up The Number) *(Apple R 5833)*

1976

March 8 **YESTERDAY**/I Should Have Known Better *(Apple R 6013)*
June 25 **BACK IN THE USSR**/Twist And Shout *(Parlophone R 6016)*

1978

September 30 **SGT. PEPPER'S LONELY HEARTS CLUB BAND**/With A Little Help From My Friends/A Day In The Life *(Parlophone R 6022)*

1982

May 24 **THE BEATLES MOVIE MEDLEY**/I'm Happy Just To Dance With You *(Parlophone R 6055)*
October 4 **LOVE ME DO**/P.S. I Love You *(RP 4949 +)*

1983

January 10 **PLEASE PLEASE ME**/Ask My Why *(RP 4983 +)*
April 11 **FROM ME TO YOU**/Thank You Girl *(RP 5015 +)*
August 22 **SHE LOVES YOU**/I'll Get You *(RP 5055 +)*
November 14 **I WANT TO HOLD YOUR HAND**/This Boy *(RP 5084 +)*

+ Re-issued as a picture disc, 20 years after original release date

EPS – THE BEATLES
Date Title/Tracks Label/Cat. No.

1963

July 12 **TWIST AND SHOUT:** Twist And Shout/A Taste Of Honey/Do You Want To Know A Secret/There's A Place *(Parlophone GEP 8882)*
September 6 **THE BEATLES' HITS:** From Me To You/Thank You Girl/Please Please Me/Love Me Do *(Parlophone GEP 8880)*
November 1 **THE BEATLES No.1:** I Saw Her Standing There/Misery/Anna/Chains *(Parlophone GEP 8883)*

1964

February 7 **ALL MY LOVING:** All My Loving/Ask Me Why/Money/P.S. I Love You *(Parlophone GEP 8891)*
June 19 **LONG TALL SALLY:** I Call Your Name/Slow Down/Long Tall Sally/Matchbox *(Parlophone GEP 8913)*
November 4 **A HARD DAY'S NIGHT NO.1 (FILM):** I Should Have Known Better/If I Fell/Tell Me Why/And I Love Her *(Parlophone GEP 8920)*
November 6 **A HARD DAY'S NIGHT No.2 (ALBUM):** Any Time At All/I'll Cry Instead/Things We Said Today/When I Get Home *(Parlophone GEP 8924)*

1965

April 6 **BEATLES FOR SALE No.1:** No Reply/I'm A Loser/Rock And Roll Music/Eight Days A Week *(Parlophone GEP 8931)*
June 4 **BEATLES FOR SALE No.2:** I'll Follow The Sun/Baby's In Black/Words Of Love/I Don't Want To Spoil The Party *(Parlophone GEP 8938)*
December 6 **THE BEATLES' MILLION SELLERS:** She Loves You/I Want To Hold Your Hand/Can't Buy Me Love/I Feel Fine *(Parlophone GEP 8946)*

1966

March 4 **YESTERDAY:** Act Naturally/You Like Me Too Much/Yesterday/It's Only Love *(Parlophone GEP 8948)*
July 8 **NOWHERE MAN:** Nowhere Man/Drive My Car/Michelle/You Won't See Me *(Parlophone GEP 8952)*

1967

December 8 **MAGICAL MYSTERY TOUR:** Magical Mystery Tour/Your Mother Should Know/I Am The Walrus/Fool On The Hill/Flying/Blue Jay Way *(Parlophone SMMT 1*2)*

1981

December 7 **THE BEATLES' EP COLLECTION:** (Box set of all thirteen EPs) *(Parlophone BEP 14)*

ALBUMS – THE BEATLES

Date Title/Tracks Label/Cat. No

1963

March 22 **PLEASE PLEASE ME:** I Saw Her Standing There/

Misery/Anna/Chains/Boys/Ask Me Why/Please Please Me/
Love Me Do/P.S. I Love You/Baby It's You/Do You Want To
Know A Secret?/A Taste Of Honey/There's A Place/Twist
And Shout *(Parlophone PCS 3042)*
November 22 **WITH THE BEATLES:** It Won't Be Long/All
I've Got To Do/All My Loving/Don't Bother Me/Little Child/
Til There Was You/Please Mr. Postman/Roll Over
Beethoven/Hold Me Tight/You Really Got A Hold On Me/I
Want To Be Your Man/Devil In Her Heart/Not A Second
Time/Money *(Parlophone PCS 3045)*

1964
August 10 **A HARD DAY'S NIGHT:** A Hard Day's Night/I
Should Have Known Better/If I Fell/I'm Just Happy To Dance
With You/And I Love Her/Tell Me Why/Can't Buy Me Love/
Any Time At All/I'll Cry Instead/Things We Said Today/
When I Get Home/You Can't Do That/I'll Be Back *(Parlophone
PCS 3058)*
December 4 **BEATLES FOR SALE:** No Reply/I'm A Loser/
Baby's In Black/Rock and Roll Music/I'll Follow The Sun/Mr.
Moonlight/Kansas City/Eight Days A Week/Words Of Love/
Honey Don't/Every Little Thing/I Don't Want To Spoil The
Party/What You're Doing/Everybody's Trying To Be My
Baby *(Parlophone PCS 3062)*

1965
August 6 **HELP!:** Help!/The Night Before/You've Got To
Hide Your Love Away/I Need You/Another Girl/You're
Gonna Lose That Girl/Ticket To Ride/Act Naturally/It's Only
Love/You Like Me Too Much/Tell Me What You See/I've Just
Seen A Face/Yesterday/Dizzy Miss Lizzy *(Parlophone PCS
3071)*
December 3 **RUBBER SOUL:** Drive My Car/Norwegian
Wood/You Won't See Me/Nowhere Man/Think For
Yourself/The Word/Michelle/What Goes On/Girl/I'm
Looking Through You/In My Life/Wait/If I Needed
Someone/Run For Your Life *(Parlophone PCS 3075)*

1966
August 5 **REVOLVER:** Taxman/Eleanor Rigby/I'm Only
Sleeping/Love You To/Here, There And Everywhere/Yellow
Submarine/She Said She Said/Good Day Sunshine/And
Your Bird Can Sing/For No One/Doctor Robert/I Want To
Tell You/Got To Get You Out Of My Life/Tomorrow Never
Knows *(Parlophone PCS 7009)*
December 10 **A COLLECTION OF BEATLES OLDIES
(BUT GOLDIES):** She Loves You/From Me To You/We Can
Work It Out/Help!/Michelle/Yesterday/I Feel Fine/Yellow
Submarine/Can't Buy Me Love/Bad Boy/Day Tripper/A
Hard Day's Night/Ticket To Ride/Paperback Writer/Eleanor
Rigby/I Want To Hold Your Hand *(Parlophone PCS 7016)*

1967
June 1 **SGT. PEPPER'S LONELY HEARTS CLUB BAND:**
Sgt. Pepper's Lonely Hearts Club Band/With A Little Help
From My Friends/Lucy In The Sky With Diamonds/Getting
Better/Fixing A Hole/She's Leaving Home/Being For The
Benefit Of Mr. Kite/Within You/Without You/When I'm
Sixty Four/Lovely Rita/Good Morning, Good Morning/A
Day In The Life *(Parlophone PCS 7027)*

1968
November 22 **THE BEATLES:** Back In The USSR/Dear
Prudence/Glass Onion/Ob-La-Di, Ob-La-Da/Wild Honey
Pie/The Continuing Story Of Bungalow Bill/While My
Guitar Gently Weeps/Happiness Is A Warm Gun/Martha My
Dear/I'm So Tired/Blackbird/Piggies/Rocky Raccoon/Don't
Pass Me By/Why Don't We Do It In The Road/I Will/Julia/
Birthday/Yer Blues/Mother nature's Son/Everybody's Got
Something To Hide Except Me And My Monkey/Sexy Sadie/
Helter Skelter/Long Long Long/Revolution 1/Honey Pie/
Savoy Truffle/Cry Baby Cry/Revolution 9/Goodnight *(Apple*

PCS 7067*8) (double)

1969
January 17 **YELLOW SUBMARINE:** Yellow Submarine/
Only A Northern Song/All Together Now/Hey, Bulldog/It's
All Too Much/All You Need Is Love/Pepperland/Sea Of
Time/Sea Of Holes/Sea Of Monsters/March Of The Meanies/
Pepperland Laid Waste/Yellow Submarine In Pepperland
(Apple PCS 7070)
September 26 **ABBEY ROAD:** Come Together/Something/
Maxwell's Silver Hammer/Oh! Darling/Octopus's Garden/I
Want You – She's So Heavy/Here Comes The Sun/Because/
You Never Give Me Your Money/Sun King/Mean Mr.
Mustard/Polythene Pam/She Came In Through The
Bedroom Window/Golden Slumbers/Carry That Weight/
The End/Her Majesty *(Apple PCS 7088)*

1970
May 8 **LET IT BE:** Two Of Us/Dig A Pony/Across The
Universe/I Me Mine/Dig It/Let It Be/Maggie May/I've Got A
Feeling/One After 909/The Long And Winding Road/For
You Blue/Get Back *(Apple PCS 7096)*

1973
April 19 **THE BEATLES 1962-1966:** Love Me Do/Please
Please Me/From Me To You/She Loves You/I Want To Hold
Your Hand/All My Loving/Can't Buy Me Love/A Hard's Day
Night/And I Love Her/Eight Days A Week/I Feel Fine/Ticket
To Ride/Yesterday/Help!/You've Got To Hide Your Love
Away/We Can Work It Out/Day Tripper/Drive My Car/
Norwegian Wood (This Bird Has Flown)/Nowhere Man/
Michelle/In My Life/Girl/Paperback Writer/Eleanor Rigby/
Yellow Submarine *(Apple PCS P717)* (double)
April 19 **THE BEATLES 1967-1970:** Strawberry Fields
Forever/Penny Lane/Sgt. Pepper's Lonely Hearts Club
Band/With A Little Help From My Friends/Lucy In The Sky
With Diamonds/A Day In The Life/All You Need Is Love/I
Am The Walrus/Hello Goodbye/The Fool On The Hill/
Magical Mystery Tour/Lady Madonna/Hey Jude/
Revolution/Back In The USSR/While My Guitar Gently
Weeps/Ob-La-Di, Ob-La-Da/Get Back/Don't Let Me Down/
The Ballad Of John & Yoko/Old Brown Shoe/Here Comes
The Sun/Come Together/Something/Octopus's Garden/Let
It Be/Across The Universe/The Long And Winding Road
(Apple PCS P718) (double)

1976
June 10 **ROCK 'N' ROLL MUSIC:** Twist And Shout/I Saw
Her Standing There/You Can't Do That/I Wanna Be Your
Man/I Call Your Name/Boys/Long Tall Sally/Rock 'n' Roll
Music/Slow Down/Kansas City/Money/Bad Boy/Matchbox/
Roll Over Beethoven/Dizzy Miss Lizzy/Anytime At All/
Drive My Car/Everybody's Trying To Be My Baby/The Night
Before/I'm Down/Revolution/Back In The USSR/Helter
Skelter/Taxman/Got To Get You Into My Life/Hey Bulldog/
Birthday/Get Back *(Parlophone PCSP 719)*
July 19 **THE BEATLES TAPES:** David Wigg interviews the
Beatles. Also music tracks: Because/Come Together/Give
Peace A Chance/Here Comes The Sun/Hey Jude/Imagine/
Octopus's Garden/Something/Yellow Submarine *(Polydor
2683 068)*

1976
November 18 **MAGICAL MYSTERY TOUR:** Magical
Mystery Tour/The Fool On The Hill/Flying/Blue Jay Way/
Your Mother Should Know/I Am The Walrus/Hello
Goodbye/Strawberry Fields Forever/Penny Lane/Baby
You're A Rich Man/All You Need Is Love *(Parlophone PCTC
255)*

1977
May 1 **THE BEATLES LIVE!:** I Saw Her Standing There/

Roll Over Beethoven/Hippy Hippy Shake/Sweet Little Sixteen/Lend Me Your Comb/Your Feets Too Big/Twist And Shout/Mr. Moonlight/A Taste Of Honey/Besame Mucho/Reminiscing/Kansas City/Ain't Nothing Shakin'/To Know Her Is To Love Her/Little Queenie/Falling In Love Again/Ask Me Why/Be-Bop-A-Lula/Hallelujah I Love Her So/Red Sails In The Sunset/Everybody's Trying To Be My Baby/Matchbox/Talkin' 'Bout You/Shimmy Shake/Long Tall Sally/I Remember You Lingasong (LNL 1) (double)
May 6 **THE BEATLES AT THE HOLLYWOOD BOWL:** Twist And Shout/She's A Woman/Dizzy Miss Lizzy/Ticket To Ride/Can't Buy Me Love/Things We Said Today/Roll Over Beethoven/Boys/A Hard's Day Night/Help!/All My Loving/She Loves You/Long Tall Sally (Parlophone EMTV 4)
November 19 **LOVE SONGS:** Yesterday/I'll Follow The Sun/I Need You/Girl/In My Life/Words Of Love/Here, There And Everywhere/Something/And I Love Her/If I Fell/I'll Be Back/Tell Me What You See/Yes It Is/Michelle/It's Only Love/You're Going To Lose That Girl/Every Little Thing/For No One/She's Leaving Home/The Long And Winding Road/This Boy/Norwegian Wood/You've Got To Hide Your Love Away/I Will/P.S. I Love You (Parlophone PCSP 721) (double)

1978
December 2 **THE BEATLES COLLECTION** (Box set of all 13 original albums) (Parlophone BC 13)

1979
May 11 **HEY JUDE:** Can't Buy Me Love/I Should Have Known Better/Paperback Writer/Rain/Lady Madonna/Revolution/Hey Jude/Old Brown Shoe/Don't Let Me Down/The Ballad Of John & Yoko (Parlophone PCS 7184)
October 12 **RARITIES:** Across The Universe/Yes It Is/This Boy/The Inner Light/I'll Get You/Thank You Girl/Komm, Gibt Mir Deine Hand/You Know My Name (Look Up The Number)/Sie Liebt Dich/Rain/She's A Woman/Matchbox/I Call Your Name/Bad Boy/Slow Down/I'm Down/Long Tall Sally (Parlophone PCM 1001)

1980
October 20 **THE BEATLES BALLADS:** Yesterday/Norwegian Wood (This Bird Has Flown)/Do You Want To Know A Secret/For No One/Michelle/Nowhere Man/You've Got To Hide Your Love Away/Across The Universe/All My Loving/Hey Jude/Something/The Fool On The Hill/Till There Was You/The Long And Winding Road/Here Comes The Sun/Blackbird/And I Love Her/She's Leaving Home/Here, There And Everywhere/Let It Be (Parlophone PCS 7214)

1982
March 12 **REEL MUSIC:** A Hard Day's Night/I Should Have Known Better/Can't Buy Me Love/And I Love Her/Help!/You've Got To Hide Your Love Away/Ticket To Ride/Magical Mystery Tour/I Am The Walrus/Yellow Submarine/All You Need Is Love/Let It Be/Get Back/The Long And Winding Road (Parlophone PCS 7218)

SINGLES – WINGS

Date Titles Label/Cat.No

1972
February 25 **GIVE IRELAND BACK TO THE IRISH/** (Version) (Apple R 5936)
May 12 **MARY HAD A LITTLE LAMB/**Little Woman Love (Apple R 5949)
December 1 **HI HI HI/**C Moon (Apple R 5973)

1973
March 23 **MY LOVE/**The Mess (Apple R 5985 *)
June 1 **LIVE AND LET DIE/**I Lie Around (Apple R 5987 *)
October 26 **HELEN WHEELS/**Country Dreamer (Apple R

5993 *)

1974
February 18 **JET/**Let Me Roll It (Apple R 5996 *)
June 28 **BAND ON THE RUN/**Zoo Gang (Apple R 5997 *)
October 25 **JUNIOR'S FARM/**Sally G (Apple R 5999 *)

1975
February 7 **SALLY G/**Junior's Farm (Apple R 5999 *)
May 16 **LISTEN TO WHAT THE MAN SAID/**Love In Song (Apple R 6006)
September 5 **LETTING GO/**You Gave Me The Answer (Capitol R 6008)
November 28 **VENUS AND MARS ROCK SHOW/**Magneto and Titanium Man (Capitol R 6010)

1976
April 30 **SILLY LOVE SONGS/**Cook Of The House (Parlophone R 6014)
July 23 **LET 'EM IN/**Beware My Love (Parlophone R 6015)

1977
February 4 **MAYBE I'M AMAZED/**Soily (Parlophone R 6017)
November 11 **MULL OF KINTYRE/GIRL'S SCHOOL** (double A-side) (Capitol R 6018)

1978
March 23 **WITH A LITTLE LUCK/**Backwards Traveller – Cuff Link (Parlophone R 6019)
June 16 **I'VE HAD ENOUGH/**Deliver Your Children (Parlophone R 6020)
September 15 **LONDON TOWN/**I'm Carrying (Parlophone R 6021)

1979
March 23 **GOODNIGHT TONIGHT/**Daytime Nightime Suffering (Parlophone R 6023)
April 3 **GOODNIGHT TONIGHT/**Daytime Nightime Suffering (12") (Parlophone 12Y R 60230
June 1 **OLD SIAM, SIR/**Spin It On (Parlophone R 60260
August 10 **GETTING CLOSER/BABY'S REQUEST** (double A-side) (Parlophone R 60270

1980
April 11 **COMING UP/**Coming Up (Live At Glasgow)/Lunch Box – Odd Sox (Parlophone R 6035 **)
*Record credited to Paul McCartney and Wings
**A-side credited to Paul McCartney, B-side to Wings

ALBUMS – WINGS

Date Title/Tracks Label/Cat. No

1971
December 3 **WINGS WILD LIFE:** Mumbo/Bip Bop/Love Is Strange/Wild Life/Some People Never Know/I Am Your Singer/Tomorrow/Dear Friend (Parlophone PCS 7142)

1973
May 3 **RED ROSE SPEEDWAY:** Big Barn Bed/My Love/Get On The Right Thing/One More Kiss/Little Lamb Dragonfly/Single Pigeon/When The Night/Loup (1st Indian On The Moon)/Hold Me Tight/Lazy Dynamite/Hands Of Love/Power Cut (EMI PCTC 251 *)
November 30 **BAND ON THE RUN:** Band On The Run/Jet/Bluebird/Mrs. Vanderbilt/Let Me Roll It/Mamunia/No Words (For My Love)/Picasso's Last Words (Drink To Me)/Nineteen Hundred And Eighty-Five (Apple PAS 10007 *)

1975
May 30 **VENUS AND MARS:** Venus And Mars/Rock

Show/Love In Song/You Gave Me The Answer/Magneto And Titanium Man/Letting Go/Venus And Mars – Reprise/ Spirits Of Ancient Egypt/Medicine Jar/Call Me Back Again/ Listen To What The Man Said/Treat Her Gently – Lonely Old People/Crossroads *(Capitol PCTC 254)*

1976
March 26 **WINGS AT THE SPEED OF SOUND:** Let 'Em In/The Note You Never Wrote/She's My Baby/Beware My Love/Wino Junko/Silly Love Songs/Cook Of The House/ Time To Hide/Must Do Something About It/San Ferry Anne/ Warm And Beautiful *(Parlophone PAS 10010)*
December 10 **WINGS OVER AMERICA:** Venus And Mars/ Rock Show/Jet/Let Me Roll It/Spirits Of Ancient Egypt/ Medicine Jar/Maybe I'm Amazed/Call Me Back Again/Lady Madonna/The Long And Winding Road/Live And Let Die/ Picasso's Last Words/Richard Cory/Bluebird/I've Just Seen A Face/Blackbird/Yesterday/You Gave Me The Answer/ Magneto And Titanium Man/Go Now/My Love/Listen To What The Man Said/Let 'Em In/Time To Hide/Silly Love Songs/Beware My Love/Letting Go/Band On The Run/Hi Hi Hi/Soily *(Parlophone PCSP 720)* (triple)

1978
March 31 **LONDON TOWN:** London Town/Cafe On The Left Bank/I'm Carrying/Backwards Traveller/Cuff Link/ Children Children/Girlfriend/I've Had Enough/With A Little Luck/Famous Groupies/Deliver Your Children/Name And Address/Don't Let It Bring You Down/Morse Moose And The Grey Goose *(Parlophone PAS 10012)*
December 1 **WINGS GREATEST:** Another Day/Silly Love Songs/Live And Let Die/Junior's Farm/With A Little Luck/ Band On The Run/Uncle Albert – Admiral Halsey/Hi Hi Hi/Let 'Em In/My Love/Jet/Mull Of Kintyre *(Parlophone PCTC 256)*

1979
June 8 **BACK TO THE EGG:** Reception/Getting Closer/ We're Open Tonight/Spin It On/Again And Again And Again/Old Siam, Sir/Arrow Through Me/Rockestra Theme/ To You/After The Ball/Million Miles/Winter Rose/Love Awake/The Broadcast/So Glad To See You Here/Baby's Request *(Parlophone PCTC 257)*
*Record credited to Paul McCartney & Wings

SINGLES – OTHER

1971
February 19 **ANOTHER DAY**/Oh Woman Oh Why – Paul McCartney *(Apple R 5889)*
August 13 **THE BACK SEAT OF MY CAR**/Heart Of The Country – Paul and Linda McCartney *(Apple R 5914)*

1974
October 18 **WALKING IN THE PARK WITH ELOISE**/ Bridge Over The River Suite – The Country Hams *(EMI 2220)*

1977
April 22 **UNCLE ALBERT – ADMIRAL HALSEY**/Eat At Home – Percy 'Thrills' Thrillington *(Regal Zonophone) (EMI 2594)*

1979
August 10 **SEASIDE WOMAN**/B-side To Seaside – Suzy & The Red Stripes *(A&M AMS 7461)*
November 16 **WONDERFUL CHRISTMAS TIME**/Rudolph The Red-Nosed Reggae – Paul McCartney *(Parlophone R 6029)*

1980
June 14 **WATERFALLS**/Check My Machine – Paul McCartney *(Parlophone R 6037)*
July 18 **SEASIDE WOMAN**/B-Side to Seaside – Linda McCartney *(A&M AMS 7548)*
July 18 **SEASIDE WOMAN/B-Side to Seaside – Linda McCartney** *(A&M AMS 7548)* (12")
September 15 **TEMPORARY SECRETARY**/Secret Friend – Paul McCartney *(Parlophone R 6039)*
September 15 **TEMPORARY SECRETARY**/Secret Friend – Paul McCartney *(Parlophone 12R 6039)* (12")

1982
March 1 **WALKING IN THE PARK WITH ELOISE**/Bridge Over The River Suite – The Country Hams *(EMI 2220)*
March 29 **EBONY AND IVORY**/Rainclouds – Paul McCartney and Stevie Wonder *(Parlophone R 6054)*
April 2 **EBONY AND IVORY**/Rainclouds/Ebony And Ivory (solo version) – Paul McCartney and Stevie Wonder *(Parlophone 12R 6054)* (12")
June 21 **TAKE IT AWAY**/I'll Give You A Ring – Paul McCartney *(Parlophone R 60560)*
July 5 **TAKE IT AWAY**/I'll Give You A Ring/Dress Me Up As A Robber – Paul McCartney *(Parlophone 12R 6056)* (12")
September 20 **TUG OF WAR**/Get It – Paul McCartney *(Parlophone R 60570)*
October 29 **THE GIRL IS MINE**/(Can't Get Outta The Rain) – Michael Jackson & Paul McCartney *(Epic EPC A2729)*
December 24 **THE GIRL IS MINE**/(Can't Get Outta The Rain) – Michael Jackson & Paul McCartney *(Epic EPC All2729)* (7" picture disc)

1983
October 3 **SAY SAY SAY**/Ode To A Koala Bear Paul McCartney & Michael Jackson *(Parlophone R 60620)*
December 5 **PIPES OF PEACE**/So Bad *(Parlophone R 60640*
Notes:
'The Country Hams' is a Paul and Linda McCartney pseudonym.
'Percy "Thrills" Thrillington' is a Paul McCartney pseudonym.
'Suzy & The Red Stripes' is a Paul, Linda & Wings pseudonym.

ALBUMS – OTHER

1970
April 17 **McCARTNEY:** The Lovely Linda/That Would Be Something/Valentine Day/Every Night/Hot As Sun/ Glasses/Junk/Man We Was Lonely/Oo You/Momma Miss America/Teddy Boys/Singalong Junk/Maybe I'm Amazed/ Kreen-Akrore *(Apple PCS 7102)* Paul McCartney

1971
May 21 **RAM:** Too Many People/3 Legs/Ram On/Dear Boy/ Uncle Albert-Admiral Halsey/Smile Away/Heart Of The Country/Monkberry Moon Delight/Eat At Home/Long Haired Lady/Ram On/The Back Seat Of My Car *(Apple PAS 10003)* Paul & Linda McCartney

1977
April 29 **THRILLINGTON:** (all instrumental tracks) Too Many People/3 Legs/Ram On/Dear Boy/Uncle Albert – Admiral Halsey/Smile Away/Heart Of The Country/ Monkberry Moon Delight/Eat At Home/Long Haired Lady/ The Back Seat Of My Car *(Regal Zonophone) (EMC 3175)* Percy 'Thrills' Thrillington *

1980
May 16 **McCARTNEY II:** Coming Up/Temporary Secretary/On The Way/Waterfalls/Nobody Knows/Front Parlour/Summer's Day Song/Frozen Jap/Bogey Music/ Darkroom/One Of These Days *(Parlophone PCTC 258)* Paul McCartney

1981

February 23 **THE McCARTNEY INTERVIEW:** An Interview by Vic Garbarin of MUSICIAN: Player & Listener Magazine *(Parlophone CHAT 1)*

April 3 **THE CONCERTS FOR KAMPUCHEA:** Four tracks only on side 4 by Wings and the Rockestra. Coming Up/ Lucille/Let It Be/Rockestra Theme *(Atlantic K 60153)* (double)

1982

April 26 **TUG OF WAR:** Tug Of War/Take It Away/ Somebody Who Cares/What's That You're Doing?/Here Today/Ballroom Dancing/The Pound Is Sinking/ Wanderlust/Get It/Be What You See (Link)/Dress Me Up As A Robber/Ebony And Ivory *(Parlophone PCTC 259)* Paul McCartney

1983

October 31 **PIPES OF PEACE:** Pipes Of Peace/Say Say Say/ The Other Me/Keep Under Cover/So Bad/The Man/Sweetest Little Show/Average Person/Hey Hey/Tug Of Peace/ Through Our Love *(Parlophone PCTC 1652301)* Paul McCartney

NOTE:
Percy 'Thrills' Thrillington is a Paul McCartney pseudonym

The Best Rock 'n' Roll Reading from Proteus

☐ **TOYAH**

An illustrated fan's eyeview much-liked by Toyah herself.
by Gaynor Evans
UK £1.95
US $3.95

☐ **REGGAE: DEEP ROOTS MUSIC**

The definitive history of reggae. A major TV tie-in.
by Howard Johnson and Jim Pines
UK £5.95
US $10.95

☐ **BOOKENDS**

The first full study of Simon and Garfunkel, their joint and solo careers.
by Patrick Humphries
UK £5.95
US $10.95

☐ **PRETENDERS**

The first full study of this powerful and turbulent band.
by Chris Salewicz
UK £3.95
US $7.95

☐ **LOU REED**

A definitive profile of this almost reclusive figure.
by Diana Clapton
UK £4.95
US $9.95.

☐ **JAMES LAST**

A fully illustrated study of this world phenomenon of popular music.
by Howard Elson
UK £4.95
US $9.95

☐ **RARE RECORDS**

A complete illustrated guide to wax trash and vinyl treasures.
by Tom Hibbert
UK £4.95
US $9.95

☐ **THE PERFECT COLLECTION**

The 200 greatest albums, the 100 greatest singles selected and discussed by leading rock journalists.
Edited by Tom Hibbert
UK £4.95
US $9.95

☐ **EARLY ROCKERS**

All the seminal figures of rock 'n' roll:
Berry, Little Richard, Jerry Lee, Presley et al.
by Howard Elson
UK £4.95
US $9.95

KATE BUSH ☐

Complete illustrated story of this unique artist.
by Paul Kerton
UK £3.95
US $7.95

BLACK SABBATH ☐

Heavy Metal Superstars.
by Chris Welch
UK £4.95
US $9.95

A-Z OF ROCK GUITARISTS ☐

First illustrated encyclopaedia of guitar greats.
by Chris Charlesworth
UK £5.95
US $10.95

A-Z OF ROCK DRUMMERS ☐

Over 300 great drummers in this companion to ROCK GUITARISTS.
by Harry Shapiro
UK £5.95
US $10.95

CHUCK BERRY ☐

The definitive biography of the original Mr Rock 'n' Roll.
by Krista Reese
UK £4.95
US $8.95

A CASE OF MADNESS ☐

A big illustrated guide for fans of this insane band.
by Mark Williams
UK only £1.95

TALKING HEADS ☐

The only illustrated book about one of the most innovative bands of the 70s and 80s.
by Krista Reese
UK £4.95
US $9.95

DURAN DURAN ☐

The best-selling illustrated biography.
UK £1.95
US $3.95

A TOURIST'S GUIDE TO JAPAN ☐

Beautifully illustrated study of Sylvian and his colleagues.
by Arthur A. Pitt.
UK £1.95
US $3.95

ILLUSTRATED POP QUIZ ☐

Over 400 impossible questions for pop geniuses only.
by Dafydd Rees and Barry Lazell
UK £2.95
US $5.95

order form overleaf